the world all of its significance. To "know thyself"; that is what matters.

The primary characteristic of all human experience, as Gentile saw it, was moral responsibility. We are responsible for what we believe about the world, just as much as for what we do in it. Moral responsibility is the essential characteristic of all rational thought.

In the individual, particularity and universality coincide. The more the individual is himself, the more closely he is identified with all men. The concrete reality of the individual is not to be found in his existence in space and time as a natural phenomenon, an object of sense, but rather in his spiritual existence as a self-conscious being. He exists as a particular person, but not as one among others; his existence is unique and therefore infinite and universal. So the real individual is not opposed to the universal — he is the universal; and the concrete universal is just the individual himself as an actual, self-conscious, determinate, unique being.

As man is conscious of himself only within society, the State is immanent in the consciousness of the individual citizen and the highest concrete expression of the moral conscience of mankind. Since the State is the universal aspect of the individual, it is bound to possess the same morality as the individual; it is not a presupposition of his existence — a limit to his liberty — but the concrete actuality of his will.

Gentile's theory of transcendental society is the foundation stone for this whole final work and unifies his discussion of ethics, the individual and character, the State, economics, religion, science, history, politics, and finally death and immortality.

H. S. HARRIS is assistant professor of philosophy at the University of Illinois. A native of England, he received his B.A. and M.A. degrees from Oxford University and his Ph.D. from the University of Illinois. His other major work is *The Social Philosophy of Giovanni Gentile*.

GENESIS AND STRUCTURE OF SOCIETY

GENESIS
AND
STRUCTURE
OF SOCIETY

by Giovanni Gentile

translated by H. S. Harris

UNIVERSITY OF ILLINOIS PRESS, URBANA, 1960

This work is translated from the posthumous edition published at Florence by G. C. Sansoni in 1946.

CONTENTS

INTRODUCTION

Gentile's Career

Giovanni Gentile was born 30 May 1875 at Castelvetrano in Sicily. He received his high-school education (*ginnasio-liceo*) at Trapani and in 1893 he won a scholarship from there to the *Scuola Normale Superiore* at Pisa. When he arrived at Pisa he seemed already destined for a distinguished career in literary studies, and he became at once a favorite pupil of the great Jewish-Italian literary scholar Alessandro D'Ancona. But at Pisa he came under the influence of Donato Jaja, a pupil of Bertrando Spaventa, the most important of the nineteenth-century Italian followers of Hegel. Gentile was an enthusiast by temperament, and to the dismay of D'Ancona, who had little use for philosophical theorizing, he became imbued with the ambition to continue and restore the idealist tradition of Spaventa in philosophy. His *tesi di laurea* on *Rosmini and Gioberti* was the first step in this program, for it was conceived as an illustration of one of Spaventa's principal theses, 'the circulation of European philosophy'; and from that time onward Gentile restricted his own scholarly researches mainly to the history of the native Italian philosophical tradition. The peculiarly 'national,' and even at times almost chauvinistic, character of his culture and his genius is one of the factors that has impeded the understanding of his work in foreign countries.

His own first steps in literary history and aesthetics brought him into epistolary contact with the young Neapolitan Benedetto

Croce, nine years his senior, and already in a fair way to establish a national reputation. But it was their mutual interest in Marx that first drew them together as friends. Gentile's interest in Marx was more philosophical than Croce's, as the published results showed; and he was already a self-conscious and critical Hegelian, whereas Croce was still feeling his way forward under the confused influences of Vico, De Sanctis, and Herbart. It seems now to be agreed by those who have access to their correspondence that in this formative period Gentile's influence on Croce was more fundamental than Croce's upon Gentile. The increasingly 'Hegelian' character of the successive volumes of the *Philosophy of the Spirit* was apparent to observers from the beginning; and Croce, in the brief "Contribution to the Criticism of Myself" which he wrote when it was completed, acknowledged that this was the result of his gradual assimilation on his own terms of Gentile's arguments about the identity of philosophy with the history of philosophy.[1]

By that time, however, Gentile had pursued his somewhat stormy academic career to the point of announcing his own 'system.' In 1898 he had begun to teach at the *liceo* at Campobasso, and in 1901 he moved to the *Regio liceo* at Naples. There he obtained a *libera docenza* at the university, and inaugurated his career as a lecturer by proclaiming "The Rebirth of Idealism" (1903).[2] He had already produced an important essay on the "Concept of Education" in 1900; and in company with Lombardo-Radice, a younger contemporary of his at Pisa, he was about to embark on a twenty-year campaign for educational reform. Gentile's lifelong concern with the theory and practice of education is the other major influence—along with his studies in the history of philosophy—that contributed to the formation of his thought.

The year 1907 was a milestone with respect to both of these interests. He was called to be Professor of the History of Philosophy at Palermo, and he was invited to prepare a report on the concept of 'lay' education for the congress of secondary-school teachers at Naples. At this congress he argued that 'lay' education was

---

[1] *An Autobiography* (tr. by R. G. Collingwood), Oxford, Clarendon, 1927, p. 105; cf. pp. 93, 96.

[2] He spoke more truly than he can possibly have realized, for 1903 was the year in which Croce founded *La critica*.

the only true education, but that on the other hand all true education must have a religious foundation. These antitheses were reconciled in the practical proposal that a definite religious creed should be taught in the elementary school *as a foundation for* the teaching of philosophy in the secondary school. In his professorial studies at Palermo he continued to reflect on the relation of religion to philosophy, gradually reformulating the Hegelian triad of Absolute Spirit—Art, Religion, and Philosophy—as "The absolute forms of the [human] spirit" (1909). At the same time his meditation on the theoretical significance of the history of philosophy led him to a 'reform of the Hegelian dialectic' through what he called 'the method of immanence'; and his new idealism was announced in a paper of 1912 on "The Act of Thought as Pure Act." By this time he was already working on his *Summary of Educational Theory* (2 vols., 1913–14) in which the new 'method' was systematically applied.

Croce expressed grave dissatisfaction about the 'method of immanence' and the conception of thought as 'pure act,' which seemed to him to reduce all theoretical distinctions to a single mystic intuition, and all practical experience to the immediacy of the present instant. But the collaboration in *La critica* went on.

In 1914 when Jaja died, Gentile returned to fill his former master's chair at Pisa. Here in 1916 he produced the *General Theory of the Spirit as Pure Act* (English translation, *The Theory of Mind as Pure Act,* 1922), the first systematic theoretical statement of his position, and the *Foundations of the Philosophy of Law,* a rather condensed and gnomic account of his practical philosophy. In 1917 there followed the first volume of his *Logic;* but the even tenor of his academic life was disturbed by the national emergency which resulted from the Italian defeat at Caporetto. Gentile had always been an 'interventionist' in his attitude toward the war, but he had hitherto felt it was his duty to stick to his last. After Caporetto he decided that the time had come to speak out, and for the next two years he produced a veritable flood of newspaper articles instinct with the spirit of patriotic conservatism.

Caporetto was avenged at Vittorio Veneto; but Italy's diplomatic defeat at Versailles and her parlous economic position kept the bitter divisions and recriminations alive; and Gentile's whole attention, even in work of an outwardly theoretical nature like the

Addresses on Religion (1920), was devoted to the problem of restoring the sense of national unity.[3] Naturally he held that the source of the trouble was in the nation's schools, and he published the outlines of a plan for their organic reform.

In 1922, disgusted at the virtual paralysis of the successive 'Liberal' governments, he joined with a group of friends in founding a review called *The New Liberal Politics*. But they were overtaken by events; before the first number appeared, Mussolini had marched to Rome and invited Gentile to become Minister of Public Instruction with full powers to reform the school system. During eight months of frenzied activity the plan for the reform was prepared. It became law in May 1923, and at the same time Gentile joined the Fascist party. His tenure of the ministry lasted only one more year. Being in too much of a hurry after so long in the wilderness, and always too certain that he was right, Gentile was not popular among politicians; it has been plausibly suggested that his resignation at the end of June 1924 was part of Mussolini's attempt to curry favor with Parliament in the Matteotti crisis. Paradoxically, his appointment to head the Commission on Constitutional Reform in August fits into this same pattern, for he was well known as a conservative with an almost religious respect for law and order, and for constitutional modes of procedure—though in the election campaign of May 1924 he had made an apologia for the blackjacks of the *squadristi* which unluckily became his most famous utterance.

In 1925 came the establishment of the dictatorship, when Mussolini's attempts to placate Parliament failed. Croce now declared against the Regime, and signalized his breach with Gentile by writing a Protest against the Manifesto which Gentile was charged to write by the Congress of Fascist Intellectuals. Croce's anti-manifesto was itself signed by many prominent intellectuals, so that in effect they became the leaders of two opposed camps in the world of Italian culture. Gentile became President of the National Fascist Institute of Culture, and embarked on a new career as the leading Fascist publicist and self-styled "philosopher of Fascism." In this same year he was appointed to direct the newly

---

[3] In 1920 he founded the *Giornale critico della filosofia italiana* as an organ for his growing 'school.' But only a few chapters from the second volume of the *Logic* appeared there from his pen. He did manage to finish the *Logic* before he became Minister of Public Instruction.

planned *Enciclopedia italiana,* which survives as the principal cultural monument of the Fascist period. *The New Liberal Politics—* retitled first *Political Education* and then *Fascist Education,* until finally a new beginning was made with the title *Fascist Civilization* in 1934—became the organ of the institute; and Gentile's work for the institute and the *Enciclopedia* occupied most of his attention for the next fifteen years. It should be noted, however, that he never ceased to fulfill his professorial duties. He had been appointed to the chair in the history of philosophy at Rome in 1917, and on the death of his elder colleague Varisco in 1928 he succeeded to the chair of theoretical philosophy, which he held until his death. In 1930 he published his *Philosophy of Art.*[4]

The conclusion of the Concordat in 1929 was the beginning of a long period of increasing disillusion for Gentile. He opposed reconciliation with the Church because it meant the admission of Church authority in education, the teaching of dogmatic religion in secondary schools, and ecclesiastical censorship over the *Enciclopedia* (cf. 92b).[5] (The Fascists had already begun to pervert his educational reform in a number of other ways.) He may have felt momentarily heartened in 1932 when Mussolini set his name to a statement of the fundamental principles of Fascism in the *Enciclopedia,* which he, Gentile, had actually written. But he continued to fight a losing battle against Party chauvinism in education and culture. His momentary enthusiasm for the Ethiopian war was soon overshadowed by the increasing influence of Nazi Germany over Fascist attitudes, which culminated in the promulgation and partial implementation of a number of racialist decrees, which were absolutely inimical to his own conception of Fascism.

In sharp contrast with his enthusiastic support of intervention in 1915, he remained silent when Mussolini joined Hitler's war in 1940. But when, through the entry of the United States and Japan, the war became truly global in its extent, he persuaded himself that there could be no question here of merely capricious decisions by individual leaders, and so once again at a moment of crisis he spoke out publicly when others were drawing back. On 24 June 1943, at the invitation of the Fascist party secretary,

---

[4] Even that work was unjustly dismissed as Party propaganda by some on account of the political animus clearly evident in his references to Croce.

[5] Numbers in parentheses refer throughout to the corresponding items in the bibliography.

he delivered a great *Address to the Italians* in Rome, calling for national unity in the face of the enemy at their gates.

When Mussolini was overthrown by a palace plot a month later, Gentile was not in the capital but in Florence. Thanks to the shamefully ungracious way in which he was publicly attacked by the new Minister of Education, he became the target of all who were anxious to display their newborn anti-Fascist zeal. It was in these circumstances that he went into virtual retirement to write the book here translated. Inevitably, therefore, it assumed something of the character of an *apologia pro vita sua.*

He had scarcely completed the manuscript when the Armistice was announced, the Germans invaded, and the Italians themselves were divided by civil war. Mussolini was rescued, and became the head of a puppet Fascist Social Republic in the North. He was naturally anxious to rally as many of his former supporters as possible, and Gentile, though he was anxious to remain in retirement, felt obliged to accept an invitation to go to see him. As a result of this interview, he accepted appointment as President of the Italian Academy, a purely symbolic expression of his allegiance, with no political significance. In January 1944, having stipulated that he must be allowed to choose his contributors freely without inquiry into their politics as long as they were not actively opposed to the Fascist government, he became editor of the *Nuova antologia.* His hope was that by appealing to the common heritage of Italian culture he might be able to do something, however little, to heal the breach in the national consciousness created by the civil war. He urged the same policy of 'pacification of hearts' in the interest of national unity on the government itself.

On 15 April 1944, as he was returning from one of his periodic visits to the police authorities in Florence to intercede for some students whose political loyalties were suspect, he was assassinated by a group of four Communist partisans. The moderate wing of the Partisan movement denounced the action immediately; and for a time rumors were current that the murder was the work of Fascist extremists who feared Gentile's moderating influence. This in itself is a sufficient comment on the political futility of the act; of its moral obliquity, no one who has studied Gentile's works and his career as intently as the present writer can yet speak with the calm of a historian. It is best, therefore, to be silent, and end by recording that as a result of direct intervention by Mussolini, his body was buried in Santa Croce.

The Study and Influence of Gentile in the Anglo-Saxon World

The Influence of Gentile in England

Actual idealism has had its students and even, here and there, an occasional adherent in the English-speaking world. But it has never been, except momentarily in the last work of Bernard Bosanquet, part of "the public domain of philosophical discussion in England"—still less in America.[6] For the most part those who have chosen to study it have either been historians, political scientists, or educational theorists, and not professional philosophers at all; or else if they were philosophers they have paid the price of their interest by alienation from the normal concerns of the great mass of their professional colleagues. Like heretics everywhere they have even tended to accentuate this alienation, and to exhibit it as if it were a badge of honor. This tendency was very apparent, for example, in the work of Collingwood, who was by far the most important and most powerful thinker to be influenced by Italian idealism.

Of course, this condition of alienation, of emotional and even at times obscurantist revolt and reaction against the prevailing temper of English philosophy, has been an abiding characteristic of the idealist tradition in England ever since the Renaissance. The "Platonic tradition in England," as Muirhead called it, was never quite snuffed out; and had Collingwood lived to fulfill his early promise, the Italian followers of Spaventa might have seen the 'circulation of European philosophy' confirmed in a new instance, by the return from Oxford of a clarified and enriched tradition

---

[6] The phrase is borrowed from J. A. Passmore's *One Hundred Years of Philosophy*, London, Duckworth, 1957, p. 7. An examination of this work will give a very fair idea of what an obscure footnote to the history of Anglo-Saxon philosophy the present essay is likely to be. It should be noted that Passmore's virtually complete neglect of Italian philosophy in his book is not the result of ignorance. The few reviews of Italian books in the *Australasian Journal* have come mainly from his pen. See especially the review of Barié: *La spiritualità dell'essere e Leibniz, Australasian Journal of Psychology and Philosophy*, XII, 1935, 236–39, for his appreciation of the varying currents in Italian idealism.

which in the first instance passed from the Florentine Academy to Cambridge. The steady disintegration of European culture since 1914 seems now to have proceeded so far that we must abandon all hope of such a consummation in the foreseeable future.

We can now see that this catastrophe had already begun by the time that actual idealism was born; but certainly the time could hardly have been more propitious for its reception in England at least. The normally recessive idealist tradition was momentarily dominant; but it was already on the retreat before the attacks of native empiricism—reborn in the form of linguistic analysis partly as a result of the verbal quibbling of the idealists themselves— so that it was quite ready to welcome reinforcement from any friendly quarter. Even at Oxford, the center of the movement, the third generation of idealists, those who had grown up under the tutelage of Bradley and Bosanquet, were dissatisfied with what their teachers had to offer. The most obvious source of their discomfort lay in the fact that, after fifty years of polemic, the problem of evolution presented itself at last in a form which even religious thinkers could no longer simply reject or evade. This was especially clear in the work of Bergson, but also in the pragmatists and modernists. The younger idealists could no longer be content to say with their masters that time was 'unreal'; and hence they were very ready to embrace a form of idealism which took its stand upon the fundamental historicity of things.

J. A. Smith, who became Professor of Metaphysics at Oxford in 1910, provides a typical example of this unrest. For him the discovery of Croce's works, while on holiday in Naples just before his election, was a turning point. He found subsequently in Gentile a solution for the problems which continued to trouble him in Croce's 'philosophy of the Spirit'; and from his inaugural lecture until his death in 1935 he remained a loyal follower of his Italian masters, especially Gentile. Presumably because he felt he had little to add to what they had already said, he published little, and then usually only where the choice did not rest with him, since publication was an inevitable corollary of his consent to read a certain paper or deliver a certain lecture.

His inaugural lecture on "Knowing and Acting" was, as he himself says, composed under the influence of Croce (12d, p. 231). But on 1 December 1913 he read a paper to the Aristotelian Society "On Feeling" (12a) which is the earliest example that I have discovered of Gentile's influence upon an English thinker.[7] He endeavors in it to reduce Croce's 'circle' of the four forms of the spirit to unity, through an analysis of the concept of 'feeling' (understood as that which is "essentially either-pleasant-or-painful," 12a, p. 51) which is clearly Gentilian in origin, though Gentile's name is not mentioned, and the first volume of the *Sommario di pedagogia* from which he must have derived his inspiration had been published only a few months previously. It is notable, however, that he defends the Gentilian claim that "Pleasure *is* Feeling, and Pain not Feeling but its opposite" by appealing to the Anglo-Hegelian (or Platonic) conception of 'reality' as equivalent to rational coherence. He appears to admit this as the fundamental or absolute sense of the term, alongside the dialectical sense in which the word 'real' has what he calls "a modified and relative meaning, which includes a modified and relative unreality" (12a, p. 74). Thus, his position is that of a mediator, not merely between Croce and Gentile, but between English and Italian idealism.

In 1916 he delivered two popular lectures on the 'idea of progress' which were immediately published. The first of these, on "Progress in Philosophy," was certainly inspired by Gentile's conception of the history of philosophy, but it was couched in such

---

[7] The earliest reference to Gentile in English was in a 1909 review by the Scottish scholar J. L. McIntyre of his work in the field of Bruno studies (95). The earliest *explicit* reference to his actual idealism was in an article by J. A. Smith for the *Quarterly Review* for April 1916 (CCXXV, 295–96), i.e. more than two years after the article here discussed. The passage is as follows:

"It is only of late that the philosophic thought of Italy has attracted much attention outside its native land. That attention may, as far as England is concerned, be said to be slight and as yet directed to writers of some interest but no great originality. But the forecast may be ventured that in time there will not fail to be discovery of that important movement of thought in Southern Italy, the freshness and vitality of which is partly hidden by its acknowledged derivation from the great German idealisms of the early 19th Century. The systematic 'Philosophy of the Spirit,' to which Benedetto Croce has given so full an expression, and the profounder though as yet somewhat formless or inarticulate 'Absolute Idealism' of Giovanni Gentile cannot long pass without recognition and study by those among us who are on the watch for help towards the deeper explanation of our present experience of man and his world."

The "writers of some interest but no great originality" here referred to are probably Aliotta (*La reazione idealistica,* translated as *The Idealistic Reaction Against Science,* 1914) and Varisco (*I massimi problemi,* translated as *The Great Problems,* 1914, and *Conosci te stesso,* as *Know Thyself,* 1915). In making his forecast Smith probably knew that Collingwood and Hannay had begun their translation of De Ruggiero's *La filosofia contemporanea* before the war (11).

general terms that almost any Hegelian could have written it (12b). But the second, on "Progress as an Ideal of Action," is much more distinctive. Having first shown that the evolutionary conception of progress in nature cannot be an ideal because if it exists it must of necessity impose itself on us as a *fact*, Smith proceeds to defend the conception of progress as an ideal of action "wholly and solely of our own making, the very thought of it self-begotten in our mind, every step to its actual existence the self-created deed of our own will" (12c, p. 301). Anticipating the objection, which Bosanquet was later to make in print against the 'new idealism,' that a progress *ad infinitum* is absurd (see 14, pp. 53 ff., 119 ff.), he takes the view that the self-realization of the spirit is a process which is at the same time a fulfillment. But again, the tendency to regard 'ideals' as having some kind of Platonic reality of their own is apparent; and there are even hints of a compromise with Bergsonian or evolutionary theism when he insists that the "Progress within us" must be congruent with "the Progress which is achieved in the Universe," or that we must 'imitate' the universal spirit (12c, pp. 308–9).

His paper for the Aristotelian Society in January 1920, specifically concerned with "The Philosophy of Giovanni Gentile," gives evidence of the thoroughness with which J. A. Smith had studied Gentile's published writings down to that time. He traces Gentile's early career, and rightly stresses the double origin of his speculation in the theoretical study of the history of philosophy on one side, and in his practical experience as a teacher and educational planner on the other. But he insists that Gentile's pedagogical concerns determined "rather the form than the substance of Gentile's thought." The 'substance' of the doctrine seems to have been for him a monism so absolute that the personality of the individual thinker was completely lost and dissolved in it (cf. 12f, pp. 16–17). His own idealism ends in a kind of mystical union which certainly deserves the label of *filosofia teologizzante*.

The existence of a conscious 'leap of faith' in all of his arguments, at the crucial point where the absolute unity of the spirit is asserted, seems to have led Smith to a conception of the philosopher's task that was very different from that of Gentile. In his own summing up (12d) he offers his philosophy as a system of "presumptions and presuppositions," "a doctrine concerning what is in itself unknown and unknowable, the inward and secret essence of Mind." His 'presumptions' are for the most part theses

which in Gentile's 'philosophy without presuppositions' are dialectical *conclusions*—that reality is a historical process but that
this process itself is eternal, that history is spiritual, etc.—but in
some places the transcendent character of his presupposed 'logos'
is apparent. Thus spirituality manifests itself "most freely and fully"
(but not, we infer, uniquely) in self-consciousness; and "Mind
. . . *as the representative of the spirit of the whole*, at once knows
and creates whatever in any sense is. Hence it at once creates and
knows all minds, and in so doing imparts to them its nature which
then is theirs" (12d, p. 243; my italics). The language here is more
akin to that of Coleridge and T. H. Green than to the strict humanism of Gentile.

Smith was perhaps closer than he realized to the final position
of Bosanquet; and if he chose to make himself the champion of
the 'new idealism' while Bosanquet set himself against it, we might
argue that this was only because the older man understood it better.[8]
Bosanquet reviewed Gentile's *Pedagogia* and his *Riforma della
dialettica* in 1920; and the *Teoria generale* (the third edition which
Wildon Carr promptly translated) as well as the *Discorsi di religione* in 1921. About the first two he said: "I differ from Prof. Smith
with the greatest hesitation and reluctance; but I must set down
the fact that as in Croce, so in Gentile . . . I am continually shocked
by what seems to me to be overstraining of undeniable truth—the
conversion of familiar platitudes into untenable paradoxes" (96–97,
p. 369). His fundamental objection was that "The conception of a
self-creative progressive real, which is pure thinking, destroys all
meaning in 'the whole'"; and he felt that if Smith was right in
claiming that 'the whole' is to be found in a thought that belongs
to the 'we' (cf. 12, pp. 77–78), "*this* is an implicit real, and the
'attualità' of the 'atto puro' is gone." Reading the *Teoria generale*
and the *Discorsi* he became convinced that Smith was right, that
Gentile's transcendental Ego was a 'group-mind' and that "the
mind and institutions of a group" with which we are in living unity
were not to be counted as presuppositions. This "emphasis on the
'We'" enabled Bosanquet to "understand in some degree . . . how
it is possible for him to refer, as it seems, the very universe itself
to the creative fact of our will and the process of our cognition"

---

[8] We should note that Smith, although fifteen years younger than Bosanquet,
was still twelve years older than Gentile.

(98a, p. 101). But he held that "from the position here recognized, that of the group-mind and communal life, an argument, we think, will run back and incorporate with our living real, all that transcends, not our experience, but only our immediacy—Plato's Forms, and Nature, and the logical idea, and the living and immanent Good" (98a, p. 99).

The link for Bosanquet's 'argument' was provided by the "mode of participation by which Gentile has explained how the finite spirit is linked with the group-mind." Gentile would have objected, of course, that he did not intend the relation between transcendental and empirical ego to be understood as a kind of Platonic 'participation.' But Bosanquet's mistake points up the necessity in actual idealism for *some* bridge between the individual and the community—a requirement which was only finally met in *Genesis and Structure of Society*.

Bosanquet's main complaints against actual idealism were two: first, that by confusing 'transcendence of experience' with 'transcendence of immediacy' it threatened to become an irrational activism; and second, that it exalted the moral point of view to the total exclusion of religion. These fundamental criticisms were repeated and developed in his last book, *The Meeting of Extremes in Contemporary Philosophy* (14). The 'meeting of extremes' referred to was in the first instance "the really startling difference and agreement between the Italian neo-idealists . . . and the English and American neo-realists" (p. viii); but in the argument of the book he is much concerned to see how far there can be a 'meeting' between the 'old' idealism (i.e. the 'absolutism' of Bradley and himself) and the 'new' extremes. The bringing together of philosophers whose aims and problems differ so widely results at times in merely verbal identities and mistaken criticisms, but since Bosanquet, in his care and sympathy, was almost a model critic, the confrontation is for the most part enlightening.[9]

On the first issue concerning the 'transcendence of immediacy' we might say that Smith, who grasped the eternal character of *pensiero pensante*, understood Gentile better. But the things that troubled Bosanquet, the 'narrow humanism,' the rejection of the Platonic forms, and still more the rejection, or at any rate devalua-

---

[9] Smith himself, with a clear recognition of the ultimate ambiguities involved, attempted to come to terms with Alexander's theory of space-time (12e); and Wildon Carr likewise worked for a 'meeting of extremes.'

tion, of nature, were consequences of Gentile's view which, as we have seen, Smith himself tried to evade. On the second issue, there can be no doubt that Bosanquet saw more clearly than Smith that acceptance of 'progressism' involves a preference for "the ethical as distinct from the religious attitude." He called this preference "one-sided" (14, p. 100) and insisted that the notion of endless moral progress was a contradiction. But since his own absolute is 'changeless' and timeless, it is hard to see how it can help us to escape from the 'one-sided' morality of our human condition. One thing that emerges from his discussion is that we cannot, in fact, compromise or hold a balance between the moral and the religious attitude. Bosanquet complains bitterly about the injustice of Gentile's treatment of mysticism. But his own Absolute has (verbally) all the characteristics of Gentile's Objective moment, and evades Gentile's criticism—if it does evade it—by being (verbally) excluded from the realm of actual existence, which is all that Gentile is concerned with, and all that, as mere men with human lives to lead, we *can* be concerned with.

The lead given by Bosanquet was followed by another primarily religious thinker, W. G. De Burgh. He was more sympathetic to historicism than Bosanquet, but he could not accept the identification of history with philosophy; and Gentile's claim that actual thinking creates being was too much for him. After the most careful and sympathetic presentation of Gentile's thesis that one could ask for within the space of a few pages, he proceeded to a searching critique of the transcendental Ego, uncovering a whole series of difficulties and inconsistencies, all of them rooted in "Gentile's identification of the Spirit with the present act of human thinking": "That there is truth in Gentile's analysis, if we confine ourselves to the actual facts of human knowing, is undeniable. . . . The only relevant criticism is that it proves on examination to be unintelligible. We have seen that Gentile fails to explain the relation of the empirical to the universal Ego, or to give a clear answer to the question: Who, in this concrete act of thinking, can truly be said to think? . . ." (22, p. 22). He recognized that Gentile claimed to solve this problem by admitting a 'concrete' multiplicity within the transcendental Ego but he found this "intrusion of the *Noi* . . . intolerably ambiguous. . . . The identification . . . must be complete; else the Spirit is transcendent of the act of thinking and has lost its title to the name *Io*" (22, p. 11). Thus, like Bosanquet, he put his finger on the difficulty that is not fully resolved until *Genesis and Structure of Society.*

Before we pass on to Collingwood and his contemporaries, there is one other figure among the elder generation of philosophers whom we must consider: Herbert Wildon Carr. Wildon Carr was a businessman who became an enthusiastic member of the London Aristotelian Society within a year or so of its very humble and nonprofessional beginnings, and whose imagination was caught by the ferment in scientific thought in the first decade of this century. He became one of the first English expositors of Bergson's philosophy and subsequently of Croce (with whose work he first became acquainted in 1908–9). After the war he shed his amateur status, becoming a professor at London in 1918; he now turned his attention largely to the philosophic implications of Einstein's relativity theory, and began to publish and expound a pluralistic idealism or 'monadology' of his own in which the different strands of evolutionism, historicism, and relativity theory were interwoven. But even while working on his own *Theory of Monads* (1922) he turned aside to make a very good translation of Gentile's *Theory of Mind as Pure Act.* The extent of Gentile's influence on a mind open to such disparate currents of thought is hard to estimate. But we can fairly say that his whole conception of the individual or monad is typically Gentilian. He himself in his own final sketch of his system declared: "While my theory of knowledge is idealistic, *and even solipsistic,* my theory of existence is vitalistic." [10] This characterization, so far as I can judge, is accurate; and the qualification that I have italicized is intended, beyond a doubt, to point to actual idealism.

The most important philosopher influenced by actual idealism was Robin George Collingwood. He was, indeed, the only English philosopher of his generation, the generation after Whitehead and Alexander, Russell and Moore, to approach greatness. It would be impossible within the scope of a few pages to give a complete account and a just estimate of his debt to Gentile (and to Croce) even if their influence were fully documented in his published works; and in fact it is not. Gentile's name does not occur in any one of his books, though there is one reference to the theory of

---

[10] *Cogitans Cogitata,* London, Favil Press, 1930, p. xi.

mind as 'pure act' in *The New Leviathan* which was, in order of writing, the last of them. Croce is fairly treated in *The Idea of History*, but in *The Principles of Art* he is mentioned only once in a footnote, as guilty of an error in the interpretation of Plato. Worse still, Collingwood maintains absolute silence about Italian influences upon his thought in his *Autobiography*, and even represents his personal friend and immediate predecessor as Professor of Metaphysics, J. A. Smith, as an idealist of the 'old school.' This fact seems to me to invalidate any hypothesis that would exonerate him from a charge of deliberate concealment.[11]

Oddly enough, the only result of his silence has been to leave him completely isolated and hence very easy to ignore. Deliberately and of set purpose he severed his own work from the philosophical discussions of his colleagues in which he joined only socratically, that is, as one having no doctrine of his own.[12] His further failure to relate his work explicitly and accurately to the Italian tradition to which it owed so much left no incentive for Italian students to read him, and made it tempting for the few English students who knew something of his sources to believe that he was trying to conceal the fact that he really did have no doctrine of his own.[13] So far no one among his few admirers has attempted to set the record in the *Autobiography* straight.[14] Here I can do no more than offer a few surmises about the picture that will result when this is done.

His *Autobiography* presents us with a picture of the young Collingwood becoming dissatisfied with the 'realism' of Cook Wilson and his other teachers, as a result of his training in archaeology—then still in its infancy as a truly historical discipline. But we need only remark that his first published labors in philosophy were translations of Croce's book on Vico and De Ruggiero's *Filosofia con-*

---

[11] We cannot grant, therefore, that his *Autobiography* is, as he pretends, *un livre de bon foi.*

[12] In G. J. Warnock's recent *British Philosophy Since 1900* his name does not even appear. He is forgotten by the new generation even in the college (Magdalen) where he held his professorship!

[13] *Experto crede.* What I say here is in large measure intended as a palinode for years of neglect, and unfair depreciation of Collingwood on my own part.

[14] To do this requires, of course, a knowledge of Italian thought as deep as Collingwood's own, which perhaps none of his English defenders have possessed. The only essay on the subject by an Italian pen is, as far as I know, that of De Ruggiero in *Filosofi del novecento*, which deals only with *Speculum Mentis* and is radically vitiated by the author's prejudice against Gentile.

temporanea [15] in order to see that his dissatisfaction and his growing concern with historical knowledge were nourished from theoretical as well as practical sources.

His first book, *Religion and Philosophy* (1916), was completed
before the war, so that it must have been written while he was
working on the translations. It is an interesting blend of the 'old'
idealism and the 'new,' with the native tradition predominating.
The forms of argument are often reminiscent of Gentile but the
positions defended and conclusions reached are closer to those of
Bosanquet and H. H. Joachim. Thus religion is identified on the
theoretical side with theology, theology is then identified with
philosophy, and philosophy with history. In the process one is often
reminded of Gentile's reduction of everything that he touched to
philosophy; but here it is religion that is regarded as the most concrete term. The purely immanent conception of God is flatly rejected; but so is the view, to which Bradley and Bosanquet appear
to give countenance, that the religious attitude transcends morality; and the explanations of error and evil offered are brilliantly
plausible interpretations of views which in Gentile's work before
1914 were expressed only in abrupt paradoxical paragraphs and
aphorisms. Indeed, the 'elimination of error by truth' (and of
evil by good, together with the associated theory of punishment
and forgiveness) were perhaps never as clearly expounded, or as
persuasively argued, by Gentile as they are here by Collingwood;
and the reason is that Collingwood utilizes the logical tradition
of Anglo-idealism that culminates in Joachim's *The Nature of Truth*.
The 'coherence theory of truth' is in a sense common ground between the two traditions; but in the English writers it is largely
divorced from the conception of thought as dialectical contradiction, the 'power of the negative.' As a result the conception of
truth in English idealism tends to be somewhat static or Platonic.
Collingwood's marriage of the two traditions gives Gentile's paradoxes the systematic background required for intelligibility, and
at the same time endows the 'coherent whole' with a genuinely
dynamic, *progressive* character.

The influence of the 'new idealism' on Collingwood's mind gradually increased in the succeeding years until in his second book,

---

[15] This was not published until 1921 (11); but it was at least *begun* before
the war.

Speculum Mentis (1924), it was unmistakably dominant.[16] In January 1921 he published an article on "Croce's Philosophy of History" in which he found Croce guilty of combining a naturalistic philosophy with a truly idealistic conception of history. He added that Croce seemed to be "not a little indebted" to Gentile for the idealistic strain in his thought, and expressed the hope that through his "desertion of philosophy for history" he might "reach the point of absolute idealism to which his successors Gentile and De Ruggiero have already carried his thought." [17] This paper was followed by another at a philosophical congress in August 1923, explaining the relation between philosophy and mysticism in Gentile and in particular defending 'actual idealism' against Bosanquet's imputation that it was a 'philosophy of change' (15, pp. 161–75). The exposition of Gentile, though necessarily very brief, illuminates his position with a clarity and an avoidance of merely verbal issues that is hardly to be found elsewhere; and Collingwood derives from it a "programme" for "modern idealistic philosophy" which is clearly taken up in *Speculum Mentis,* which he must at this time have virtually completed.

Speculum Mentis or *The Map of Knowledge* is a phenomenological study of the growth of the spirit through five phases: Art, Religion, Science, History, and Philosophy. Each phase is developed to the point at which through the manifestation of its inadequacy it generates its successor; and this process of development is held to occur in the history of European culture as well as in the life of the individual. From this point of view the book seems to resemble most nearly Vico's *New Science* and Hegel's *Phenomenology.* Further, Collingwood claims that the phases are autonomous as 'lives'; and in this way he accounts for the mutual hostility of artist,

---

[16] Collingwood seems to have feared—not without good reason—that if he acknowledged this, his book would be dismissed without the critical examination it deserved. His Preface contains a half-denial that is an implicit confession: "if the reader feels that my thesis reminds him of things that other people have said, I shall not be disappointed: on the contrary, what will really disappoint me is to be treated as the vendor of new-fangled paradoxes and given some silly name like that of 'New Idealist' " (p. 13).

[17] *Hibbert Journal,* XIX, 1920/21, 276, 278. This article forms a companion piece to that of Romolo Murri, "Religion and Idealism as Presented by Giovanni Gentile" (13), which precedes it in the same issue. It is the one and only place in which Gentile's influence on Croce is explicitly referred to in English. The general assumption was, and continued to be, that Gentile was the most gifted 'follower' of Croce.

man of faith, scientist, etc. Here we may perhaps detect the influence of Croce.

But when he faces the question of why there should be just these five forms of experience, Collingwood seems inclined to say that his 'quincunx' is only an empirically convenient selection from the infinite number of categories applicable to experience. This echo of Gentile makes nonsense both of their 'autonomy' and of Collingwood's careful logical-historical deduction of their unity; and his uneasiness on the point is strong enough to prevent him from adequately developing the application of the quincunx to European cultural history, which because of its extreme sketchiness appears unduly 'forced.' The actual account of the five phases is a blending of Crocean and Gentilian arguments; and when we examine the quincunx more carefully we discover that it is really a doubling of Gentile's absolute triad thus:

Art (Subjective or imaginative and 'supposing' moment)
Religion (Objective or 'assertive' moment)
Knowledge (Subjective or questioning moment—Science)
      (Objective or answering moment—History)
      (Absolute synthesis—Philosophy)

What is genuinely novel in the book is the analysis of the 'act of thinking' as a dialectic not of subject and object, but of question and answer. This became the foundation of most of Collingwood's later work.[18] In *Speculum Mentis* it makes it possible for him to treat many views with sympathy, which Croce and Gentile either flatly contradict or simply ignore—especially in the field of science and scientific or dogmatic philosophy.

The following years were given over mainly to work on the archaeology and inscriptions of Roman Britain, and when Collingwood turns again to philosophy in the *Essay on Philosophical Method* (1933) Italian influence is no longer apparent on the surface. But, as Passmore points out,[19] the task and method proposed for philosophy—to discover the ideal form by reference to which the imperfect embodiment of a concept can be 'placed' on a 'scale of forms'[20]—is exemplified in *Speculum Mentis*. We should also

---

[18] In his *Autobiography* he claims to have developed his logic of question and answer in a manuscript of 1917; having made this claim he destroyed the manuscript.

[19] *Op. cit.*, p. 306.

[20] The contrast of the 'method of science' with the 'method of philosophy'

notice that the first application of his new 'method' was in *The Idea of Nature* (lectures 1934, published 1945); this was then followed by *The Idea of History* (lectures 1936, published 1946) and the *Essay on Metaphysics* (1940). The *Principles of Art* (1938) intervened, and we might say that religion in its most self-conscious form, i.e. theology, is dealt with in the *Essay on Metaphysics*. The pattern of the quincunx is surely unmistakable.

If now we look at these later works as in some sense the fulfillment of a program provided by *Speculum Mentis,* the apparent absence of Italian influence in some of them becomes explicable almost to the point of being explained away. Croce and Gentile had, as their critics among the English idealists complained, no concrete conception of nature and no sympathy for naturalistic philosophy. For them the word 'nature' meant the Newtonian-mechanical world view which was received into dialectical idealism at its inception by Kant and Fichte. Collingwood set himself against this unhistorical abstraction even as early as *Religion and Philosophy.* From his appreciation there of the continuity between spiritual idealism and the 'higher materialism,' it was a simple step to the recognition that though 'nature' itself can hardly have a history, the 'idea of nature' certainly does. Thus we might surmise that having arrived in *Speculum Mentis* at a Gentilian 'philosophy without presuppositions,' he conceived it to be the proper task of that philosophy to re-examine and reconcile to itself ("place on the scale of forms") the various phases of experience which involve presuppositions. For this purpose his conception of the act of thinking as a dialectic of question and answer was ideally suited. He sought to complement Gentile's essentially negative critique of experience with its appropriate positive counterpart.[21] Whether this hypothesis is his-

---

makes the *Essay on Philosophical Method* a distant cousin of Gentile's *Logic.* But in Collingwood's 'concrete logic' the unity of opposites is achieved through conceptions like 'continuity' and 'overlapping'—typical of Anglo-idealism—rather than through dialectical synthesis as in the orthodox Hegelian tradition.

[21] Even in history—where the attitude of Croce and Gentile may seem far from negative—the contrast is there. Collingwood explicated the Gentilian thesis that "all history is the history of thought" by applying it to archaeology, whereas Croce and Gentile seem to have concluded from it that the proper business of the historian is the history of higher intellectual culture. The truth in Collingwood's account of his development in the *Autobiography* lies in the fact that his archaeological experience taught him the correct, fully concrete significance of the doctrines he found in the Italians.

torically correct or not, it does, I think, represent correctly the ideal relation between them.

The *Autobiography* and *The New Leviathan* represent a new departure arising from the pressure of political events. Once more the starting point was Gentilian. The *Autobiography* shows how the concrete significance of his doctrine of the 'unity of thought and action' only began to come home to Collingwood during the Spanish Civil War. In *The New Leviathan* he continues the attempt begun in the *Principles of Art* to provide a positive evaluation from the point of view of actual consciousness of the revolution in psychology associated with the name of Freud. The dry bones of the dialectic of sense experience in the first volume of Gentile's *Pedagogia* were thereby developed and enriched almost as much as his abstract concept of nature had been earlier. Collingwood makes an oblique reference to the source of his inspiration and indicates his attitude toward it when he says:

A study of mind on the historical method . . . renounces with Locke all 'science of substance'. It does not ask what mind is, it asks only what mind does [9:16].

You can have your cake and eat it too by holding that mind is 'pure act', so that the question *what mind is* resolves itself without residue into the question *what mind does;* but whether this is defensible I shall not ask [9:17].

But in point of fact he has already made this resolution, for in his first chapter he stipulates that "Man as mind is *whatever he is conscious of being*" (1:84). All that he wished to reject, or at least to leave aside, was the metaphysical, semitheological, interpretation of the 'pure act.' For him the theory was not in itself a kind of absolute knowledge, but a method for the study and clarification of human experience. The kinship of his 'method' to that of Gentile is more apparent than usual in his analysis of human society, because he allows the dialectical opposition and synthesis of 'force' and 'reason' to coexist beside and indeed to preponderate over the gradualism proper to his own 'scale of forms.' This confusion was probably produced by the violence of his own political 'conversion'; and although it makes his doctrine harder to grasp at times, it does make it easier for us to perceive the process of its genesis.

An account of social experience explicitly modeled on the Anglo-idealist "coherence theory of truth" was given by H. J. Paton in

The Good Will (1927),[22] which was subtitled "A Study in the Coherence Theory of Goodness." J. A. Smith was Paton's tutor, and in his Preface he acknowledged his debt to Italian idealism thus:

Among foreign writers I am much indebted to Monsieur Bergson, and still more to Signor Croce and Signor Gentile, the two pioneers of modern Italian idealism. In many passages I am either consciously agreeing or consciously disagreeing with one or other of these two writers, and it may be that this has made my thinking in some places a little obscure; but I believe that much of what value my book may have is derived from them, and also that my agreement with them goes very much deeper than my disagreement.

Having made this general acknowledgment he hardly mentions names in the course of the book. But his conception of the self and of thought are Gentilian,[23] and he even stands for a moment on the verge of the doctrine of transcendental society:

. . . it is probable that we become aware of ourselves only as we become aware of others. It is at least questionable whether there could be a self, that is a self-conscious self, except in a society. What we begin with must be a whole within which self and world, myself and other selves become gradually discriminated. And *as we develop there is still a sense in which we are the whole within which we make the distinctions of subject and object, of myself and other selves.* But these high matters are not our concern. . . .[24]

Paton avoided "these high matters" because he was anxious to show that the coherence theory of goodness could stand on its own feet, and did not depend on an idealistic theory of experience. He seems to have accepted the 'method of immanence' himself, but his desire to let sleeping dogs lie caused him to stop short in applying it, as soon as he was sure that he had established the practical point he wished to make. For instance, he stigmatizes statements which "postulate entities outside of the actual process of living" as "mythological"; but he does not mind putting things 'mythologically' himself to make things easier for his readers.[25] In the end, however, he

---

[22] This book, which seems to have been the swan song of the Anglo-Hegelians —and no unworthy one—is one of the few important publications that escaped the notice of Passmore, who discusses only Paton's later Kantian studies. Paton devoted himself to Kant as the other survivor, G. R. G. Mure, did to Hegel. Mure apparently found Croce interesting but not Gentile (cf. *A Study of Hegel's Logic*, Oxford, Clarendon, 1950, p. 348, and 108b).

[23] See *The Good Will*, London, Allen and Unwin, 1927, pp. 63, 65, 72, 108; cf. "The Idea of the Self," in *University of California Publications in Philosophy*, VIII, 1926, 73–105.

[24] *The Good Will*, p. 303 (my italics); cf. p. 285.

[25] *Ibid.*, p. 166; cf. p. 115 and contrast pp. 218–25, 431–34.

does very tentatively put forward "the doctrine that reality is nothing other than the spirit itself, which overcomes the abstract antithesis of subject and object" [26] as suggested by his ethical view.

None of the English idealists felt moved to write a systematic critical study of Gentile's work or any aspect of it [27]—though J. A. Smith did expound it in courses of lectures. Only two such studies— one general and one specific—were produced in England, the first by an Italian, the second by a Frenchwoman; but in their different ways they both reflect the fundamentally religious concern which Gentile excited in all of the English thinkers whom he influenced.[28] Angelo Crespi produced a scathing critique of actual idealism from the vantage point of a rather eclectic Christian spiritualism; and Aline Lion defended 'the idealistic conception of religion' in a book remarkable for the enthusiasm lavished equally on Gentile and on the Catholic faith.

It was perhaps unfortunate that Professor Tudor Jones should have chosen Crespi to do the volume on Italy in his "Library of Contemporary Thought." An introductory survey of this sort should be made by one who is basically sympathetic to the main trend that he is surveying. But probably there was no one else who could have performed the task adequately without the assistance of a translator. In any case Crespi could not help making his work "the first attempt, in the English language, towards a systematic criticism of Italian Hegelianism" (17, p. vi). Whereas the English critics usually fastened on Gentile's denial of transcendence and his theoretical insistence on unity as premises for the deduction of unpleasant consequences, Crespi attacked from the other side. For him the basic premise was 'the union of theory and practice,' and his conclusion was that 'actualism' is synonymous with 'activism.' The

---

[26] *Ibid.*, p. 428.

[27] The only exception seems to be the three expository articles (21, 24, 60) by Miss Valmai Evans.

[28] The fact that Gentile gave more sympathetic and serious consideration to religion and theology than Croce was one of the principal reasons for the attention that was paid to him. This is reflected, for example, in the essays of Murri (13) and Pellizzi (31). Among the English only Collingwood passed on beyond the 'theological' phase, and only De Ruggiero (20) among the Italian observers presented the 'theologizing' tendency in Gentile and his 'school' as an evil.

foundation stone for his interpretation was provided by Gentile's support of Fascism, and especially by the *filosofia del manganello:*

. . . just as Actual Idealism is the celebration of Truth as consisting not in any relation between my present thinking and any past or external reality, but in the mere fact that I am by such thinking achieving a new realization of myself: so Fascism is just activity for activity's sake, the negation of any standard of truth beyond the capacity of being and doing all that one succeeds in being and doing at any moment. It is the apotheosis of immediacy, of passing impulse, of uncriticized and uncriticizable self-assertion considered as synonymous with absolute freedom [17, p. 200].

This is of course a shameful caricature of everything that Gentile lived and worked for. But anyone who wishes to defend Gentile must remember that it is not his personal beliefs and ideals but the logic of his views that is at issue. If this reflection helps him to control his feelings better than Crespi, he will find amid the welter of misunderstanding and misrepresentation some problems that deserve serious consideration.

Miss Lion, having studied with Gentile in Rome and translated the *Teoria generale dello spirito* into French (1925), went to Oxford in 1926 to write a thesis on Gentile's philosophy of religion under the guidance of J. A. Smith. Her work was published as *The Idealistic Conception of Religion: Vico, Hegel, Gentile* (33) by the University Press in 1932, with a preface by yet another Anglo-idealist, Professor C. C. J. Webb, the most prominent philosopher of religion among them. In it Gentile's attitude toward religion is traced from his essays on Marxism in 1898 to the essay on "The absolute Forms of the Spirit" (1909). The *Discorsi di religione* are then rather slightingly mentioned, but are passed over in favor of the Fascist University lecture of 1927 on "Il problema religioso in Italia." The resulting picture of Gentile's position is demonstrably inaccurate and unreliable, in spite of Miss Lion's detailed knowledge of his works, and the impression that she gives of possessing personal knowledge of his views. She allots the part of villain to Hegel for treating religion merely as an inferior form of philosophy; and her primary concern is to prove that Gentile is not tainted by this heresy. She insists rightly that for Gentile Religion is not just a phase, but an eternal moment in the dialectic of actual consciousness. But the full vindication of her thesis requires her to dismiss Gentile's argument for religious education in primary but not in secondary schools ("The Lay School," 1907) as a momentary aberration. To accept such a view would mean dismissing Gentile's whole career as an educational reformer as incoherent with his speculative theory.

The trouble arises from the fact that Miss Lion's reflections on *Il modernismo e i rapporti tra religione e filosofia* ("modernism and the relations between religion and philosophy") led her to a very definite conception of what Gentile's philosophy of religion *ought* to be. To all intents and purposes she developed the outlines of a philosophy of religion of her own, for which she sought against the weight of the evidence to give the credit to Gentile.[29] She might now claim that her work was prophetic, for Gentile certainly came closer to her position in his lecture of 1943 on "My Religion" than he was when she wrote. But even there he reaffirms the 'Hegelian' thesis of "The Lay School." On balance it seems as clear now as in 1932 that his attack on modernism was more of an aberration than the report of 1907.

The Study of Gentile in the United States

In England Gentile's speculations seriously influenced the thought of a small minority of thinkers; but precisely because the influence was genuine they preferred to state their own conclusions, rather than to summarize his for a wider audience. In the United States the case was different. Here, as far as can be seen, he influenced no one. But two factors combined to produce a steady trickle of published studies of the different aspects of his work: first, the emphasis on publication as a condition of academic advancement, and second, the existence of a large minority whose interest in Italy and things Italian was sustained by ties of blood and sentiment.

We might say that the possibility of Gentile's having any influence in America perished when Royce died at the age of sixty-one in 1916. Idealism in America was already virtually submerged in the rising tides of pragmatism and naturalism; but Royce in his last years had begun to develop a historicist philosophy of his own from premises supplied by Peirce, the acknowledged founder of pragmatism. His thought continued to be plagued by the ambiguity

---

[29] Of her reviewers, only John Laird, who had no sympathy with Gentile at all, was sufficiently knowledgeable to realize that her own position needed to be distinguished from his (33d). But then Laird had earlier written a most generous and perceptive review of the *Theory of Mind as Pure Act* (98b).

which had been remarked by critics from the beginning, arising from his religious desire for a real (transcendent) Absolute, where his philosophical reasoning would yield only a transcendental ideal. But in a semiconscious way he was an actual idealist himself, and had he lived another ten years he would have had the opportunity to face the fact and go either forward or back from it.

Inevitably one of the main centers for the study of Gentile was the Casa Italiana at Columbia University. In 1922 Dino Bigongiari translated the "Discorsi ai maestri di Trieste" for J. E. Spingarn's "Library of European Culture" (3). Gentile rewrote the first chapter and Croce contributed a valuable introduction; but the book passed unnoticed in philosophical and educational journals. The philosophy of education is scarcely even a Cinderella in the minds of Anglo-Saxon philosophers. Only in the *Church Quarterly Review* (London), and after an interval of four years, was it finally submitted to friendly but searching criticism by a practicing secondary-school teacher (45). The translation is a little freer than Wildon Carr's *Theory of Mind as Pure Act*, but as an introduction to Gentile it cannot be bettered.

In the United States, even the *Theory of Mind as Pure Act* had to wait until 1926[30] to receive the attention of a competent judge in the *Journal of Philosophy*. Boas' article on "Gentile and the Hegelian Invasion of Italy" (18) was presented by the editors as "a review of several recent translations of Gentile's works"; but only the English and French translations of the *Teoria generale* were mentioned, together with Spirito's *L'idealismo italiano*. It was not really a review at all, but an attempt to characterize the new idealism, and to decide why it had taken Italy by storm. Boas, like Crespi, found the key in Gentile's association with Fascism; and unlike Crespi he cannot be dismissed as a prejudiced witness when he calls Gentile's philosophy "the latest incarnation of the Scotistic will" (18a, p. 428).

The trickle of academic studies began at Columbia in 1929 with P. M. Riccio's doctoral thesis, rather misleadingly entitled *On the*

---

[30] By which time its fame had even reached Australia, where it was carefully analyzed and criticized from a psychological point of view by A. C. Garnett, now a professor at the University of Wisconsin (19). His criticism of Gentile's conception of evil seems to foreshadow Collingwood's 'scale of forms' (though the terms in which it was couched had already been criticized by Collingwood in *Religion and Philosophy*).

Threshold of Fascism (23). The book is dedicated to Bigongiari, and is in fact a study of the cultural ferment in Italy before 1914, focused especially on the review *La voce*. The relations of Croce and Gentile with the *Voce* group are discussed in an incidental way, but a whole chapter is given over to the "agitation for educational reform," ending with a brief account of the reform itself. The 'Fascism' of which we are 'on the threshold' is very clearly the fascism of optimistic idealists like Gentile; and despite his own youthful enthusiasm and the inevitable overstraining of the links between *La voce* and Mussolini, the author did half recognize that the revolution was still more a hope than a reality. He was careful not to misrepresent the ambiguous and uncertain attitude of Prezzolini himself toward the new movement. Thus, though there are signs of distorted judgment he cannot justly be accused of propagandist bias.

Apart from its Italian connections, Columbia University was also the center from which John Dewey's enormous influence radiated over the whole sphere of social studies. The experimentalists had naturally little sympathy with the idealist tradition from which they considered themselves emancipated, and the virtual monopoly which they have to a great extent maintained to this day in the philosophy of education was one of the more important reasons why so little attention was paid to Gentile's philosophy of education.[31] It was therefore not from New York but from Los Angeles that the only serious study of Gentile's educational philosophy was to come. After the death of Royce, Boston and Los Angeles were the only places in which actual idealism might possibly have hoped for a sympathetic hearing. In these two centers, and especially in the latter, the tradition of 'personalism' deriving mainly from the work of B. P. Bowne (1847–1910) has continued down to the present day.

---

[31] Although they had little interest in opposing *theories*, the experimentalists were always curious about *practical* experiments of all kinds, and the various Fascist innovations came in for a due share of their attention. Insofar as their studies touched on Gentile's practical career and achievements they will be dealt with in the next section. But we must notice here the good work done by Kandel, as editor of the *Educational Yearbook* of the International Institute of Columbia University Teachers College, in presenting American educationists with authoritative accounts of the philosophical and historical antecedents of the Gentile reform, written by the reformers themselves (40, 49, 51, 56, 67, 69, 71). (Professor G. N. G. Orsini of the Department of Comparative Literature at the University of Wisconsin has recently drawn my attention to the quite sympathetic and acute criticism of the *Theory of Mind as Pure Act* in Charles Morris' *Six Theories of Mind* (24 bis, pp. 88–101). Since Morris was one of the most important pupils of G. H. Mead, it cannot be said that *all* instrumentalists were indifferent to the theoretical issues of actual idealism.)

The hope was a slender one, however, for Bowne's personalism was a pluralistic or monadic idealism which derived its inspiration from Lotze rather than from Fichte or Hegel, and his theology was in all essentials a traditional Christian theism consciously and deliberately opposed to all forms of Hegelian absolutism. The fact that the Italian correspondent of the *Personalist* was the Catholic theologian Mario Puglisi did not help matters.[32] When Italian idealism was at last presented to them through the mouth of Wildon Carr, who found a sympathetic audience for his own monadism at Los Angeles in his last years after his tenure of the professorship at London ended, the leaders of the group were unimpressed.

It is possible, however, that M. M. Thompson's doctoral thesis on *The Educational Philosophy of Giovanni Gentile* was a legacy or result of Wildon Carr's influence.[33] Against this hypothesis we must set the fact that Thompson's understanding of Gentile's idealism is not very deep, or to put it more accurately, not very secure. He approaches Gentile from three points of view which he calls the 'practical' (through study of the Gentile reform), the 'historical' (though study of the history of philosophy), and the 'social' (through study of Gentile's Fascism). But in his first approach he does not see the need to distinguish Gentile's work from that of his successors; and his second merely reveals his lack of the necessary equipment for the task. He specifically renounces any attempt at detailed criticism, and when he proceeds to analyze the *Sommario di pedagogia*[34] he does not ask how far the theory is consistent

---

[32] Puglisi himself contributed to the American *Journal of Religion* an article on "Religious Teaching in Italian Schools" (37) which, though it gave a useful account of the tradition that formed Gentile's attitude, shamefully misrepresented Gentile's own position. In his survey of "The Present State of Philosophy in Italy" for the *Personalist* in 1924 he discussed the school of De Sarlo and the Neo-Scholastics before coming to the Idealists. Having confessed that "today there is not a single young man of culture who, although no disciple of Gentile, fails to keep in touch with the latter's mode of thought," he went on to claim that "Gentile's system has suppressed every distinction between good and evil, and remains outside every religious or irreligious category" (37a, pp. 166–67). How much more fortunate were the English idealists in having men like Murri and Pellizzi as their informants!

[33] Thompson did his work not in the school of philosophy but in education, and Wildon Carr was dead before he can have well begun. But his connection with the personalist school is clear. For years now he has been making heroic efforts to survey the whole range of philosophical publications in Italian and Spanish for the readers of the *Personalist*.

[34] A ninety-page analytical summary of the *Sommario* is given in an appendix to his work. This method of treatment emphasizes the arid logic of much of Gentile's argument, and loses the concreteness of living experience which so

with the reform or with the Fascism that he has examined. Every-thing—the *Sommario,* Fascist propaganda by Gentile and others, the statements of critics, etc.—is carefully recorded on the same plane. The result is that when he comes at the end to state in sum-mary form eleven points of appreciation and criticism, his genuine insights—for his is clearly a labor of love and he has moments of real vision—are found embedded in a background of misunderstand-ings and false premises.

Thompson's very awareness of his limitations in philosophy and philosophical criticism was a more serious impediment than the limi-tations themselves. But his interest in Gentile did not die with the publication of his thesis, and the advance of years gave him the courage to use his own critical judgment a little more. In his article of 1944 on "Personalism in Education" (75) he used Gentile as the 'type' of personalism, and considered how far Dewey could be shown to conform to the standard thus established; and in review-ing *Genesi e struttura della società* in 1956 he finally ventured the hesitant judgment that "the actual governing powers of Italy during the Fascist regime and Gentile may never have really understood one another" (108c, p. 105).

In 1937 Roger Holmes published his masterly examination of the *Sistema di logica;* and Patrick Romanell completed and submitted for approval as a Ph.D. thesis at Columbia his "Inquiry into Gen-tile's Conception of Experience" (26 and 27). Were they truly comparable in caliber, these two books would complement one an-other beautifully, since Holmes concentrates his whole attention on the central sections of the *Logic* while Romanell attempts to de-scribe and characterize the whole sweep of Gentile's work. But in fact the gulf between them is such that when called on to review

---

often enlivens it. One cannot help regretting that Thompson did not translate the work, instead of devoting so much care to removing the flesh from the skeleton. (Since this book went to press Dr. Harry S. Broudy of the College of Education at the University of Illinois has kindly brought to my attention an article by Thompson in *Educational Forum* entitled "A Neglected Educator" (77 bis). The article is not of much consequence in itself, being too cursory to be very enlightening, but a footnote to the title explains that it "is taken largely from the translator's Preface to Giovanni Gentile's *Dynamic Idealism as a Philosophy of Education,* an unpublished translation of his *Sommario di Pe-dagogia";* and the last sentence echoes the regret expressed above that Gentile's philosophy of education "is so little known and cannot be made available to the students of education in the United States." The fault therefore lies no longer with Thompson but with the educational publishers.)

Holmes's book, Romanell showed himself scarcely able to appreciate what Holmes had tried to do. The *Journal of Philosophy* delivered each to the tender mercies of the other; and the quickest and simplest way to see what each was trying to do is to examine his evaluation of the other's work. Romanell attempts to refute Holmes's careful analysis of what, in conformity with his own logical and critical principles, Gentile *ought* to say by quoting what Gentile *does* say, and even what his Italian interpreters and apologists say. He does not seem to realize that to expound Gentile's philosophy in English means to translate it into the sort of English that Anglo-Saxon philosophers habitually use. That Holmes succeeded in doing this is the measure of his achievement—though one of his reviewers complained ungratefully that he had only "made a beginning of the task" of interpreting Gentile to the English-speaking world (26d, p. 359), and another accused him of being "soliloquistic" (26f, p. 75)—and one must suppose that it was primarily the intellectual challenge involved that drew him to the attempt, for he does not write as one whose emotions are deeply engaged. He is not 'committed' either for or against Gentile[35] but views his work with all the calm of a Platonic 'spectator' as a possible alternative to the two previously existing "doctrines with regard to the *Logos:* that it transcends the act of thinking, and that it does not exist" (26, p. 228). His 'logocentric' reconstruction of actual idealism gives a positive rather than a negative significance to the criticisms of the Gentilian Ego made by Bosanquet and De Burgh. I believe myself, with Romanell, that "if one recalls Gentile's interest in education and remembers that the problems of pedagogy have profoundly colored his thought, any attempt to depersonalize his philosophy is bound to kill its spirit" (26c, p. 415). But the question of whether Gentile's *Logic* requires him to commit this spiritual suicide cannot simply be set aside.[36]

On the other side Holmes is almost too generous to Romanell's

---

[35] The anonymous reviewer in the London *Times Literary Supplement*—who betrays his hostility to Gentile in every sentence in which he lauds Holmes—remarks that "his high achievement has about it this much of irony, in the Socratic sense, that the reader is sometimes left wondering whether Mr. Holmes is Gentile's defender, even on the comparatively rare occasions when he purports to be . . ." (26a). But no one who has read Holmes's concluding paragraphs can doubt that he has a genuine sympathy for Gentile's humanism (cf. the quotation in n37 below).

[36] For a full discussion of Holmes's reconstruction of the logic of *pensiero pensante* see my *Social Philosophy of Giovanni Gentile,* Chapters 2 and 9.

book as a faithful exposition of Gentile's thought in his own linguistic idiom. The statement that it "makes available material essential to an understanding of idealism" (27a, p. 418) must be read in the light of T. E. Jessup's comment: "I do not think, however, that Gentile lends himself well to summary exposition: with so uncompromising and pontifical a thinker, what we need is less summary and more explanation" (27b, p. 243). But about Romanell's attempt at a critical 'appraisal' of Gentile, Holmes's summing up cannot be bettered:

His argument is simply a restatement of the description in Professor Montague's *Ways of Knowing* of the seven stages of subjectivism, actual idealism being employed as an illustration of the seventh stage. . . . In philosophy it is fruitless to stand in one corner and forswear your opponent because he is in another. You must meet him in the center of the room and open up anew the whole problem of the relative merits of corners. Dr. Romanelli's "appraisal of Gentile's actual idealism" is neither an appraisal nor is it directed especially at Gentile. It is a summary account of idealism as seen through the eyes of a realist [27a, p. 420].

Not to put too fine a point on it, Holmes's book is the most serious and careful attempt to judge Gentile by the standards that he himself applies to others known to me in any language; and it *must* therefore be read by all who wish to criticize or defend him adequately. Whereas Romanell's book can safely be ignored by anyone who is able to read Gentile for himself. But Romanell's concern lest the 'impersonal' interpretation of Gentile put forward by Holmes be confused with Gentile's own position was justified by events.[37] The veteran personalist E. S. Brightman, Bowne Professor at Boston, was so far misled by his own prejudices as to write: ". . . Holmes shows that Gentile . . . omits the ego or person, leaving only impersonal acts of thought which are their own objects.

---

[37] The general unpreparedness of American philosophers to seize the opportunity for discussion offered by Holmes can be judged from the fact that the only serious attempt to debate the issues raised by his book appeared in *Isis* (the organ of the History of Science Society) from the pen of the Italian historian of science Giorgio de Santillana (28). Holmes must have appreciated receiving a sympathetic hearing in this quarter for his own concluding words are: "The doctrine that only the act of thinking is real is the broadest rather than the narrowest of doctrines. Poetry, because it is the expression of the inner self, has always been human. Since the time of Spinoza and Leibniz we have humanized religion, and the gain to our understanding has been incalculable. When the final fortress has fallen, when science has been humanized and taken its true and important place in human life and given up the claim to be everything, then humanism will be supreme. Then philosophy will exhibit that harmony and temperance which are its very soul" (26, p. 245).

. . . A sane and objective refutation of Gentile [*such as Holmes's book*] is also a real service to idealism. It would be a scandal if such views were supposed to be in any way essential to idealism" (26e, p. 444).

Holmes seems not to have pursued his interest in Gentile any further (though he subsequently reviewed a few Italian books for the *Philosophical Review*). But an odd concatenation of circumstances led Romanell to publish in 1946 a slim volume entitled *Croce versus Gentile* ("A Dialogue on Contemporary Italian Philosophy"). This was originally written for the volume on Croce planned by Professor Schilpp of Northwestern University for his "Library of Living Philosophers." The plan was complete and most of the essays allocated when the war supervened. When communication was restored Croce refused even to consider the publication of any such essay in a volume devoted to his work, so that Romanell was compelled to publish his already completed dialogue independently. But since the pressure of his political and other obligations made it impossible for Croce to collaborate in the way required by the basic conception of Schilpp's "Library" the whole project eventually collapsed in any case.[38]

Romanell's decision to use the dialogue form in this case can only be described as a disastrous blunder. Free explanatory discussion of the issues involved becomes impossible when such a method is adopted, for one cannot make the speakers talk in an idiom which is alien to them. Romanell would presumably retort that the only way to secure an unbiased presentation of a controversy is to let the subjects speak for themselves; but by the logic of that view he should have confined himself to the direct translation of carefully chosen passages with a full documentation and bibliography.[39] Such a collection of documents would be preferable to his manufactured dialogue. But even so it would be a classic example of the *reductio ad absurdum* of his view of philosophical exegesis. For in the controversy between Croce and Gentile, especially when it developed into a polemic, the real issues were hidden behind a mass of verbal distinctions and petty squabbling over

---

[38] Nicolini published his two essays in Italy before communication was restored. I do not know that any of the other essays have so far appeared anywhere.

[39] He does in fact supply a select bibliography of the explicitly polemical utterances of his two protagonists.

terminology. Anyone who wishes to understand the relation between the two thinkers must penetrate the smoke screen behind
which they attempted to hide how much they had learned and were
still learning from each other. This smoke screen appears to have
deceived Romanell; but at least one can say that in his presentation
its true nature becomes apparent to a critical reader. T. V. Smith,
who certainly had no special knowledge of the topic before he read
the book, ended his brief critical note thus:

But, worst of all, the dialogue moves at so high a conceptual level that
the meaning is sterilized. Only those who know already the technical
doctrines of both Croce and Gentile, and the major differences between
them, will be able to understand what is moving between the lines of
name-calling and concept-wagging. As Gentile is made to say to Croce:
"But calling names does not settle arguments." We may add: "Calling
concepts does not enlighten readers, unless they are already enlightened"
[30a].

The record does not quite end here, however, for in 1950 Mario
Rossi contributed to the *Journal of Philosophy* a review of *Genesi e
struttura della società*, which for all its brevity is one of the most
important contributions to Gentile studies in English. It is important first for the biographical details that it supplies concerning the
period in which the book was written, and the circumstances of
Gentile's death. But much more important is the critical estimate of
the book itself which is seen as "the crowning of Gentile's system
and even . . . the ultimate expression and best possible solution
that can be given to one of the basic problems of idealism in general" (108a, p. 218). This problem is the one that vexed De Burgh
in England and inspired Holmes in the United States—the problem
of mediating between the one infinite transcendental Ego and the
many finite empirical persons. Hence we have here the testimony of
an independent witness, one "who is in general strongly opposed to
any sort of idealism," that *Genesis and Structure of Society* provides
the solution to the gravest problems encountered in our survey.

[The attention of American literary critics has recently been drawn
to Gentile's *Philosophy of Art* by Giovanni Gullace's article, "Gentile versus Croce: A Comparison of Two Rival Aesthetic Systems"
(30 bis). His discussion is rather pedestrian on the theoretical side,
but the contrasts that he draws in the practical application of the
two theories are very interesting and should in fact lead to a re-
valuation and revision of some of the orthodox theoretical oppositions that he sets forth. One can only lament that Carritt's transla-

tion of the *Philosophy of Art* (8) languishes unpublished like Thompson's work mentioned in n34 above.]

Estimates of Gentile's Political Career

Gentile's work as Minister of Education and his subsequent prominence in the cultural world of Fascist Italy meant that everyone who seriously wished to understand the new Regime had to arrive at some estimate of his work and his influence. For the apologists and sympathizers he was a perfect witness, often quoted though less often understood, author of "the most Fascist of the reforms" and acknowledged authority on the aims and purposes of Fascism. For enemies and opponents of the Regime he was, at best, a Quixotic puppet-figure used as window dressing by men more cynical than he, a philosopher drunk on his own rhetoric, or at worst a hypocritical timeserver.[40]

The ambiguity of the relations between the Fascist party and the idealist reformers of education was pointed out by some observers quite early. In his little book on *Fascism* (82)—the best of the early analyses, written in 1924—Prezzolini drew attention to the fact that the congress of the Fascist party had voted against the *esame di Stato* shortly before the March on Rome—a decision which contrasted oddly with the claim that the *Riforma Gentile* was "perfectly fascist." Nonetheless it continued to be generally assumed that the educational aims and ideals of the Gentile school were identical with those of the Party, and even Prezzolini himself in an article of 1927 ascribed to Gentile the aim of 'fascistization' (47).

As we remarked earlier, American students were furnished with regular and authoritative statements of the views and aims of the idealists through the *Yearbook* of the International Institute at Columbia, edited by Kandel. But, as far as I can discover, Kandel himself was the only person to make a critical and discriminating use of the source material thus made available. In an article of 1930 he distinguished the 'national' spirit of Gentile's reform from the 'nationalist' spirit of the Party organizations, adding the gloomy

---

[40] Those who seriously presented him as a conscious and deliberate defender of tyranny (following in the footsteps of his diabolical master Hegel) betrayed in all cases either their ignorance of what he had written and done, or—like the exiles "William Elwin" (84) and "N. Travi" (92c)—their own invincible prejudices.

forecast—which was hardly a forecast even then—that the latter would inevitably become dominant in the end (52). The sections on Italy in his *Comparative Education* (1933, 61) were the first attempt in English at a genuinely critical survey of the Fascist educational system.[41]

The only student of Italian education both able and willing to work on the original sources was, for a long time, Howard R. Marraro; and even if one cannot rate highly his critical acumen, one cannot but admire the industry which his enthusiasm sustained. The bibliographies in his two books (44, 68) contain a large number of items which to the profane eye seem to have nothing to do with Italy—or even at times with education—but they are the best available on the subject and this section of the present survey is largely based on a careful sifting of them. Of Marraro's own work, Minio-Paluello, when he came to write his definitive study, said: "The point of view is that of the Fascist reformers themselves, especially of Professor E. Codignola" (76, p. 227). But this verdict is unjust to "the Fascist reformers." For although he makes occasional references to the views of opponents and critics (whose work is listed with scrupulous care in his bibliographies), Marraro's view is always and only the official view of the Ministry of Education in Rome. There is never any suggestion in his work of divergence between the views of the government and those of "the reformers themselves"—though the existence of divergences can occasionally be gathered even from the necessarily guarded remarks of Marraro's supposed mentor Codignola in his contributions to the *Yearbook* (cf. 56, 71).

I have not traced anything from Marraro's pen after his five-hundred-page book on *The New Education in Italy* in 1936 (68). But the De Vecchi reforms were reported in the *Yearbook* (69) and Kandel himself published the text of Bottai's School Charter with a brief comment on its relation to the Gentile reform (72). During the war the *Yearbook* was of course cut off from its Italian correspondents, but for his last volume in 1944 Kandel asked an exiled Italian scholar to treat the problem of postwar educational reconstruction. The essay he received (74) began with a violently hos-

---

[41] This statement must be understood in a restricted sense. Schneider and Clough made a very good survey of the whole business of forming political opinion in Fascist Italy, including of course the infiltration of Fascist doctrine in the schools, in 1929 (48).

tile, but nevertheless brilliant, critique of educational policy in the Fascist period. The author, Lamberto Borghi, is cruelly unfair to Gentile (and for that matter to Bottai also) as far as his conscious aims were concerned, but by concentrating severely on the over-all pattern of policy that emerges from what was actually done, he does reveal clearly the antidemocratic undercurrent that was always, so to speak, potentially present or available for development in Gentile's work.

At about the same time the Royal Institute of International Affairs in London commissioned Luigi Minio-Paluello to write a survey of the whole topic.[42] His work (76) can safely be regarded as definitive. It supersedes virtually everything that had previously appeared on the subject in English. Beginning from the *Lex Casati* in 1859 he describes first the situation before Gentile's reform. Then, in the Fascist period he distinguishes three phases: the Gentile reform, 'fascistization,' and the School Charter. His account of Gentile's work is a model of critical objectivity, and even on the difficult topic of 'Fascist doctrine'—where perhaps agreement on what constitutes objective criticism is scarcely to be hoped for—few people would wish to quarrel, unless from motives of personal apologia, with his summing up.[43]

It fell to De Ruggiero to begin the task of reconstructing the Italian educational system during the period of Allied military occupation. From the articles by himself (77) and A. Vesselo (77a) in the London University *Yearbook of Education* [44] for 1948, one gets the impression that he conceived his task to be, at least tem-

---

[42] *Education in Fascist Italy* was not published until 1946, but the author informs us in his Preface that it "was partly written before the fall of Fascism, and finished before any direct source of information on what happened in Italy during the war was accessible" (p. xi).

[43] The statement that Gentile "became a much-followed master of verbose pseudo-philosophical compromise" (p. 127) can scarcely be called objective in the light of the events and decisions that brought him to his death—about which Minio-Paluello was still very imperfectly informed (p. xi). But a careful reading of the context reveals, I think, that the sting of the epithets is directed more at the 'followers' than at the 'master.' No one can deny that Gentile was habitually 'verbose'; and it would be hard to defend some of his Fascist pronouncements against the charge of being 'pseudo-philosophical.' But I do not think that Minio-Paluello's general picture of Gentile himself is one of 'compromise.'

[44] The London *Yearbook*, like its Columbia namesake (now merged with it), provided periodic reports on education in Italy. But except in the 1948 issue these are much less interesting (57, 70).

porarily, the restoration as far as possible of the original Gentile
reform by the removal of later Fascist accretions. Coming as it does
from the pen of one who had no cause to love Gentile personally,
and had for years criticized his philosophy bitterly, De Ruggiero's
article is a marked tribute to Gentile as an educational reformer.

The breach between Gentile and Croce, which became symbolic
of a corresponding breach in the national life because it was expressed in the "Manifesto of the Fascist Intellectuals" on one side,
and a "Protest" signed not just by Croce but by a long list of prominent non-Fascist intellectuals on the other, was widely reported in
the Anglo-Saxon world. Very soon, as some of the anti-Fascist intellectuals went into exile, and Fascism itself began to collect ad-
herents abroad, the same division was repeated on an international
scale among those who concerned themselves with the new movement. But fortunately for our present purpose not very many of
these admirers and detractors were philosophically inclined.

Among the admirers of Fascism, one of the most serious, and for
us the most important, was Miss Lion, whose book on *The Idealistic
Conception of Religion* we have already discussed. Not long after
her arrival in England she set to work to expound for English readers
the philosophical background and significance of the Italian revolution. As an enthusiastic pupil of Gentile she naturally accepted his
view of Fascism, and proceeded to supply it with a most impressive
'pedigree' in the history of political thought (81). The *Times Literary Supplement* commented a little sourly that her "popular essay," far from being popular, was in fact very technical. It is divided into two parts, "Political Antecedents" and "Philosophical
Antecedents"—the first tracing the political history of Italy from
the Risorgimento, and the second the history of philosophy in Europe from the Renaissance. For Miss Lion Fascism is identical with
actual idealism, and the two parts of her book are each based on
views expressed in fragmentary fashion in Gentile's early Fascist
essays. Had it been written five years later it would have been
what the title of Gentile's own most authoritative work on Fascism
promised but did not produce—a systematic treatise on 'the origins
and doctrine of Fascism' from the idealist point of view.

If anyone needed to be told that Miss Lion's idealist version of
Fascism was not the only one current among its supporters, they

were soon enlightened. Major Barnes in 1928 employed "the scholastic method . . . to expound the political Philosophy underlying Fascism." He received assistance from a professor of dogmatic theology at the Gregorian University, and the *Duce's* imprimatur in the shape of a commendatory preface. He expresses "the very greatest respect for Professor Gentile" but adds cautiously, "I confess I find great difficulty myself in always following his thought, and when I do, I by no means always find myself in agreement with him" (84, pp. xiv–xv). His few references to Gentile are for the most part restricted to bare assertions that he is not really a Hegelian, that he has "purged" Hegel's theses of their "gross materialism," that his school is "gradually sifting the truth from the falsehood," etc. The "falsehood" is "Historical Fatalism," and Hegel derived it from Vico; Major Barnes assures his readers that "the notion of the State as an end in itself forms no part whatever of orthodox Fascism" (84, pp. 94–95). He devotes a single paragraph in a chapter entitled "Heterogeneous Legislation" to the *Riforma Gentile,* and it is worthy of note that he there ascribes to it with full approval the reactionary antidemocratic aims for which Borghi castigated it in 1944: "Gentile's great Education Act . . . made it more difficult for unnecessary numbers of boys and girls to obtain the required qualifications at the expense of the State in order to compete for 'black-coated' employment" (84, p. 184).

Both of these views were set in perspective by H. W. Schneider's *Making the Fascist State* (1928). Schneider, being a philosopher trained in the school of Dewey, was well fitted to appreciate the experimental pathfinding character of Fascism. His "guiding aim," as he says,

was to investigate the construction of fascist theories in terms of the varying practical situations into which the movement was forced by dint of circumstances. The fascist mind and imagination hold the foreground of this picture, while enough of the political history and economic problems of the movement is brought into the background to make clear how the *fascisti* intended their ideas to be applied. The interaction between fact and philosophic fiction, between practical exigencies and social theories, between mind and body, forms the dominant theme of the following interpretation of fascism. To the practical politicians both within and without the movement the greater part of this ideology is mere froth. But to the student of the workings of the human mind such froth is not negligible. Philosophies may not reveal the ultimate and universal nature of things, nor are they prime movers; but they are significant symptoms of social pathology and entertaining forms of human energy [83, p. v].

His plan is brilliantly carried out, mainly through well-chosen quotations from the various ideologists.[45] A selection of more important documents and specimens of Fascist thought is supplied in the Appendix—including sizable extracts from *Che cosa è il fascismo* (4). Gentile is given his due place as one of the most "significant symptoms" of Fascism: "Gentile and his disciples are the most conspicuous and the most distinguished group of fascist thinkers and have succeeded in giving the impression very widely that their particular brand of idealist philosophy is also the official philosophy of fascism. Though this is not true and though fascism has no single philosophic content, the idealists are certainly predominant and far above any other philosophical group both in numbers and in philosophic erudition" (83, p. 344). Schneider refrains from critical judgment, save insofar as it is necessary for the disentangling of his historical skeleton. But this disentangling does lead him to grant that Gentile's philosophy was more than "froth" or "entertainment," since the educational reform was an attempt "to lay the foundations for the new culture" (83, p. 235); and in the subsequent volume *Making Fascists* by Schneider and Clough, the reform is examined in some detail. In this book the focus of concern is not so much the Fascist climate of opinion as the growing system of institutions by which that opinion was created and maintained.

Schneider regarded Gentile's educational policy as a move toward the secularization of religion—"The Church lost its monopoly and religion lost its preeminence" (83, p. 221). But he saw that Gentile's successors had not understood his policy, so that "if politicians rather than educators should get control of the educational system . . . neoscholasticism rather than national idealism may become the official theology of the fascist faith. But for the present this hardly seems probable." In this respect his book was soon overtaken by events. The polemics between Gentile and the Vatican

---

[45] One must be thankful that he performed his self-appointed task so well, since his book became the stand-by of all students who, lacking knowledge of Italian, wished to pursue the study of 'Fascist thought' beyond the *Enciclopedia* article. For example, Sabine's account of Fascism in his *History of Political Theory* (90) owes much to it. (Gentile's essay on "L'essenza del fascismo" (B.948) was neatly condensed and translated in *Foreign Affairs*, January 1928 (5). This, together with Alfredo Rocco's "Political Doctrine of Fascism," tr. by D. Bigongiari in *International Conciliation*, No. 223, completes the list of available material. Miss Lion's book does not seem to have been widely known; and in any case it was too far removed from practical realities.)

were recounted to readers of the *Quarterly Review* by Villari even as the Lateran Accords were being signed (32). But it was some years before this turn of events came to be carefully analyzed. An attempt to survey the whole problem of Church and State in the history of Italy as a nation was made by S. W. Halperin of the University of Chicago in 1937 (34). He was under the mistaken impression that Gentile "had supported Mussolini during the latter's swift ascent to power," but otherwise gives a fairly accurate summary of his views.

Just about the time that Halperin's little book was published, the Irish legal historian D. A. Binchy began to work on the same problem for the Royal Institute of International Affairs; and when his magisterial volume of nearly eight hundred pages was published in 1941 it was immediately recognized as the definitive treatment of the whole subject.[46] Writing from a Catholic viewpoint, he was naturally hostile to Gentile, but he neither minimized nor misrepresented the extent and nature of Gentile's influence even after the Concordat, pointing out that "Whatever be his present position in the Party hierarchy, it is his system of philosophy that is still taught in more than three-quarters of the secondary schools of Italy. . . . Actual Idealism, then, remains a powerful factor in the spiritual formation of the Fascist *élite*. . . . Mussolini has borrowed heavily from Gentile, notably in those portions of his official 'Doctrine' which most concern us here" (35, p. 322).

For himself he accepted Father Chiocchetti's verdict that actual idealism was "the liquidation of Christianity." But he made every effort to present the philosophy and work of its author fairly, reserving his bitterest strictures for the 'Catholic' Fascists—especially foreign sympathizers like Major Barnes. Only once is he less than just to Gentile, when he refers to the article written after the Accords were published as "an ignoble expression of servility . . . in which this arch-opponent of Reconciliation recanted everything that he had been preaching for the past three years." In point of fact, as I have argued elsewhere, Gentile recanted nothing.[47]

We cannot do better than to close this survey with a reference to Herman Finer's *Mussolini's Italy* (1935) which is, I think by com-

---

[46] In his Preface Binchy tells us that he found himself obliged to condense his original draft on the history of the *dissidio* before Fascism from seven chapters to two. It is perhaps a pity that he chose to do this, for to judge from what he has given us his book might well have been the authoritative history of Italy from a Catholic viewpoint in English.

[47] See my *Social Philosophy of Giovanni Gentile*, Chapter 6, pp. 198–200.

mon consent, "by far the best and most objective work on Fascism
in general that has appeared in English" (Binchy). Finer's primary
concern was, of course, with the emerging pattern of Fascist institutions. But he devoted nearly seventy pages to a commentary on
the "Fundamental Ideas" section of the *Enciclopedia* article on
"Fascismo." Knowing as we do that Gentile was the real author
of this section, we may be tempted to discount his reflections when
we find him discovering not merely Gentile's influence, but in some
places that of Rocco as well, for as Finer himself emphasizes, Gentile and Rocco were poles apart.[48] But this would be a mistake. For
the fact that, in the mouth of Mussolini, Gentile's words could be
mistaken for Rocco's by the most competent observer of Mussolini's
work is an eloquent commentary on the ambiguous situation in
which Gentile himself was involved through his adhesion to Fascism. In my view Finer's interpretation is essentially a correct account of what Mussolini thought the article meant when he signed it.

Finer himself was very conscious of the ambiguity of Gentile's
position, being clearly much impressed by his character and ideals,
but unable like every other observer who was not himself an enthusiastic Fascist to see any connection between those ideals and
the actual situation. He did not attempt to deal with Gentile's
strictly philosophical work, but from a surprisingly comprehensive
knowledge of Gentile's various Fascist essays [49] he gathered a
much fairer conception of "Gentile's free-will idealism" than many
of the more academic critics ever achieved. He gives a full account
of Gentile's conception of the Party and the Institutes of Fascist
Culture, but his conclusion is sadly ironical: "John Stuart Mill himself would not have been dissatisfied with the full implications of
Gentile's arguments in favour of doubt and criticism. They do honour
to Gentile; if they were in being they would scarcely give continued
life to Fascism" (88, p. 424). Therefore in his final estimate Gentile

---

[48] "Comparative examination of the Fundamental Ideas show[s] marked
traces of Gentile's influence, even to similarities of phrase: and this is a good
sign for the future of Italy. The debt to Rocco is as weighty on its practical side
as it is full on the spiritual. And whereas Gentile taught an idealism which
soars above the Nation and includes individual self-development, Rocco taught
Nationalism which makes the Nation paramount over the individual and in
international relations. There is charity in Gentile's teaching, and misanthropy
in Rocco's. The latter has triumphed" (88, p. 166).

[49] He even quotes at length from one that escaped the notice of Bellezza
(the inaugural address to the Second Congress of the Institutes of Culture,
Rome, November 1931—*Educazione fascista*, December 1931).

was foredoomed to failure as a Fascist. He was "squeezed dry and the peel thrown away" (88, p. 470) even before the establishment of the dictatorship, and his fatal decision to work for a new 'Fascist' culture. Of course the "peel" was actually useful to the Party. Finer explains "thrown away" with the footnote "Made editor of the *Enciclopedia Italiana,* and President of the Institute of Fascist Culture." But with this qualification the verdict was confirmed in 1938 by Ascoli in his balanced if rather impressionist account of "The Press and the Universities in Italy" (91) [50] and again by Minio-Paluello in 1946 (76, p. 67). The circumstances of his assassination—first described to English readers by Rossi in 1950 (108a)—would seem to make his death no more than an apt epitome of the essential tragedy of his whole political career.

Gentile's Philosophy and the Present Book

To provide a brief introduction to *Genesis and Structure of Society* is virtually impossible. The full understanding of it presupposes a knowledge of the whole of Gentile's previous work. I have endeavored to provide an adequate introduction to it in another book; and, even if I were willing to repeat myself, I could not summarize the results of that work here.[51] On the other hand it is clearly necessary to say something in justification of this attempt to interest English-speaking readers in the social philosophy of an author whose own attempts to put it into practice resulted only in ambiguity, disappointment, and personal tragedy. I shall end therefore by sketching an interpretation of actual idealism which will enable the reader to make sense enough—not the only possible sense, nor perhaps the full sense, but nonetheless some sense—out of Gentile's fundamental position, to appreciate what I conceive

---

[50] "The situation of Gentile and his followers is not substantially different from that of the rest of their colleagues. Since Gentile left the Ministry of Education in 1924 he has been given several positions of honor and prestige. He is at the head of the Italian Encyclopedia, of the Fascist Institute of Culture, and so forth. From time to time he seems to have fallen into utter disgrace, and after a while he enjoys a 'comeback.' For the present ruling class he is too much of a philosopher, sometimes too outspoken—as for instance in his opposition to the Lateran Treaties—too ready to rescue fellow scholars from political difficulties. But no other Fascist intellectual can command such respect as he does. He is considered an irreplaceable nuisance that the regime must stoically bear" (91, p. 252).

[51] See my *Social Philosophy of Giovanni Gentile.*

to be important in his last book. I am assuming, of course, that the reader wishes to make sense of it, and not simply to make fun of it or to refute it—alternatives which are superficially easy and certainly very tempting.

The 'method of immanence' requires that in the analysis of his experience the philosopher should presuppose nothing, and adhere strictly to the task of making his actual consciousness as clear and as systematically coherent as possible. It results in the view that the act of thinking is a 'pure' act—i.e. a self-creative act, an act whose existence is its essence—because it is only by taking our own act of thinking as the foundation of our world that we can avoid *presupposing* a world having an independent foundation.

But, after all, it may be asked, why should we *not* presuppose a world, if an analysis of our experience as unprejudiced as we can make it seems to lead to this presupposition as the best way to make our experience coherent? What is so sacred about the ideal of self-sufficiency, that a philosopher must sacrifice all for it as Gentile did? Why *must* philosophy be 'without presuppositions'? The answer to this question reveals the moral imperative at the root of all of Gentile's philosophizing. The primary characteristic of *all* human experience as he saw it was *moral responsibility*. We are responsible for what we believe about the world, just as much as for what we do in it; and in any case responsibility, even if it be limited to the sphere of what is ordinarily called 'moral action,' presupposes freedom of choice. Thus the philosopher, in his endeavor to make his experience coherent, has among other things to make intelligible the part played in it by moral freedom. But 'to make freedom intelligible' means to show how it is rooted in the universal nature of things; and, for Gentile, Kant's philosophy was sufficient proof that freedom could have no intelligible place in a world whose independent reality was presupposed. The principal result of his own conception of thought as 'pure act' was to rescue moral freedom from the noumenal world to which Kant had been obliged to exile it. It must be conceded that, since throughout this revolution his own conception of science and scientific knowledge remained severely Kantian, his philosophy acquired something of the character of a polemic against science; but it must equally be emphasized that this was an accidental result of his own ignorance of science, and not a necessary corollary of his theory.

In the present climate of philosophical opinion in the Anglo-

Saxon world, it is more than likely that an objection will here be raised against the presentation of 'determinism' and 'freedom' as if they were absolute and exclusive alternatives. It will be urged that after all an agent may be 'responsible' whether his act was 'determined' or not, or that an act may be 'free' from one point of view yet 'determined' from another, and so on. I am myself in general sympathy with a pragmatic approach of this kind, though occasionally I cannot help suspecting that some of the analyses of ethical terms which appeal to 'ordinary usage' are evasions of the basic moral question as to when and why we have a *right* to use a given ethical term like 'responsible.' But I think that against Gentile the objection is in any case mistaken, since his problem is not how words like 'freedom' and 'responsibility' are used in ordinary speech, but rather what usage to treat as fundamental in order to give a rational account of moral experience; and I cannot myself dissent from his contention that moral responsibility is the essential character of all rational thought. That there are other valid usages more 'ordinary' than his own he does not for a moment deny—though he does perhaps unduly depreciate them for their 'abstractness.'

If now the first hurdle has been safely negotiated, and we are prepared to admit that there are valid reasons for adopting the 'method of immanence,' we must face a new and still more serious objection. For with the best will in the world—and not simply as a 'move in the game'—a critic may say that he does not understand what can possibly be meant by the assertion that the act of thinking *creates* its own world. "Which of you by taking thought can add one cubit to his stature?" The proposed moral justification of Gentile's method is null and void if his results are unintelligible.

His use of language does indeed willfully court comparison with the first chapter of Genesis; and the image called up in the mind of ordinary men by the theological doctrine that God created the world *out of nothing* is that of a material universe springing into existence where there was only a void before. But clearly this interpretation will not do for Gentile any more than it will for the theologians, the primary reason in both cases being that it is not radical enough. The act of thought 'creates' the space in which the world is; indeed, this aspect of the theological doctrine—which the ordinary man overlooks—is more easily assimilated to Gentile's view than the aspect which the ordinary man seizes on. The 'external world' which the ordinary man conceives God as 'creating' is not, so far as I can understand Gentile, created at all, because it is not anything positive, but only a limit concept, the not-self which is essential to the process of thinking in order that it may have always new worlds to conquer. Gentile insists that the act of thinking creates (or 'posits') even this limit; but that is only to say that the limit is not fixed and immovable. To 'create' a limit is precisely to 'posit' it, to put it in position or decide where it shall be. I do not by my thinking create the 'external world,' precisely because by definition it is external to my world. But I do decide where to draw the line between my world and the external world; and should I decide that it is important to add a cubit to *human* stature (it is admitted that I cannot do it for myself as an 'empirical ego' except in some sophistic sense such as 'by wearing stilts,' and if *that* will serve my purpose I shall not be troubled much about the sophistry), then clearly I must devote myself to that body of organized thinking known as experimental genetics. At least this much can be said: that there is no *other* way to add a cubit to one's stature than 'by taking thought.' And if it be now objected that it may in fact prove to be impossible even then, that perhaps the 'external' world does *impose* an *absolute* limit at some point, and is not indefinitely patient of our molding, the answer must be given on methodological rather than ontological grounds. We must say that the existence of a final limit at any point can never be taken for granted. There clearly is, for example, *some* limit to the speed at which an athlete can run a mile; but this will not prevent, nor should it prevent, every generation of athletes from attempting to break the record set by its predecessors.

The 'self' and the 'not-self' are correlative terms. My 'self' is clearly not my 'body' even as a minimum, for I have to 'conquer' my own body in the first instance, and control of it may be wrested from me by paralytic disease or accident. There is no finally assignable lower limit any more than there is an assignable upper limit. It was not so long ago that no man dared to interfere with the workings of the heart and brain so that these organs constituted, as it were, a minimal body. They *were* minimal then. But the achievements of modern surgery forbid us to say that they are minimal in principle; and just because there is nothing that can safely be consigned finally to the 'external' world we *cannot* ask (in any philosophical or absolute sense) what the external world is in itself. Since Gentile is interested only in this 'absolute' sense, he is right to define 'Nature' as a limit posited by the act of thought itself.

The scientist, straining after an ideal of objectivity which will give his results perfect reproducibility, may ask what the natural process he is studying is 'in itself.' But there are two things to be noted about this. In the first place, he can ask this question meaningfully only when he can fully isolate his problem, so as to define perfectly what it is 'in itself.' But he never, in fact, does have a perfectly defined problem—the 'definition' of the problem is identical with the discovery of a method for its solution. Secondly, he asks the question only as a moment in the process of conquering nature, so that science as an institution survives, like Kronos, by devouring the 'results' which are its own children.

The self that 'creates' itself is a world of meanings. My 'self,' the world that I create by my own thought, and for which I am morally responsible, is precisely my personal interpretation of *the* world, that is to say it is all the meaning and significance, all the value, that the world has or can have for me. But even if this account of Gentile's *autoctisi* be accepted as both true and comprehensible there are still two alternative objections that can be brought against it; and with these objections we come finally to the book here translated.

The objection offered by rugged common sense will be that my 'self,' the values and significances that the world has for me, is a product of my education, that I am, at least to a very large extent, what my culture makes me. Gentile's answer to this objection would probably be shorter and ruder than it deserves. But I will try to answer it for him as gently and moderately as I can. Gentile insists that "all education is self-education," that one cannot learn anything from any other person or institution unless one has the will to learn it. Whatever modicum of truth there may be in this, it is essentially an evasion, as anyone can see who reflects on the importance that is accorded to the organized social group ('the State'), and to the teacher as mouthpiece of the human cultural tradition, the 'patrimony of humanity,' in his thought. The fact is that though one can only learn if one has the will to learn, the will itself can only become enlightened by learning, so that in the first instance one has no choice but to accept what one is offered, and the choices made subsequently will be those suggested or at any rate left open by the historical and cultural situation in which one finds oneself. This is the limitation of the 'empirical ego.' The Ego that is truly free is the universal consciousness of the whole cultural complex, which is what Gentile calls *lo Stato*. But this 'State' is not in his view an empirically existent community for any but the moral weakling. The moral man has an ideal community, his membership of which constitutes for him his very self-hood. He is not a man who claims as an alibi that he acted as he had been taught, or that he only did what everyone does, or worst of all that he obeyed the orders of his superiors—this last is an excuse valid only for the Aristotelian slave, a person not admitted to the rights of citizenship. The moral man is one who says, like Luther, "Here I stand. I cannot do otherwise." When we are faced, for example, with the defenses offered by German civil servants to the war-crimes tribunals, we must from a sympathetic awareness of our own weakness say, "There, but for the Grace of God, go I"; but we can hardly fail to recognize at the same time the moral inadequacy of the theory of cultural determinism.

In rejecting the objection of the ordinary man who refuses to accept responsibility for his society as a whole, however, we have impaled ourselves seemingly upon the opposite horn of a dilemma. For how shall we face the objection raised by technical philosophy that Gentile's view is tantamount to solipsism? It might seem as if, just as we have simply rejected the common-sense objection, so we must simply accept the philosophical one. That was the view of Roger Holmes, who described Gentile's system as "the attempt to develop a complete solipsism" (26, p. 120). But it is morally as unacceptable as the view that we have rejected. If we cannot admire the man who pleads always his own weakness, neither can we tolerate the one who trusts implicitly in his own strength (his 'strength' here means the coherence of his own vision of human society). The moral man may, as we said above, be one who says "Here I stand," but this is not to say that anyone who says "Here I stand" is a moral man, let alone that he is beyond moral criticism. Himmler was, as far as I can discover, a self-respecting and in many ways outwardly respectable man, as gentle and humane in his personal feelings as any of the civil servants who obeyed his orders. But the fact that though he may, abstractly speaking, have regretted some of the orders he felt obliged to give, he never for a moment doubted that they ought to be given and obeyed, does not make him more, but rather less, moral than those of his subordinates who were tormented in their obedience by moral doubts or guilts.

The man who cannot tolerate doubts and ambiguities in himself or his fellows cannot be allowed to exercise power in a society that wishes to remain healthy. The worst weakness discoverable in Gentile's own character was his inability in practical matters to tolerate his own doubts and uncertainties, or to remain patient when he found himself in an ambiguous situation. The emphasis on the *unity* of the spirit, noticeable in all of his early writings, and amounting almost to idolatry, is the corresponding flaw in his theory. It reaches its height in some passages in his *Logic* where he exalts the 'transcendental loneliness' of thought, and it provides the justification of Holmes's interpretation. But it is a one-sided emphasis, and it is corrected in his last book.

Rossi says (108a) that *Genesis and Structure of Society* shows why Gentile could not stand aside when Italy was divided—he felt morally obliged to decide which state was 'his.' But from a theoretical point of view this interpretation is quite invalid. Gentile was no more obliged by his theory to choose between the Royal Government in the South and the Fascist Social Republic in the North than his hero Mazzini was obliged to opt for one of the existing princedoms as the nucleus of his Italy of the future. The stand that Gentile took was taken in the name of a Nation above the party strife; and his choice of a place in which to make that stand was governed, at least partly, by empirical calculations as to where his influence would be most effective. One side was willing to listen or at least pretend to listen to him, the other was not. But it is arguable that he could have spoken for the Nation better had he refused to join either side. This, however, would have left him in an ambiguous position, subject, as he was when he wrote *Genesis and Structure of Society*, to attack from all sides, and to the further accusation of being a fence-sitter. The fact that this last accusation was false ought to have made it endurable; but it had just the opposite effect. Gentile had not had the twenty-year schooling of Croce in the difficult art of 'making himself a party of one.'

What is needed in order to provide us with a way through the horns of our dilemma is a social theory of the act of thinking itself. This would preserve the moral freedom and responsibility of the individual, without condemning him to 'transcendental loneliness' or allowing him to indulge in egocentric megalomania. Such a theory is what is offered in *Genesis and Structure of Society*. The view that the individual himself is a society, that his being lies in his communicating, is not new. It was used as a methodological principle by Plato, and as a metaphysical one by Hegel, by Peirce, by Royce, and by Mead. In Mead it even reaches a form which seems virtually identical with the theory expounded by Gentile.[52] But in all of these thinkers the social theory of individuality since it was not subjected to the 'method of immanence' involved a decision to presuppose society, to regard it as ontologically or temporally prior to the individual. In Royce the priority seems to be mainly ontological; faith in God as the true interpreter of all interpretations and guarantor of objective truth, and faith in the Beloved Community or Kingdom of Heaven, is conceived as necessary in order to make a rationally coherent existence possible for the human individual. In Mead the priority is clearly temporal: self-conscious individuals can only come into existence through a behavioral process within an existing social context.

Let us take Mead's evolutionary theory first. I do not think there is anything in it that Gentile ought to deny, though he would certainly reject it as 'empirical' and might therefore be tempted to heap unjust scorn on it (as he appears to be doing with evolutionary theories of the a priori in Chapter 12, section 7, herein). The weakness in Mead's view lies in the fact that both the individual and the social process are conceived naturalistically, that is as a struggle to meet certain needs that are naturally given and unchangeable. Man is, according to Mead, the form in which evolution has at last become master of itself; but when we ask "how then is it to express this mastery?" or "what are we to do with ourselves?" there is no answer except "fulfill your needs more efficiently." But the only 'need' of life as such is to go on; and for this all that is necessary is the establishment of a comfortable environment and its maintenance in a stable equilibrium. Thus the conscious individual is speedily swallowed again in the social process that has produced him; and the nemesis of Dewey's long dominance over the educational scene, with his emphasis on the experimental study and satisfaction of individual needs, is an educational system dedicated to the typically Platonic ideal of 'life adjustment,' a sys-

---

[52] For a comparison of Gentile's views with those of Peirce, Royce, and Mead see my *Social Philosophy of Giovanni Gentile*, Chapter 8, pp. 258–63.

tem in which conformity is regarded as a good because it is undeniably a comfort, but which has lost sight of everything that
could make conscious individuality worth struggling for. The man-
agerial classes are our guardians and the psychologists our phi-
losopher-kings.

Such a fate could never overtake Royce's individual. For he
knows that his nature is 'fallen' and that he can only be saved by
his 'community'; and he knows further that his community is a
history in the past or in the future, a 'community of memory' or
a 'community of hope.' He will not awaken only to fall asleep again,
because he has always something to fight for and his own sinful
nature to fight against. The nemesis of Royce's view is not the
happy pig, but the religious fanatic who sought to take Socrates'
unhappiness from him.

Of course it was no more part of Royce's intention to justify
the dogmatic religious crusader than it was Dewey's intention to
produce a nation of contented television viewers. But it is a logical
consequence of his belief that the rationality of the world is a necessary presupposition; and in the present situation it may yet prove
a more disastrous legacy than Dewey's. For salvation is asserted
to depend on loyalty to the 'Beloved Community'; but there is
no discoverable community to which we are all loyal. If it is asserted that, despite appearances, there really is a mystic Church
to which all good men are loyal, the way is opened for an argument of the following sort: My membership of this community
is the source of grace for me; and even though there may be other
good communities, it is certain that any community basically opposed to mine must be evil, and should be destroyed. It is useless
to protest that this is a perversion of Royce's view. For if the community cannot be identified as definitely as the individual, how
can it have *any* practical importance, let alone the saving grace
that Royce attributes to it? Thus we arrive at the nauseating rub-
bish that one reads every day in the newspapers about 'the free
world' and 'the enslaved peoples'; one only has to read those same
newspapers to discover that the 'free world' contains horror and
shame and even slavery as terrible as anything reliably reported
among the 'enslaved peoples.' That we can still read this is the one
thing that really distinguishes those diminishing areas of the world
that are genuinely free. But it needs no great wit to see that the
nearer we come to a crusading mentality, the less of this freedom

we shall possess. On the day that we set out to 'save' the 'enslaved peoples' we shall ourselves finally be 'lost,' for we shall no longer recognize how very like them we are, and because of this we shall be no longer merely 'like' but indistinguishable from them. Far from being saved by our community, it is we who must save it, by saving ourselves in it and to a certain extent *from* it.

This is what Gentile's conception of our social nature will enable us to do. There can be no logical justification in his view for the swallowing of the individual by society, since the self-consciousness of the individual is seen as the transcendental ground of all empirical society; and there can be no justification for fanaticism, since the 'method of immanence' forbids us to assume the reality of any community that we do not ourselves actually create, or of any truth that we do not ourselves successfully interpret. Both the megalomania and the impotence of 'transcendental loneliness' are undermined by this conception. Having recently suffered much from megalomaniacs, the self-conscious members of our society are now oppressed by a sense of their own impotence, and we hear a great deal about the impossibility of communication. But the degree of *Angst* in their railing against fate is in direct proportion to the intensity of their own supposed self-awareness; and if they are indeed self-conscious they are already communicating successfully with their own 'internal other.' Yet the one and only proof that we are able to understand ourselves is that we can make ourselves understood by others; everyday experience assures us, even apart from the findings of the psychoanalysts, that there are many occasions when we communicate more successfully with others than with ourselves, and even occasions when we should not understand ourselves at all if we did not understand what others tell us about ourselves.

Bosanquet accused Gentile of offering us a "unity without a universe" (14, p. 159). In the light of his last work we might reply for Gentile in the words of Fichte: *Die Welt ist meine Pflicht.* This is indeed much less paradoxical in Gentile than in Fichte, for the notion of 'duty' is shorn of its associations with Newtonian scientific law, and gains its meaning directly from the conception of the world as an *actual* community in process of becoming. "To know oneself; that is what matters," concludes Gentile. But to know oneself is to communicate successfully with oneself, and one's true self is the whole universe of which one is conscious. Thus to know oneself is to create a universe of successful communication; and we can say of something that its truth or its value is genuinely established when it passes current throughout this universe. We have no *right* to assert categorically that anything is 'true,' or that there *is* a universe, when experience informs us that there is virtually no event that is not in fact differently interpreted by different communities. The very concept of an 'event' itself becomes ambiguous to the point of vanishing. We may *believe* that certain things are 'true'—that is that they *ought* to pass current: this 'belief' itself entails, or perhaps we should say it is identical with, our obligation to communicate the 'truth,' to make it pass current. But communication is a reciprocal affair: the opposite face of our duty to communicate our beliefs is contained in the precept *audi alteram partem*. The test of our essential sincerity is found in the fact that the force of our belief itself ought to lead us to set it in abeyance in order to 'hear the other side.' By violence or intolerance one communicates only one's own fear, because that is all that one seeks to create in the other. Such 'truth' as there is in our world today, as for instance the commonly agreed truths of physics, rests largely on the universal community of fear. We approach the subatomic world with a common aim and therefore we arrive rapidly (despite our best attempts to impede one another) at a common interpretation. The best hope of the world now lies in the possibility that the unmistakable fearfulness of the spirits we have called from the vasty deep to allay the fears we have so busily communicated to each other while masking them as far as possible from ourselves may finally cause us to face those fears and conquer them through a slow and painful process of learning mutual trust. Nothing can help us more in this process than the initial recognition that truth is not guaranteed by revelation or by our faith, still less by 'the scientifically ascertained facts,' but only by our ability to communicate it. Truth of revelation or of fact is only conceivable, if it is conceivable at all, as a 'mystery' passing our understanding. It becomes truth actually for us only so far as we can successfully interpret and communicate it.

Note on the Translation

Traduttore, traditore, says the Italian proverb with its brutal frankness. I wish I could be certain that it does not apply in this case. Having had occasion to use many translations myself at different times, I have learned to value faithfulness to the original very highly. But in translating Gentile I have often seemed to have before me only a choice of betrayals. My first attempt to translate this book was so faithfully literal as to be virtually unintelligible. Progressive revisions have made it increasingly free, but I hope also somewhat easier to understand. Gentile wrote the book in a great hurry, and in places where he is repeating views stated in earlier works his style becomes almost telegraphic; furthermore, the basic vocabulary that he uses has in English an unnatural and often repellent effect. Hence I have often felt obliged to link together and slightly expand his more staccato sentences; and at least some of the time I have offered an interpretation rather than a simple translation of sentences containing terms like *spirito, atto, sintesi, dialettica,* etc. I hope that the frequent citation of the original text in such cases will obviate most of the dangers inherent in this practice.

BIBLIOGRAPHY OF GENTILE STUDIES
IN ENGLISH

Writings of Gentile in Translation

1. "Hegel," in *The Encyclopedia and Dictionary of Education*, ed. by FOSTER WATSON, London, Pitman, 1921, II, 791–92.

2. *The Theory of Mind as Pure Act*, tr. from the 3rd ed. with an introduction by H. WILDON CARR, London, Macmillan, 1922, xxviii + 280 pp. (B.660.[1] Translation of *Teoria generale dello spirito come atto puro*, 1920, B.560. Readers should take note that the *last two* chapters are a defense of Gentile's views in their earliest formulation (1913, B.297) against the criticisms of Croce. These chapters were thus written three years *earlier* than the body of the book to which they are now appended.)

3. *The Reform of Education*, tr. by DINO BIGONGIARI, with an introduction by BENEDETTO CROCE, New York, Harcourt, 1922 (and London, Ernest Benn, 1923), xi + 250 pp. (B.659. Translation of *La riforma dell'educazione: Discorsi ai maestri di Trieste*, 1920, B.557, the first chapter being specially revised by Gentile for this edition.)

4. Fragments of *Che cosa è il fascismo* (1925) under the heading "Gentile's Version of Fascism," tr. by H. W. SCHNEIDER in his book, *Making the Fascist State*, New York, Oxford, 1928, pp. 344–53. (See also pp. 321–25 for fragments of Gentile's report on constitutional reform. Other fragments are scattered throughout the text of the book, which is adequately indexed. All are from B.818.)

5. "The Philosophic Basis of Fascism," *Foreign Affairs*, VI, No. 2 (January 1928), pp. 290–304. (B.941. Translation of a condensed version of B.948. It is now known that Gentile was the real author of the

---

[1] Numbers prefixed by B identify the corresponding entries in V. A. BELLEZZA, *Bibliografia degli scritti di Giovanni Gentile*, Florence, Sansoni, 1950.

first part of the article on Fascism (1932) in the *Italian Encyclopedia* which was signed by Mussolini. This article (authorized translation by JANE SOAMES) exists in numerous English editions. Gentile's section of it can be found, together with an extensive commentary, in HERMAN FINER, *Mussolini's Italy*, London, V. Gollancz, 1935, Part III. See also item 106 below.)

6. "The Philosophy of the Modern State," *The Spectator* (London), 3 November 1928 (centennial issue supplement), pp. 36–37. (B.947.)

7. "The Italian Encyclopedia," in *What Is Fascism and Why?* ed. by T. SILLANI, London, Ernest Benn, 1931, pp. 169–73. (B.1031. Translation of B.990, 1930.)

8. Fragments from *La filosofia dell'arte*, tr. by E. F. CARRITT in his anthology, *Philosophies of Beauty*, Oxford, Clarendon, 1931, pp. 320–30. (Carritt translated the whole work for E. W. Titus of Paris but it was never published. The translator's page proof, with an autograph letter from Gentile approving the translation, is in the Bodleian Library at Oxford. The title page bears the date 1932. The proof contains 7 unnumbered and 377 numbered leaves.)

9. "The Transcending of Time in History," tr. by E. F. CARRITT, in *Philosophy and History, Essays Presented to Ernst Cassirer*, ed. by H. J. PATON and R. KLIBANSKY, Oxford, Clarendon, 1936, pp. 91–105.

10. "The Thought of Leonardo," in *Leonardo da Vinci*, New York, Reynal, [1957?] (and London, Cresset, 1957), pp. 163–74. (Translation of B.1204.

Books and Articles on Gentile

General Philosophical and Historical Discussion

11. G. DE RUGGIERO, *Modern Philosophy*, tr. by A. H. HANNAY and R. G. COLLINGWOOD, London, Allen and Unwin, 1921, 402 pp. (This book was published in Italy in 1913 when Gentile's idealism was scarcely hatched. On Gentile see especially pp. 357–62, but the whole work expresses the attitude of the new movement.)

12. J. A. SMITH, "The Philosophy of Giovanni Gentile," *Proceedings of the Aristotelian Society*, XX, 1919/20, 63–78. See also:
   (a) "On Feeling," *Proceedings of the Aristotelian Society*, XIV, 1913/14, 49–75.
   (b) "Progress in Philosophy," in F. S. MARVIN (ed.): *Progress and History*, London, Oxford, 1916, pp. 273–94.
   (c) "Progress as an Ideal of Action," in *ibid.*, pp. 295–314.
   (d) "Philosophy as the Development of the Notion and Reality of Self-consciousness," in J. H. MUIRHEAD (ed.): *Contemporary British Philosophy*, second series, London, Allen and Unwin, 1924, pp. 225–44.

(e) "Professor Alexander's Notion of Space-Time," *Proceedings of the Aristotelian Society*, XXV, 1924/25, 41–60.

(f) "The Issue Between Monism and Pluralism," *ibid.*, XXVI, 1925/26, 1–24.

13. ROMOLO MURRI, "Religion and Idealism as Presented by Giovanni Gentile," *Hibbert Journal*, XIX, 1920/21, 249–62.

14. BERNARD BOSANQUET, *The Meeting of Extremes in Contemporary Philosophy*, London, Macmillan, 1921, xxviii + 220 pp. (Neither the index nor the analytical table of contents is a satisfactory guide. See pp. 20–26, 32–33, 52–62, 70, 101–2, 104–6, 110–13, 118–26, 127, 157–67, 186, 197, 200, 203–10, 212, 216.) See also items 96, 97, 98a, 100a below; and for Bosanquet's last word, the note in *Contemporary British Philosophy* (see item 12d), first series, pp. 68–69.

15. E. UNDERHILL, R. G. COLLINGWOOD, and W. R. INGE (symposium), "Can the New Idealism Dispense with Mysticism?" *Aristotelian Society Supplementary Volume* III, 1923, 148–84. (The contribution by Miss Underhill belongs properly to the next subsection, but that by Collingwood is of general philosophical interest. The brief eruption by Dean Inge is philosophically negligible.)

15 bis. CYRIL E. M. JOAD, *Introduction to Modern Philosophy*, London, Oxford, 1924, 112 pp. (See pp. 37 ff., especially pp. 56–66.) Cf. also:
(a) *Matter, Life and Value*, London, Oxford, 1929, xviii + 416 pp. (See index.)

16. ANGELO CRESPI, "Actual Idealism, an Exposition of Gentile's Philosophy and of Its Practical Effects," *Hibbert Journal*, XXIV, 1925/26, 250–63. (Cf. the note to item 45.)

17. ANGELO CRESPI, *Contemporary Thought of Italy*, London, Williams and Norgate (and New York, Knopf), 1926, 249 pp. (Only Chapter 4, pp. 149–211, is specifically concerned with Gentile; but the book should be read as a whole. I have not discovered any reviews of this book in philosophical periodicals, but see: ANON. in *Times Literary Supplement* (London), XXVI, 1927, 75.)

18. GEORGE BOAS, "Gentile and the Hegelian Invasion of Italy," *Journal of Philosophy*, XXIII, 1926, 184–88. (Officially a review of item 2 above.) See also:
(a) *The Major Traditions of European Philosophy*, New York, Harper, 1929, pp. 424–28.
(b) *Dominant Themes of Modern Philosophy*, New York, Ronald, 1957, pp. 566–67. (For Boas' last word.)

19. A. C. GARNETT, "Giovanni Gentile," *Australasian Journal of Psychology and Philosophy*, IV, 1926, 8–17. (Expository and critical article on item 2 above.)

20. G. DE RUGGIERO, "Main Currents of Contemporary Philosophy in Italy," *Philosophy*, I, 1926, 320–32.

21. VALMAI B. EVANS, "The Ethics of Giovanni Gentile," *Ethics*, XXXIX,

1928/29, 205–16. (Pure exposition. Pedestrian and rather superficial except for some useful remarks on Gentile's treatment of the free-will problem.)

22. W. G. DE BURGH, "Gentile's Philosophy of the Spirit," *Philosophy*, IV, 1929, 3–22; reprinted as Chapter 5 of *Towards a Religious Philosophy*, London, Macdonald and Evans, 1937. See also:

    (a) "On Historical Greatness," *Aristotelian Society Supplementary Volume* XI, 1932, 1–22.

    (b) "Philosophy and History," *Hibbert Journal*, XXXV, 1936/37, 40–52.

23. PETER M. RICCIO, *On the Threshold of Fascism*, New York, Casa Italiana of Columbia University, 1929, 261 pp.

24. VALMAI B. EVANS, "The Philosophy of Giovanni Gentile," *Personalist*, XI, 1930, 185–92. (Expository on a cliché level.)

24 bis. CHARLES W. MORRIS, *Six Theories of Mind*, University of Chicago Press, 1932, xi + 337 pp. (See pp. 88–101 and index. This item was brought to my attention by Professor G. N. G. Orsini.)

25. ROGER W. HOLMES, "Gentile's *Sistema di Logica*," *Philosophical Review*, XL, 1937, 393–401. (Condensed extract from following item.)

26. ROGER W. HOLMES, *The Idealism of Giovanni Gentile*, New York, Macmillan, 1937, xvi + 264 pp. See item 28 below and also the following reviews:

    (a) ANON. in *Times Literary Supplement* (London), XXXVII, 1938, 22.

    (b) CLIFFORD BARRETT in *Ethics*, XLVIII, 1937/38, 459.

    (c) PATRICK ROMANELL in *Journal of Philosophy*, XXXV, 1938, 412–17.

    (d) H. A. HODGES in *Philosophy*, XIII, 1938, 358–59.

    (e) EDGAR S. BRIGHTMAN in *Personalist*, XIX, 1938, 443–44.

    (f) STEPHEN EMERY in *Philosophical Review*, XLIX, 1940, 75–77.

27. PATRICK ROMANELL (PASQUALE ROMANELLI), *The Philosophy of Giovanni Gentile, an Inquiry into Gentile's Conception of Experience*, New York, S. F. Vanni, 1938, x + 190 pp. (Published first as a Ph.D. thesis, 1937.) See the following reviews:

    (a) ROGER W. HOLMES in *Journal of Philosophy*, XXXV, 1938, 417–20.

    (b) T. E. JESSUP in *Philosophy*, XIV, 1939, 242–43.

28. GIORGIO DE SANTILLANA, "The Idealism of Giovanni Gentile," *Isis*, XXIX, 1938, 366–76. (Occasioned by the appearance of item 15, but more than a review.)

29. PETER M. RICCIO, *Italian Authors of Today*, New York, S. F. Vanni, 1938. (Contains a trivial essay on Gentile.)

30. PATRICK ROMANELL, *Croce versus Gentile, a Dialogue on Contemporary Italian Philosophy*, New York, S. F. Vanni, 1946, 62 pp. See the following reviews:

    (a) T. V. S[MITH] in *Ethics*, LVII, 1946/47, 231–32.

    (b) S. M. MC MURRIN in *Personalist*, XXIX, 1948, 308.

30 bis. GIOVANNI GULLACE, "Gentile versus Croce: A Comparison of Two Rival Aesthetic Systems," *Symposium*, XI, 1957, 75–91. (I owe this item also to Professor Orsini.)

Philosophy and Religion

31. CAMILLO PELLIZZI, "The Problems of Religion for the Modern Italian Idealists," *Proceedings of the Aristotelian Society*, XXIV, 1923/24, 153–68. (Cf. on this subject items 13 and 15 above.)

32. LUIGI VILLARI, "New Developments in the Relations Between the Papacy and the State," *Quarterly Review*, CCLII, January 1929, 15–31. (See pp. 26–31 for Gentile's part in the polemic preceding the Concordat.)

33. ALINE A. LION, *The Idealistic Conception of Religion: Vico, Hegel, Gentile*, Oxford, Clarendon, 1932, xvi + 208 pp. See the following reviews:
    (a) E. S. WATERHOUSE in *Philosophy*, VIII, 1933, 113.
    (b) R. B. WINN in *Personalist*, XIV, 1933, 211–12.
    (c) D. C. MACKINTOSH in *Philosophical Review*, XLIII, 1934, 434.
    (d) JOHN LAIRD in *Mind*, XLII, 1933, 530.

34. S. W. HALPERIN, *The Separation of Church and State in Italian Thought from Cavour to Mussolini*, University of Chicago Press, 1937, 115 pp. (See pp. 93–97.)

35. DANIEL A. BINCHY, *Church and State in Fascist Italy*, London, Oxford, 1941, x + 774 pp. (See index s.v. Gentile.)

Philosophy and Education [2]

36. ANON., "Conditions in Italy" and "The New Curriculum in Italy," *Times Educational Supplement* (London), XIV, March 1924, 85, 121. (The latter article is an interesting three-column interpretation of the "Spirit" of the *Riforma Gentile*.)

37. MARIO PUGLISI, "Religious Teaching in Italian Schools," *Journal of Religion*, IV, 1924, 479–91. See item 73 below and also:
    (a) "Present State of Philosophy in Italy," *Personalist*, V, 1924, 162–70.

38. PIERO REBORA, "Educational Reforms in Italy," *Journal of Education* (London), LVI, September 1924, 609–12; reprinted in F. J. C. HEARNSHAW (ed.): *Educational Advancement Abroad*, London, G. G. Harrap, 1925, pp. 135–51. (A well-informed summary of the results of Gentile's ministry.)

39. ERNEST GRILLO, "Educational Reform in Italy," *Education Outlook* (London), LXXVI, July 1924, 267. (Valueless.)

40. UGO SPIRITO, "Educational Developments in 1924: Italy," tr. by HOWARD R. MARRARO, *Educational Yearbook* of the International Institute, Teachers College, Columbia University, New York, Macmillan, 1925, pp. 329–52. (This and the subsequent articles in the

---

[2] This section is far from complete.

Yearbook—items 49, 51, 56, 67, 69, 71 below—are the most important source for the views of the "Gentile reformers" themselves available in English.)

41. L. A. WILLIAMS, "Reform of Secondary Education in Italy," *School Review* (Chicago), XXXIII, 1925, 201–7. (Translation of an article in *Giornale d'Italia*, 28 April 1923, summarizing the reforms.)

42. ADOLF E. MEYER, "Education in Modern Italy," *School and Society*, XXII, July 1925, 96–99. (Very slight value.)

43. HOWARD R. MARRARO, "Education in Italy Under Mussolini," *Current History*, XXXIII, February 1926, 705–9.

44. HOWARD R. MARRARO, *Nationalism in Italian Education*, New York, Italian Digest and News Service, 1927, xxviii + 161 pp. (Introduction by UGO SPIRITO.)

45. F. R. G. DUCKWORTH, "Gentile on the Teaching of Literature and Language," *Church Quarterly Review*, CIII, January 1927, 201–15. (Valuable critical article on *The Reform of Education* (item 3 above). Thompson (item 66) followed by Marraro (item 68) and Romanell (item 27) give this reference for an article by Crespi: "An Italian Philosophy of Absolute Immanence," which I cannot trace. I suspect it is simply item 16.)

46. ALFRED IACUZZI, "The Italian Elementary School Reforms," *School and Society*, XXV, January 1927, 74–76. (Impressions of elementary schools in the Palermo region. Brings out the economic reason for Gentile's emphasis on the 'spirit' of education.)

47. GIUSEPPE PREZZOLINI, "School and Church Under Fascism," *Survey*, LVII, March 1927, 710–11, 756–57. (See the remark on p. 33 herein—otherwise accurate.)

48. H. W. SCHNEIDER and S. B. CLOUGH, *Making Fascists*, University of Chicago Press, 1929, xv + 211 pp. (Especially Chapter 5.)

49. ERNESTO CODIGNOLA, "The Philosophy Underlying the National System of Education in Italy," tr. by JOSEPH A. SIMONE, *Educational Yearbook* of the International Institute, New York, Bureau of Publications, Teachers College, Columbia University, 1929, pp. 317–425. (History of Italian educational theory and practice from the actual idealist point of view. Fundamental.)

50. STEPHEN P. DUGGAN, "The Fascist Conception of Education," *News Bulletin* of the Institute of International Education, IV, No. 6, March 1929; and in *Historical Outlook*, XX, May 1929, 224–25. (Valueless.)

51. ERNESTO CODIGNOLA, "Expansion of Secondary Education: Italy," tr. by ANTHONY GISOLFI, *Educational Yearbook* (see item 49), 1930, pp. 343–86.

52. ISAAC L. KANDEL, "Nationalism and Education in Italy," *Educational Outlook*, IV, 1930, 65–71; also in *Essays in Comparative Education*, New York, Bureau of Publications, Teachers College, Columbia University, 1930, pp. 108–17.

53. E. A. MILLER, "Il Fascismo, Italian Education and the Church," *School Review* (Chicago), XXXVIII, 1930, 510–24. (Contains translation of Gentile's letter of adherence to the P.N.F., B.723.)

54. BALBINO GIULIANO, "Italian National Education and the 'Ballilla' Organization," in *What Is Fascism and Why?* (see item 7), pp. 152–62. (Official propaganda by the Minister of Education.)

55. PIETRO GERBORE, "Education in Fascist Italy," in *Health Section Report* 1931, World Federation of Education Associations, New York, American Child Health Association and Metropolitan Life Insurance Co., 1932, pp. 76–79. (Irrelevant propaganda injected into the conference at Denver by the Italian consul.)

56. ERNESTO CODIGNOLA, "Relation of the State to Religious Education: Italy," tr. by MARTHA F. SCACCIAFERRO, *Educational Yearbook* (see item 49), 1932, pp. 295–314. (Contains translation of Gentile's circular of 5 January 1924 on the topic (B.787 minus first paragraph). Exhibits discreetly but clearly the idealist reformers' hostility to the Concordat.)

57. MARINO LAZZARI, "Education in Italy," *Yearbook of Education*, 1932, London, Evans Bros., pp. 858–77. (A factual account of the reform as revised to 1932, with some flag waving.)

58. "The Oath of the University Professors," in *Italy Today* (published by the "Friends of Italian Freedom"), London, February 1932. (Not examined. According to Borghi (74, p. 194) this item contains extracts translated from a speech by Gentile which I cannot identify in Bellezza.) On the oath see also: "Oath of Allegiance to Fascism in Italian Universities," *School and Society*, XXXV, 9 January 1932, 47–48.

59. CHARLES E. LITTLE, "The Italians and Their Schools," *Peabody Journal of Education*, X, 1932/33, 72–86, 128–54, 206–44, 257–80. (Curious mélange of guidebook history, travelogue impressions and facts from official sources; Part II has perhaps some interest for students of the reform.)

60. VALMAI B. EVANS, "Education in the Philosophy of Giovanni Gentile," *Ethics*, XLIII, 1932/33, 210–17. (Sound but pedestrian on the theoretical side.)

61. ISAAC L. KANDEL, *Comparative Education*, Boston, Houghton, 1933, pp. 297–308, 455–77.

62. E. D. GRIZZELL, "Secondary Education in Italy," *Educational Outlook*, VII, 1932/33, 65–76. (No apparent awareness of 'fascistization,' but some critical insights.)

63. HOWARD R. MARRARO, "The New Education in Italy," *Current History*, XXXVII, February 1933, 571–76.

64. HOWARD R. MARRARO, "Education in Italy," *School and Home*, XV, November 1933, 209–19.

65. HOWARD R. MARRARO, *Handbook for American Students in Italy*, Institute of International Education Bulletins, Series 14, No. 2, New York, 1933, 58 pp. (Dedicated to Gentile.)

66. MERRITT M. THOMPSON, *The Educational Philosophy of Giovanni Gentile*, Los Angeles, University of Southern California, 1934, ix + 217 pp. (Southern California Education Monographs, Series 1933–34, No. 1). Brief laudatory review by:
    (a) W[ILBUR] L[ONG] in *Personalist*, XVII, 1936, 101–2.

67. ERNESTO CODIGNOLA, "Teachers' Associations: Italy," *Educational Yearbook* (see item 49), 1935, pp. 351–67. (Includes account of the *Fascio di Educazione Nazionale*.)

68. HOWARD R. MARRARO, *The New Education in Italy*, New York, S. F. Vanni, 1936, xvi + 506 pp. (Most of the items in this subsection are derived from a rechecking of the copious bibliography in this book, which contains some errors and a mass of completely irrelevant material.)

69. ERNESTO CODIGNOLA, "Educational Developments: Italy," *Educational Yearbook* (see item 49), 1937, pp. 319–35. (On the De Vecchi reforms.)

70. SALVATORE VALITUTTI, "Elementary Education in Italy," *Yearbook of Education* (see item 57), 1937, pp. 790–801.

71. ERNESTO CODIGNOLA, "The Meaning of a Liberal Education: Italy," *Educational Yearbook* (see item 49), 1939, pp. 221–36. (The shadow of the School Charter lends point to the perceptible bias against manual work. Gentile's name is not mentioned.)

72. ISAAC L. KANDEL, "Education in Italy," *Educational Forum*, IV, 1939/40, 206–12. (Text of the School Charter.) See also:
    (a) J. F. ABEL in *School Life* (Washington), XXV, October 1939, 15–16, 29.
    (b) M. A. JOHNSTONE in *Journal of Education* (London), XLI, 1939, 550–51.
    (c) KANDEL, *The End of an Era* (*Educational Yearbook*, 1941), index s.v. Gentile.

73. H. E. GOAD and G. CATALANO, *Education in Italy*, Rome, Laboremus, 1939, 64 pp. (Not examined. I can no longer trace the source from which I derived this item.)

74. LAMBERTO BORGHI, "Postwar Reconstruction in Italy," *Educational Yearbook* (see item 49), 1944, pp. 173–216.

75. MERRITT M. THOMPSON, "Personalism in Education," *Personalist*, XXV, 1944, 40–53.

76. LUIGI MINIO-PALUELLO, *Education in Fascist Italy*, London, Oxford, 1946, xiv + 236 pp.

77. G. DE RUGGIERO, "Italy: Education Under Fascism," *Yearbook of Education* (see item 57), 1948, pp. 566–77. See also:
    (a) A. VESSELO, "Education Under Allied Military Government," *ibid.*, pp. 578–91.

77 bis. MERRITT M. THOMPSON, "A Neglected Educator," *Educational Forum*, XXIV, 1959/60, 49–57. (Originally intended as an intro-

duction to his translation of Gentile's *Sommario di pedagogia*, for which a publisher has not yet been found.)

Philosophy and Fascism [3]

78. ANON., "Italian Philosophers at Odds," *New Statesman and Nation* (London), XXV, May 1925, 131–32. (Report on breach between Gentile and Croce from Rome correspondent. Search would doubtless reveal many more such reports in serious newspapers and journals.)

79. ANON., "Croce and Gentile," *Living Age*, CCCXXVI, September 1925, 637–38; reprinted from *Manchester Guardian*, 18 August 1925. (Largely devoted to Tilgher's *Spaccio del bestione trionfante*.)

80. ALINE A. LION, "Fascism: What It Believes in and Aims at," *Hibbert Journal*, XXV, 1926/27, 208–28. (Cf. the following item.)

81. ALINE A. LION, *The Pedigree of Fascism, a Popular Essay on the Western Philosophy of Politics*, London, Sheed and Ward, 1927, 236 pp. See the brief review:
    (a) ANON. in *Times Literary Supplement* (London), XXVII, 1928, p. 15.

82. GIUSEPPE PREZZOLINI, *Fascism*, tr. by KATHLEEN MACMILLAN, London, J. M. Dent (and New York, Dutton), n.d. (but 1927), xv + 201 pp. (See index s.v. Gentile; cf. also item 47.)

83. H. W. SCHNEIDER, *Making the Fascist State*, New York, Oxford, 1928, xi + 392 pp. (See index and item 4 above.)

84. JAMES S. BARNES, *The Universal Aspects of Fascism*, London, Williams and Norgate, 1928, xxi + 267 pp. (See index.)

85. "LA DIREZIONE," "The National Fascist Institute of Culture," in *What Is Fascism and Why?* (see item 7), pp. 167–68.

86. "WILLIAM ELWIN," *Fascism at Work*, London, Martin Hopkinson, 1934, 320 pp. (See index. Written by an Italian exile. Vitriolic.)

87. MARIO PUGLISI, "The Third Hegelian Congress," *Personalist*, XV, 1934, 66–69. (A Catholic account of the congress with references to the *Caso Orestano*.)

88. HERMAN FINER, *Mussolini's Italy*, London, V. Gollancz (and New York, H. Holt), 1935, 564 pp. (See index and the note to item 6 above.)

89. G. A. BORGESE, *Goliath, the March of Fascism*, New York, Viking, 1937, ix + 483 pp. (See pp. 242, 295–304, 334–42. Marred by journalistic statement of rumors as fact, and general aversion to documentation.)

90. GEORGE H. SABINE, *A History of Political Theory*, New York, H. Holt, 1937, pp. 747–70 (and London, G. G. Harrap, pp. 627–48).

91. MAX ASCOLI, "The Press and the Universities in Italy," *Annals of the*

---

[3] This section also is far from complete.

American Academy of Political and Social Science, CC, November 1938, 235–54 (and in part in item 92, pp. 107–20). (Very moderate in tone.)

92. FRANCES KEENE (ed.), *Neither Liberty nor Bread: The Meaning and Tragedy of Fascism*, New York, Harper, 1940, xiii + 358 pp. Apart from item 91 (q.v.) the following are of interest:
    (a) G. SALVEMINI, "Benedetto Croce," pp. 124–26.
    (b) G. SALVEMINI, "Censorship of Books," pp. 126–27. (Factual.)
    (c) "N. TRAVI," "Italian Culture Under Fascism," pp. 136–38. (The last word in prejudice.)

93. HERBERT MARCUSE, *Reason and Revolution*, New York, Oxford, 1941 (2nd ed., Humanities Press, 1955), pp. 402–9. (An attempt to force the *Theory of Mind as Pure Act* (item 2) into accord with Marcuse's interpretation of the *Grundlagen des Faschismus*, B.1142.)

94. HERBERT L. MATTHEWS, *The Fruits of Fascism*, New York, Harcourt, 1943, 341 pp. (See index. 'Good reportage.')

Reviews of Books by Gentile

95. *Giordano Bruno nella storia della cultura* (1907, B.153) with BRUNO: *Opere italiane* (1907–8, B.155 and B.184).
    (a) By J. L. MC INTYRE in *Mind*, XVIII, 1909, 149. (The earliest appearance of Gentile's name in English that I have discovered.)

96. *Riforma della dialettica hegeliana* (1913, B.290).
    (a) By BERNARD BOSANQUET in *Mind*, XXIX, 1920, 367–70.

97. *Sommario di pedagogia* (1913/14, B.292 and B.305).
    (a) By BERNARD BOSANQUET in *Mind*, XXIX, 1920, 367–70.

98. *Discorsi di religione* (1920, B.556, and 1934, B.1100).
    (a) By BERNARD BOSANQUET in *Mind*, XXX, 1921, 98–101.
    (b) By SALVATORE RUSSO in *Philosophical Review*, XLV, 1936, 638.

99. *Giordano Bruno e il pensiero del Rinascimento* (1920, B.558).
    (a) By J. L. M[C INTYRE] in *Mind*, XXX, 1921, 489.

100. *Teoria generale dello spirito come atto puro* (3rd ed., 1920, B.560) and *Theory of Mind as Pure Act* (1922, B.660).
    (a) By BERNARD BOSANQUET in *Mind*, XXX, 1921, 96–98.
    (b) By JOHN LAIRD in *Ethics*, XXXIII, 1922/23, 213–16.
    (c) By WARNER FITE in *Philosophical Review*, XXXII, 1923, 548. (Cf. also items 18, 19 above.)

101. *The Reform of Education* (1922, B.659).
    (a) See item 45 above. No reviews in philosophical periodicals.
    (b) By ROY I. JOHNSON in *School Review* (Chicago), XXXI, 1923, 395–96.
    (A thorough search might reveal other reviews in educational periodicals.)

102. *Il fascismo al governo della scuola* (1924, B.776).
  (a) ANON. in *Times Literary Supplement* (London), XXXIII (special Italian issue), 21 June 1934, iii.
103. *Che cosa è il fascismo* (1925, B.818).
  (a) ANON. in *Times Literary Supplement* (London), XXV, 1926, 347.
104. *Storia della filosofia italiana dal Genovesi al Galluppi* (2nd ed., 1930, B.985).
  (a) By GEORGE BOAS in *Journal of Philosophy*, XXVII, 1930, 715–19.
  (b) By G. DE RUGGIERO in *Philosophy*, VI, 1931, 491.
  (c) By R. A. TSANOFF in *Philosophical Review*, XLI, 1932, 326.
105. *La filosofia dell'arte* (1931, B.1012) and *Filosofia dell'arte in compendio* (1934, B.1102).
  (a) By G. DE RUGGIERO in *Philosophy*, VI, 1931, 493.
  (b) By GEORGE BOAS in *Journal of Philosophy*, XXVIII, 1931, 698–99.
  (c) (The *Compendio*) by SALVATORE RUSSO in *Philosophical Review*, XLV, 1936, 638.
106. *Origini e dottrina del fascismo* (1934, B.1104).
  (a) ANON. in *Times Literary Supplement* (London), XXXIII (special Italian issue), 21 June 1934, i–ii. (Deals also with 'Mussolini's' *Enciclopedia* article.)
107. *Il pensiero italiano del Rinascimento* (1940, B.1223).
  (a) By ROGER W. HOLMES in *Philosophical Review*, L, 1941, 647.
108. *Genesi e struttura della società* (1946, B.1288).
  (a) By MARIO M. ROSSI in *Journal of Philosophy*, XLVII, 1950, 217–22. (A short article of considerable importance.)
  (b) By G. R. G. MURE in *Philosophical Quarterly*, I, 1950, 83.
  (c) By MERRITT M. THOMPSON in *Personalist*, XXXVII, 1956, 104–5. (On the edition published by Mondadori ed. by V. A. BELLEZZA. On pp. 101–2 is a notice of Bellezza's *L'esistenzialismo positivo di Giovanni Gentile* and an account of the *Fondazione Gentile*.)
109. *Rosmini e Gioberti* (2nd ed., 1955).
  (a) By MERRITT M. THOMPSON in *Personalist*, XXXVII, 1956, 102–4.

GENESIS AND STRUCTURE OF SOCIETY

PREFACE

The writing of this book was a relief to my mind in days full of anxiety for all Italians, and the fulfillment of a civil duty, since I saw no other course open to me in my concern for that Italy of the future for which I have always lived and worked.

In it the reader will find many echoes of views expounded in my earlier books. In particular I have taken up and developed further the discussion of 'the State' and of 'Politics' in my *Foundations of the Philosophy of Law*,[a] and the discussion of the connections between economics and ethics in *Italian Memorials*.[b] But this familiar material now brings with it something new, for the fourth chapter contains a thesis which has not previously been stated either by me or by anyone else—a thesis that appears to me to be not without importance. Like all of my speculations this book was born in the schoolroom; it summarizes a series of lectures on "The Transcendental Theory of the Will and of Society" given during the past year (1942–43) at the University of Rome.

G.G.

Troghi (Florence), 25 September 1943.

This book arose out of a university course and was written in one burst during August and early September 1943 at Troghi. The author had time to look over the proof sheets and approve them for publication, but like the manuscript and the typescript they show no signs of revision or correction.

Publisher's note

---

[a] 3rd ed., Florence, Sansoni, 1937, pp. 103–31. [Letters are used throughout for the author's footnotes, and numbers for those added by the translator—Tr.]
[b] Florence, Sansoni, 1936, pp. 271–94.

I

ETHICS AS LAW

1. Discipline

Discipline is the governance of custom. Any concept of it presupposes the repetition of acts which by way of the repetition become habits or mores; and this implies (1) that an act can be repeated, and (2) that we can perform many acts.

Neither postulate can be granted. In the life of the spirit there is no repetition, for repetition is a mechanical thing. Looking at things superficially we do speak of 'repeating' an action in our conscious life; but the 'repetition' is always really a new act in relation to the changed being of the agent who is no longer what he was before precisely because he has already done a certain action.

Nor can we conceive a multiplicity of conscious acts. The act of the spirit is infinite because it is free, and unique because it is infinite. When we speak of many acts we are not talking precisely. We should say not *acts* but *facts*—things without liberty or spiritual value. And when 'act' declines into 'fact' all ethical interest disappears.

2. Positivism and empiricism

The positivists [1] did in fact try to abolish ethics by talking always of 'moral facts' and closing their eyes to the spiritual character of

---

[1] The reference here is to the followers of Auguste Comte—especially Roberto Ardigò and his school—rather than to the more recent analytical empiricism. Italian writers habitually lump all modern analytical philosophy together under the heading 'neopositivism.'

the moral action. But the very assumption of positivism or of any form of empiricism is absurd; for no presupposition is allowable on the level of 'empirical facts.' Where values no longer exist, and every fact is justified by the conditions to which it is naturally subordinate, everything is fact; but the assertion that everything is fact cannot itself be a fact. And the act of assertion is not simply an act which has its own kind of freedom and its own kind of value, but is itself a *moral* act. For as we shall see, morality is not the property of a special activity of the spirit; it belongs to conscious life as a whole, including theoretical knowledge as long as that knowledge is not thought of in abstract objectivity, but in its real relation to the life of the thinking subject who constructs it.

3. Law

The ethical character of an act involves, of course, a law in conformity with which the moral act is what it ought to be; and it can only be what it ought to be insofar as it is not naturally determined and therefore necessitated, but is *free*.

But if the act is to be free while yet the law remains the principle which gives it value, the law cannot be something external to the act, imposed as it were by coercion from without. It must coincide with the inner essence of the act itself. The moral law is in fact nothing but the very character of the act as free; or in other words its character as an act which is not impulsive [2] but arises consciously and spontaneously by its own power [3]—for that is what we mean when we say that an action is what it ought to be.

4. Pragmatism

This conception of morality as spontaneity and freedom of action is not identical with the irrational pragmatism or activism which

---

[2] *Immediato.*

[3] *Ex se.* (In saying that a free act is not 'immediate' but is yet 'spontaneous' Gentile may perhaps appear to contradict himself. What he means is that the act is not part of a natural chain of events but is independently conceived and is thus its own cause (*ex se*). In traditional Aristotelian terminology we could say that the explanation for it must be sought not in terms of efficient but in terms of final causation. One might be tempted to object that being thus self-caused is not enough to make an action moral. But Gentile, following the Kantian tradition, would say that an immoral action is not really self-caused but produced by the power of natural impulse. Of course, he does also want to insist that *all* conscious action is *in some measure* free and therefore moral.)

properly incurs the disapproval of all who believe in genuine freedom of action and hence in moral responsibility. Historicism has
aroused and indeed still arouses apprehensions of this kind. The
answer lies in distinguishing two different sorts of historicism: on
the one hand an empirical mechanistic mode of thought, and on
the other a true speculative idealism. An act can be conceived as a
simple object for conscious knowledge; and as such it is something
as irrational and necessary as a natural phenomenon since it is external to the spirit which considers it. But the inward act of the
spirit is the act which cannot be thus objectified and for which the
first act forms a purely factual content. This internal act which here
concerns us is not an objective datum presented to self-consciousness from outside. It is the very act of self-consciousness; a conscious act or rather an act which *consists in* consciousness. It is not
'thing' but spirit, the process of consciousness itself, not the immediate 'something' which is its starting point.

If we wish to contrast the brute irrationality of mere fact with
the liberty of consciousness there is only one way: we must set
brute fact against the actual rationality of self-consciousness with
its resultant freedom.[4] We must compare brute fact with the act
which has value because it contains its own law within itself.

5. Theory and practice

This act is certainly not pure will as distinct from intelligence, in
the sense in which the distinction is made by those philosophers who
cannot grasp the unity of theory and practice, but go on arguing
about the 'two forms of spiritual activity' as if they were irreducible:
volition that is not intelligence, and intelligence that is not volition.

Great efforts have certainly been made to define this dualism; but
none of them has ever been crowned with speculative success. I say
'speculative' success because, if we leave things all muddled up and
rest content with the easy arguments of lazy common sense, victory
over all difficulties arising from a dualism of this kind becomes a
simple matter. The difficulty only emerges and proves insurmountable when we want to define exactly what is meant by a will that
is not theoretical or a knowledge that is not practical.

---

[4] *Opporre il fatto al'atto, che è logicità concreta (consapevolezza) e quindi
libertà.*

It will be best, however, to leave aside for the moment the term 'theory,' which, like such notions as 'vision' or 'intuition,' is purely metaphorical and fanciful; for it implies such a naively realistic conception of the relation between the knowing subject and the object known that no one has been able to take it seriously—at least not in the last two thousand years and more.

Let us consider rather the concept of 'practice' or 'volition,' the most striking and important characteristic of which has attracted attention ever since it was contraposed to 'theory' by Aristotle. It was precisely because of this characteristic that the need to contrast willing and knowing was felt. For whereas in knowing the object of consciousness seemed to be an antecedent of its activity, in willing it was manifestly and undeniably a consequent. In fact, it was recognized straightaway that the object of human willing is everything which, whether good or bad, would not exist at all apart from the productive activity of the will. The crucial problem, therefore, is to understand the nature of this object that owes its existence to volitional activity.

6. The object of the will

The object of volition presents itself at first as one object among others, having its own place in space and time like any other object of sense. The earth appears to be full of natural phenomena such as mountains, plants, and animals, which exist independently of the human will, and therefore condition its activity, but it is also full of houses and cities and all the other products of human invention which are inconceivable apart from the constructive operation of the will. Before our very eyes we see among the living the murdered victims of human wickedness—and so on. But little by little we learn to distinguish the matter in which the human will is incarnated from that novel element of its own which it imports into it; until at last we come to recognize that what can properly be regarded as the result of human activity, even in the world of sensible and material things, is really something spiritual—which is why we make it an object of moral judgment and treat it as 'good' or 'evil'; and we realize that what a man can do in this world, and what he is in fact always called to account for, is good and evil; which can never be something existing in the outside world, the world of space and time, but is rather an act of the will. Praise and blame, rewards and punishments are reserved for voluntary actions; indeed, we are so much inclined to withdraw morality inward away from the external world that we make a distinction even within the same moral event, between the *intention* and the *execution* of the act. But here we go too far, for the 'intention' in which we think to preserve that *inward* aspect of the act, to which moral value properly belongs, is itself already a moral resolution. It is already an act; and in cases where the *execution* can really be distinguished from the pure *intention*, it is a different act. So that the product of the will cannot be made to consist in anything but the will itself, that same act, good or not so good, upon which we exercise our moral judgment; and, certainly, this is something that would not exist in the world but for our free will. For we might have existed, or at least we can imagine ourselves as existing, as part of a natural order created by God, with God Himself at the head of it and the Devil as the seducer in Eden—with everything in short that goes to make up the scene of human action; and yet without the spark of the human will there would be not so much as a shadow of good or evil in all heaven and earth. And though the religious conception of the world may lead us, on reflection, to admit a divine intervention in that work of creating good which is the life of the world, no theological doctrine will ever induce us to abolish human responsibility in the world, a responsibility which implies that man is somehow free and capable of creating something which but for him would never exist in all eternity.

7. Volition as self-constitution [5]

The object of human creativity is man himself. The will is not a faculty that exists independently, having the capacity to do good works but not in fact doing them. Doing good requires a determinate will which, when it really exists, is itself the good that is desired. The great harvest to which the good farmer aspires is the harvest of the good will; and the supreme prayer of the Gospel asks likewise that "Thy Will be done."

---

[5] *Volontà = autoctisi.* The word *autoctisi* was coined by Spaventa from the Greek κτίσις, which the Church Fathers used to describe the creation of the world out of nothing. It means literally 'self-founding.' Gentile often speaks of the spirit as creating itself, and *autoctisis* is his technical name for this self-creation. But, perhaps because it is such a fundamental conception in his thought, it is hard to define precisely what is meant by it (see Introduction, pp. 43–45).

The product of the will is not external to it but within it and identical with it. The will is not the cause of good and evil; if it is the cause of anything it is the cause of itself [*causa sui ipsius*]. That is why it was said that the reward of virtue is not something added to virtue itself—*praemium virtutis ipsamet virtus.*[6] It is indeed a dangerous turning along a path beset with errors disastrous to the moral life, that we take every time we separate reward or punishment from the act which is good or bad, and continue to treat someone who proves to be unworthy of an act that he once performed in a moment of exceptional heroism as deserving of respect and honor, while leaving another to bear a heavy burden of dishonor although he has reformed. (God pardons so much for one act of mercy!)

In short, the will as a spiritual activity produces only itself: it is self-constitution. Here we have the strictest possible definition of the will.

8. The practical character of knowledge

If we accept this definition, how can we exclude the process of knowing from it, once we have rid ourselves of all the prejudices of realism and intellectualism? What is knowing but self-consciousness and hence self-concept? What else is the object of knowledge but the subject himself, revealed to himself and so made conscious?

One simple consideration is here enough to free us from every 'realistic' prejudice: if the knowing subject had before him something metaphysically external and antecedent, he would be limited by it, and so would not be free; and in that case he could not even have knowledge, if to know is to choose the truth—an act of liberty.

If it be true—as indeed it is true—that all knowing is self-consciousness, that the subject is either self-consciousness or nothing, then clearly, with self-consciousness there comes into being something which no one (neither a natural nor a supernatural being) could ever create in any other way: the thought which is the great light of the world and the source of every good which we seek in it.

---

[6] The proverb was given this form by Pomponazzi. See *De immortalitate animae,* Chapter 14 (ed. by Gentile, Milan-Messina, Principato, 1925, p. 100); cf. also the English translation by W. H. Hay in E. Cassirer *et al., The Renaissance Philosophy of Man,* University of Chicago Press, 1948, p. 361.

9. The unity of theory and practice

In our concept of self-constitution, therefore, knowing coincides with willing. Everywhere we find only the self-creative activity of the spirit; Art, Religion, Science, Economics, Philosophy, everything arises from this self-constitution. And since self-constitution means moral responsibility—or freedom—every aspect of conscious life is subject to moral law; there is no corner of the earth, no moment of the day in which man can escape from the imperious voice of duty. He cannot escape from the moral world that surrounds him on every side by taking refuge in the free world of abstract speculation or of his own imagination, for the care that makes the poet "lean through the long years" [7] is a torturing passion that compels him to strive after perfection in his art, and the rigorous logic of speculative thought is a more severe constraint upon the seeker after truth than any law of the State. Within the soul of man there is a still small voice that is never silent, and will not let him rest but spurs him ever onward. Onward toward what? Toward himself—toward the ideal self that he ought to be.

In reality, an ordinary action in everyday life [8] seen from the point of view of the agent is always the solution of a problem that presses closely upon him because it concerns his own life, and his own being requires its solution. It is vital to draw a clear distinction between *abstract thought,* which seems to stand opposed to us, completely objective and independent of our relation to it (thought as it is in the logic of the abstract), and *concrete thought,* which is the only thought that really exists—our own thought about our own lives, our problems and their solution. Our problems and solutions are bound to be practical in character: the unending sequence of problems that make up our experience of life, an experience that takes on the form of an object presented to thought, gives rise to an infinity of difficulties. There is discord between acts of an apparently theoretical character, and corresponding acts which appear to be purely and simply practical; and from this root spring all the familiar divergences between 'word' and 'deed,' pure theory as opposed to actual practice. But we can dispose of this everyday experience with

---

[7] *Per più anni macro* (Dante, *Paradiso,* XXV, 3).
[8] *Un atto pratico.*

just one simple remark: the empty 'word' that is never translated
into 'deed' is generally recognized as an act of moral laziness and
a true and proper object of moral condemnation. Generally speaking
we can say that whatever appears as purely theoretical and not
practical does so only through comparison with some different activity, but not when considered in itself.

Every attempt to draw a dividing line between thought and action is really inspired by the desire to free thought from the burden
of responsibility that attaches to action by conferring on it some incomprehensible necessity which is passed off as logical—and yet
this necessity is erroneously supposed to allow of liberty. In point
of fact the same 'necessity' is to be found in moral activity, and we
may properly speak of the logic of action; everywhere, moreover, it
is the necessity of liberty. It involves responsibility and a rare kind
of moral sensibility; a man who possesses this sensibility in a high
degree is eternally vigilant (even, one might say, in his sleep),
spying on himself and marking the slightest ripple of feeling, the
faintest flicker of an idea that emerges from the depth of consciousness—he prefers to go too far in this respect rather than fall
short. Manzoni, for example, does not intrude his own moral scruples
into his art, but he cannot keep art and morality really separate; he
feels that morality is immanent in art and vital to its existence. For
art cannot exist unless it is inspired by the supreme law of the life
of the spirit.

10. The act

The essence of ethics then is to be found in the act of thought—
the whole world of morals lies within it. The act of thought is what
we have called 'self-consciousness'; it is the self-concept—an identity of opposites, the unification of subject and object in an a priori
synthesis. This unification comes about through the self-alienation
of the subject in the object which is other than it, and its return to
itself from thence. This is the process of its being, the being of
man, the only being that can say "I."

This Ego is what man is and wills to be, but he never succeeds
entirely in attaining to it; so that the object remains object still,
forever opposed and irreducible. And hence hatred creeps back
again into the love that flowers at the spirit's return to itself (or at
the identification of the 'other' with itself); and man is tempted to
seal himself off in egoism, halting his spiritual advance because he

is weary of the effort to dematerialize and assimilate his experience. This halting is the laziness that makes us accept things as they are; [9] it is a sense of bewilderment in the face of an object which remains impervious and repulsive. In our ignorance we are suspicious; we remain unaware of the spirit which is there before us; and hence it forms a limit for our own spiritual life.

Be it a man or a book or a problem that faces us, it is all one. Within the book or the problem there is the same spiritual power as in the man—that *other* through whose conquest we must achieve the conquest of our own higher selves.

We need therefore to understand who and what we are. We must grasp the significance of our individuality.

---

[9] *L'immediato essere naturale.*

II

THE INDIVIDUAL

1. 'Individuality' in the realistic and the idealistic sense

The ordinary sense of the term 'individual' is that given to it by Aristotle, who made it the foundation stone of his opposition to Platonism and hence of his own originality. He was deeply conscious that reality cannot be conceived as the universal Idea in which Plato believed, since the individual thing, in which the universal is presented always as a particular, remains excluded from the world of Ideas. The individual thing is a form incorporated in a given matter, which is susceptible in the abstract of all possible forms, but which has attained to actual existence because it has taken upon itself a single one among all the forms possible. To say nothing of the fact that the Platonic Idea is Pure Being and hence eternal; while all the individual things that the Idea was invented to explain pass in and out of existence, and therefore fall within the realm of space and time—they are mortal and finite.

The individual which Aristotle sets up as a real substance in place of the Idea is any and every determinate unity of matter and form existing in the world of Nature. In this world things are born, grow to maturity, and die, while Nature remains always one through the endless cycle of change. Everything that enters our experience in the natural world, having both matter and form, is an individual. The individual is there before us, a natural entity, existing of itself as a presupposition of our thought, which affirms its individuality only in virtue of its pre-existence. It exists as a *thing* (*res,* an object of thought) quite independent of the relation to us into which it enters when it is known. This conception of individuality meets the standard of that realism which is the essential mode of all Greek philosophical thought—in Plato, Aristotle, and their opponents all alike—and which remains the basis of ordinary 'common sense' today, though it is many centuries since Christianity first taught us the spiritual nature of the real, and the consequent impossibility of a reality-in-itself, antecedent to the spirit that knows and wills it. 'Naive' realism, 'scientific' realism, 'philosophical' realism: despite all the pretenses of its most obstinate defenders, all forms of realism are very naive, since very little reflection is needed to realize that whatever we can discover, invent, or construct by means of thought cannot itself be anything but thought.

In the modern era, however, a new conception of individuality has developed, since the difficulties that emerged in the traditional conception proved insuperable. In this modern conception the individual is no longer an object of thought, a natural entity. The unity that properly belongs to it will not allow of our seeking it in the natural world, where, if we abstract from its relatedness, there is nothing but multiplicity; the relatedness is indeed a kind of unity, but unlike anything that is truly natural it is not spatial or sensible but ideal, and, in substance, spiritual. Unity belongs to the spirit, to the Ego which confers its own unity on everything opposed to it, binding everything in an indivisible nexus which is the system of consciousness or of thought. And anyone who turns his attention inward and speaks of 'himself,' abstracting from all the other objects about which he can think, finds in himself first and foremost the unmultipliable unity that makes every man unique. His unity is quite different from the unity that belongs equally to every individual 'thing' in realistic philosophy. The unity of a thing is finite and hence it is inconceivable except in relation to and together with other units; the thing is a particular unit which forms part of the higher unity constituted by the complex of all the subordinate units. But the unity of the Ego cannot be transcended; it is infinite, universal, and absolute. When we think of the Ego as face to face with 'others,' these others reassemble within it and exist within it, since it cannot issue from itself. Its being consists in its activity (thought, feeling, or whatever we choose to call it), and this is never confined within the limits of the particular, for the Ego cannot think or feel or real-

ize itself in any way that is not universal. It thinks of everything
in and along with itself: in its feeling the feeling of the whole universe is gathered up and concentrated; nor can it separate itself in
any way from the rest of the world and consider itself as a part only.
Every time that man achieves a fuller awareness of the Whole,[1]
what he feels "no mortal tongue can utter,"[2] for his voice echoes
within him as the voice of all men, of the Whole, the voice of the
eternal and the infinite.

The individual, in short, is not the object of experience but its
subject. The true individual (*in-dividuus*, a whole that is unique
and indivisible) is man himself, not the things amid which he lives,
which are what they are in relation to him and, as is obvious in
many cases, as a result of his work.

2. The individual and society

But man lives in society; to use a famous phrase, he is a 'political animal.' And it appears that within society he must be thought
of as one individual thing among others, a particular, finite, unit
which is transcended in the social system that he along with other
men helps to establish.

There is no one possessed of an active conscience who would not
rebel against a political and social atomism of this kind, which
smashes and destroys the substantial unity of human community,
making it no more than an accident and depriving it of value as an
end in itself [3]—the only kind of value that matters. Social atomism,
like every other variety of atomism, is really only materialism; and
materialism means the collapse of all morality and even of value
in general—for any talk of 'value' implies liberty, and materialism
starts by uprooting liberty and everything that follows from it.
People who claim in the name of morality that the particular individual man must be recognized as free or as substantially independent of the social aggregation through which he also becomes a
member of society [4] do not realize what they are saying; they are

----

[1] *Il Tutto dell'uomo si allarga ad un ampio respiro.*

[2] *Lingua mortal non dice* (Leopardi, *Canti*, XXI ("A Silvia"), l. 26). This
citation was traced for me at the *Fondazione Gentile* through the courtesy of
Professor Spirito.

[3] *Ogni valore che sia un valore assoluto.*

[4] *Sostanza indipendente dalla sociale aggregazione che ne fa in un secondo
momento un membro della società.*

already on the point of falling into that dreaded materialism which they intend to resist with all their might, fighting *pro aris et focis*. The idea of society as a mechanical aggregate of unrelated units, each independent of the rest, is materialistic; and the notion of the individual in this view is still more so. For if the individual is limited in this way he is bound to be conditioned and determined; he cannot possess the liberty which is attributed to him in words but denied him in fact.

The conception of the individual as a social atom is a pure fiction of the imagination based on an analogy with material composites whose parts exist prior to their composition. But is there any such thing as a human individual who is really human and really an individual, who recognizes a given society as *his* society, and himself as the subject of relations holding between himself and society, but whom experience shows to be one particular unit among others?

Man's experience of his humanity is an experience of the Ego that speaks and sings, thinks and feels, desires and wills, and in general constitutes its own reality through its continual activity. For example a man speaks; and his language is, of course, individual and completely his own because *he* created it, even when he seems to have accepted what has come down to him in a tradition. He sets the seal of his own soul upon it always, giving it an accent of his own, expressive of his actual inward life which, whether it be powerful or feeble, is always new and original, and never to be repeated. There is nothing that brings out or sets off more clearly the unique and indestructible individuality of the spiritual life than language or art in general; for this individuality is just the originality, the personality of the artist, which is really there even when in ordinary parlance we say that it is not. A dull and boring phrase is always the expression of an individual personality; it can be recognized even from afar as typical and indicative of the essential character of the dull and boring individual who utters it.

Yet no one talks in a way so peculiar to himself that what he says does not raise echoes all round him as a human expression of some human experience, accepted and recognized by everyone as a contribution to that spiritual life in which all men, of all times and in all places, have a share. Herein lies the value of poetry, the value of all art and all language. Anyone who dares to open his mouth puts his trust in a community of human feeling, which may be slow to mature but which cannot be entirely absent. He follows and applauds his own words, judging them not according to his private bias but as a man possessing the faculty of judgment that is common and proper to all men—the universal power of reason that belongs alike to gods and men, to the dead, the living, and the still unborn. For a man can talk to the dead without fearing that what he says may be incomprehensible to them; and men unborn will one day hear his words and understand them.

The language that every man uses is that of his fathers, the language of his tribe or of his clan, of his city or his nation. It is his and yet not his; and he cannot use it to say "This is *my* view" unless at the same time he can say "This is *our* view." For at the root of the "I" there is a "We." The community to which an individual belongs is the basis of his spiritual existence; it speaks through his mouth, feels with his heart, and thinks with his brain.

3. Community immanent in the individual as his law

Membership of this community is the law of existence for every man in every aspect of his actual spiritual life: an internal law to which his every word, his every action must conform at the moment of utterance or performance. For everyone says only what, at the moment of speech, he feels he has to say, and does only what, at the moment of action, he regards as conforming to a law which is law for him because it is law for all who belong to the community to which he may at a given moment have reference. Even when he does not actually open his mouth an individual can only go on living by talking to himself in secret; and in his silent inward colloquy he cannot but use the language that serves also to communicate his thoughts to others. There is no code or cipher without a key; and the key has value for the user of codes and ciphers only because it can have the same value for all who participate in the same sphere of ideas and interests. As for the man who rebels against the law, in his very act of rebellion, by doing what is forbidden, he "turns pleasure to permission in *his* law"[5] as Dante has it: he sets up a law for himself and observes it at that moment as one which ought to be universally valid;[a] though when the deed

---

[5] *Libito fa licito in sua legge* (*Inferno*, V, 56).

[a] This must be the case at that moment, for, as that 'logically inclined' devil points out to Guido da Montefeltro, it is impossible to will something and to repent for it at the same time [Dante, *Inferno*, XXVII, 119]. The sinner sins, and in the act of sinning he does not and cannot repent. *Peccat fortiter,* he sins resolutely as Luther wished; in his mind the world takes on a form and

is done and his passion spent, he is bound to recognize that he was deceived, whether because, as Kant so acutely remarked, it is absurd to tell a lie, and will that all men should do likewise, or because experience teaches him the error involved in conceiving as universally possible the crime which society in its own defense forbids, and annuls through its penal sanction.

4. The ideal community and the desire for glory

The sense of community exists first of all as a law within the individual; but it exists also empirically in the general consensus and social approval of his contemporaries and of posterity, which serve as it were to confirm him in the resolution with which he has observed his own law. He is ambitious for their applause because there was an implicit promise of it in his sense of the conformity between his act and the law, or in the guarantee which the *ideal* community already present and active in his mind gave to his action. What else is the thirst for glory, the desire that our name may be celebrated among men who will speak of our time as ancient, but the hope that in our writings and our deeds we have performed our part perfectly; that we have written what the universal spirit of humanity, rather than our own private bias, dictated, and served the deepest interests of all men in our actions? The community to which we look for applause in everyday experience is really identical with that inner community to which we pay such close heed when we are on the point of speech or action. The applause may indeed be lacking, for it may happen that the real empirical community is for a time out of step with the ideal community which the agent had in mind. In this situation the weaklings lose faith in themselves; but there are those on the other hand who feel strong enough to make the proud affirmation of Heraclitus: "One man for me is worth more than ten thousand." But in any case we must distinguish here between what is *de facto* and what is *de jure;* between the community as it is and the community as it ought to be, and as an unconquerable moral conviction assures us that in the end it will be. For in the end *vox populi vox Dei.* But only in the end.[6]

---

aspect that make his sin a duty. Criticism comes later (and here others can help him but never take his place) to show him that the world he thought he saw was an empty illusion.

[6] This whole section is fairly clearly a reflection by Gentile on his own situation at the time of writing. He was being attacked on all sides for his public

5. Vox populi

The people have two 'voices.' There is one that is only the *ratio cognoscendi* of truth and of all value—a sign but not an argument. This is the Ciceronian *consensus gentium*. But there is another that is rather the *ratio essendi* of the truth, and this is the one that matters, the only one that can serve as the norm for a man's conduct: the voice of an ideal people immanent within him, which speaks to him without leave, without delay, and without hesitation, giving him courage to live, to speak, and to act, and sustaining him from within as the source of his own strength—the voice of the ideal Church that every believer has within him, completely at one with his own soul. Without this inner *vox populi* which sets its seal on our every resolve how should we dare to face a problem which concerned our own life, or that of our country, or of all humanity—and when we think about it this covers all the problems there are—and say firmly: "It is so"? In our unhesitating affirmation, it is the voice of the people, the voice of God, which speaks. Or in other words no one can feel differently, in spite of all the errors scattered through the history of human assertions; for no one, while he is actually thinking something, will ever think that it might be held that his thought is not the truth—the truth that everyone sooner or later is bound to accept, because although it was he who did the thinking he was only acting as the faithful interpreter of all men. The Italian who feels that he is an Italian speaks for all Italy; and the man for mankind; the father for all fathers, the son for all sons, the soldier for all soldiers, and so on—each for all.

It may seem that the contrary is really true; but only if we look at things empirically. For, as we have remarked, the existence of an ideal community within the individual does not abolish his indi-

career as a Fascist, and the speech of 1924 in which he justified the violence of the Fascist Militia was often quoted. The position which he here adopts cannot be dismissed as a mere apologia, however, for he makes the same distinction between the real and the ideal community in the dedicatory letter to *Scuola e filosofia* (1908) and in many other places. The most interesting thing about it is the reference to the Heraclitus fragment (*fr.* 49, Diels-Kranz) which foreshadows his eventual adherence to the Fascist Social Republic. For there can be no doubt that in his eyes, Mussolini was the one who was worth more than a myriad. (Cf. C. A. Biggini in *Civiltà fascista*, May 1944, p. 22, where Gentile is reported to have said "Either Italy saves herself with him or she is lost for several centuries" after his interview with Mussolini in November 1943.)

viduality or his absolute independence of tradition, and of every-thing—customs, institutions, or what you will—that may appear to be the actually existent [7] form of the community. Let us take language as our example again, for in this field the life of the spirit has been most carefully explored. It is obvious that every writer completely renews his linguistic material, molding it through the originality of his style into a shape of his own; and not strictly abiding by the usage of the ancients, as the purists do, nor yet by that of the so-called living language employed by the modernists—a usage already defined in the dictionaries and rule books that contain the linguistic patrimony of a nation. And what happens with language happens with everything else that enters into the life of the spirit. There is no imitation or repetition and nothing is preserved intact; everything is renewed. The man who lives a truly human life [8] is bound to be an innovator, a creator who lets nothing leave his forge, as it were, that does not bear the stamp of his own personality.

But when we say that every "I" is really "We," and that an ideal community is present and active in every individual, we do not mean that there is a plurality of persons already in existence prior to the act of the individual, or that the community is a legacy from the past. We are dealing with a plurality and a community that attains life only in the act of the individual. For although speaking empirically and very roughly we may talk of our community as existing in the Italian language for example, when it is gathered in appropriate dictionaries,[b] or in the whole of past history down to the present moment, the truth is that this language and history are not prior but posterior to the conscious activity [9] of the writer or of any individual.

To sum up then: in the individual, particularity and universality coincide. The more he is himself the more closely he is identified with all men.

---

[7] *Concreta.*

[8] *L'individuo che è il soggetto della vita spirituale.*

[b] Even the dictionaries only exist for people who read them, and study them, and get right inside them as it were. The same might be said of the 'classical authors' or of the 'people' to whom the purists or modernists would have us refer for our *norma dicendi;* and of the whole of history, which is there in the past certainly, but only if we seek it out, understand it, and so reconstruct it—though of course we must do so with the most scrupulous objectivity.

[9] *Attualità spirituale.*

6. The concrete reality of the individual

The concrete reality of the individual is not to be found in his existence in space and time as a natural phenomenon, an object of sense, but rather in his spiritual existence as a self-conscious being. He exists as a particular person, but not as one among others; his existence is unique and therefore infinite and universal. So the real individual is not opposed to the universal—he *is* the universal; and the concrete universal is just the individual himself as an actual, self-conscious, determinate, unique being.

If one wishes to grasp the essence of this spiritual individuality, it is vital not to slip back into conceiving the individual as one physical object among others in experience. That is just the old Aristotelian, realistic conception, an illusion from which we have to free ourselves. The individual qua self-consciousness is not a natural entity in space and time; he contains space, time and nature, all within himself. Only in this way can he have the unconditioned freedom that is his.

It should also be noted that when once the individual is thought of in this way, the relation that we generally imagine to exist between the individual and the community is overthrown. Instead of the community containing the individual, it is the individual who contains—or rather establishes—the community, within his own act of self-consciousness. And here again we must not think of that natural physical community that the imagination suggests to us, but of the spiritual community which is its soul and essence.[10] For example, the language or the law that establishes brotherhood and equality—nay more than equality, even identity—between individuals who are naturally diverse; the bond of feeling which they recognize as creating a unique reciprocal relation between them, the essence of which is not divided among them but exists whole and perfect in each one. Not the imaginary community that we think of as resulting from the accidental meeting of a number of individuals, but the community that is the constitutive principle of society and makes life in common possible. The community that is universality—for universality could not be the end toward which the individual strives if it were not first of all the fount from which individuality arises.

Indeed, we should never attain to universality if we did not

---

[10] *Ciò che fa comunità la comunità.*

possess it from the beginning. This primitive universality is what becomes splendidly manifest in genius: a sort of natural or divine universality that man discovers in himself not as a result of labor but like a gift of grace, springing from a clear fountain in which his humanity is wholly at one with nature. Man seems to halt on the threshold of the spirit, and draw a great breath of primitive feeling which pours forth in song, moving, attracting, and enchanting his fellows, and uniting a thousand hearts in one—*cor cordium.* The secret of art with its miraculous power lies beyond art, in the world of study and reflection where this spontaneity, this quasi-immediate universality, is captured and dragged into the light of consciousness to be criticized and fully comprehended. Thus it becomes civilization, the living patrimony of humanity; and if civilization is not to stiffen into an empty and artificial façade without any human substance, it must always remain in contact with and sensitive to this original feeling. We must realize that civilization is just the consciousness of feeling—in other words it is self-consciousness; and where reflection is diverted from its object, and loses contact with the feeling from which the rhythm of the inner life springs, thought is bereft of its living warmth and becomes analysis, a sterile game played by the intellect with categories and verbal counters. This is the birth of pedantry, the dissipation and death of the spirit.

7. The conquest of values

The universality that is both the starting point and the goal of spiritual life is a conquest achieved through self-consciousness; for, as we shall never tire of repeating, the consciousness of self is not an immediate attribute of the spirit but the product of its eternal labor—the bread that is earned only in the sweat of the brow. Through this consciousness and this conquest man gains possession of universal values; we might say that he discovers God in the depths of his own heart. For God is there to be discovered; but He is there to be found only because He is sought for. He is there only if man feels His presence and seeks Him. A *Deus absconditus* to be discovered, the God who weighs on the soul of the Unnamed, making him tremble in agitation and torment, but does not yet reveal Himself.[11]

---

[11] See Manzoni's *Promessi sposi,* Chapter 21 ff. (English translation by Archibald Colquhoun, London, J. M. Dent, 1951, pp. 300 ff.).

This sense of divinity is the pure feeling which is best described as nonactual.[12]

8. The process of individuality

So then, the individual is not a datum: for the conscious possession of the universal is not immediately given. To be an individual it is not enough just to be born; rabbits and chickens are born but they never become individuals except insofar as man assimilates the animals to himself, especially the domesticated ones, and they share to a minimal degree in a kind of rudimentary society. When we treat newborn babies as individuals, possessing rights, although at first they seem incapable of self-consciousness or at least give no sign of it, it is because we foresee that in the future they will give proof of their individuality and creative capacity. We extend to them a kind of credit; and sometimes, of course, our foresight proves to have been at fault—indeed it is never entirely justified. For this reason it is necessary to limit the rights even of adults, or to confine social recognition of their individuality within convenient limits.

9. The particularity of the individual in space and time

Empirically speaking, the individual is born in space and time as a particular being; but just for this reason he is not an individual when he is born. In order to become one he must gradually bring the whole of his particular existence—time and space and everything that falls under their determination—under the control of his consciousness, as one element in that complex of objects which breaks up into a multiplicity of material things as soon as he, the conscious subject, abstracts from his own unifying activity in consider-

---

[12] Feeling is only one moment in the synthesis of actual consciousness (*pensiero pensante*). Hence *pure* feeling never actually exists and must be called *non*actual, though it plays a very important role in Gentile's aesthetic theory as the ideal limit of sheer inspiration, the perfect spontaneity and immediacy toward which the artist strives (see the *Philosophy of Art*, Part I, Chapter 2). But it is also, Gentile seems to be saying here, identical with that opposite ideal limit, the God with whom the mystic seeks union. At several points in this book the moment of pure subjectivity and the moment of pure objectivity are both treated as religious (cf. Chapter 8, secs. 1–2, and Chapter 6, sec. 8, herein). This reconciliation or coincidence of art with religion is achieved through the conception of 'genius' as a gift of nature or divine inspiration (cf. Chapter 12, sec. 12, herein).

ing it; but which is actually penetrated and assimilated ever more completely by his consciousness, which resolves all particularity in its own native universality.

As long as the individual has not dissolved and ideally destroyed his own particularity through the power of this inner universality— and strictly speaking he has always destroyed it and yet never succeeds in destroying it—he has not yet found himself, he is not a true individual; he has not earned the rights that chance to be attributed to him, and he loses them easily because he does not really possess them. He has still to enter into himself from outside, as it were, changing from object to subject within his own consciousness and so becoming actually self-conscious. But this attainment of actuality does not mean that the element of particularity in the individual is completely annulled, for it is both canceled and preserved. Without this indestructible particularity, the development of individuality through moral and legal relations would cease; for these relations always presuppose the particularity of the subject as something that has to be resolved in the universality of moral or legal right. And here, too, is rooted that more profound particularity which constitutes the uniqueness of individual existence and prevents it from flying off into a merely 'possible' universality of the abstract intellect, like the entities of traditional metaphysics. The fact that the individual's 'body' (space, time, the whole of nature), which is the basis of his particularity, is canceled and absorbed in his universal humanity does not mean that it is not an essential and necessary element in his constitution. For the individual is certainly universal, but this universality must in its turn be conceived as a process of universalization; and this process would be unintelligible if there were not something particular to be universalized, just as one cannot light a fire unless there is something to burn.

In this dialectic of individuality the immanence of community in the individual becomes manifest; for he cannot set his feet on the solid earth of the particular without raising his head in the free air of universality and establishing himself in the world of liberty.

III

CHARACTER

1. Velleity, will, and character

Character is constancy of will: a constancy (*constantia*) which endows human willing with unity, necessity, rationality, universality. In its primary sense this constancy must be thought of as an intrinsic quality of the unique act of the will; only then shall we be able to understand the use of the word in an extrinsic empirical way to mean the conformity of all the separate acts of the will to a single unchanging maxim. At different levels of discourse each of these two uses is quite legitimate; and they are mutually illuminating, since 'extrinsic' constancy must be defined as a consequence or demonstration in experience of the intrinsic constancy that is primitive and fundamental.

It is in fact important to bear in mind that even in the sphere of the unique volitional act, strictly conceived, there is a kind of firmness and energy analogous to the consistency which we hope to find in everyday experience in all the actions which go to make up an individual's 'conduct.' This firmness and energy are what distinguish true volition from mere 'velleity.' Velleity may be defined as failure of will or volitional self-contradiction, 'changing one's mind' and giving up in the face of difficulties, instead of remaining steadfast and overcoming them as one should, so that the will never achieves its proper fulfillment in a completed action. Velleity is not finishing what one has begun, making plans and doing nothing, building up theories and never putting them into practice. It is fruitless, as human activity always is, when it lacks the complete and absolute conviction that gives life its meaning.[1] The 'perfectly resolute will' of Alfieri [2] is just will pure and simple, without any adjective; but it is rigorously conceived as a will that does not contradict itself, does not abandon its purpose before it is fulfilled in action, does not destroy the synthesis through which the act of self-consciousness completes its circle and establishes its place in the real world. When such a will becomes manifest in the action or even in the speech of a man who is plainly in earnest and believes in what he says and does, we are led to exclaim, "That man has real character"—and he excites a feeling of admiration in us as an outstanding example of humanity.

2. Character as revealed in outward conduct

Constancy of character would seem to involve the consistency of a plurality of different acts which all conform to a standard that does not change with the changing circumstances and content of the action. So that we might well hold that 'character' is a conception that is appropriate at the level of ordinary experience, where we encounter a multiplicity of actions or volitions such as might exhibit this consistency, but that it is not transferable to the transcendental plane which is the metaphysical ground and origin of experience.

The fact is, however, that if we consider 'ordinary experience' alone, without reference to its transcendental ground and origin, we shall not find either volition or the 'character' that is to be attributed to it. Experience contains nothing but the spirit (which for present purposes means the will) in objectified form, a mere object of knowledge fixated at the stage of the abstract logos [3] where the

---

[1] *Infeconda com' è sempre l'attività dello spirito che non si spiega nella compiuta e assoluta energia creatrice della realtà spirituale.* The translation is here an attempt to interpret what Gentile means when he speaks of 'creating spiritual reality.'

[2] The reference is to the remark "volli, e volli sempre, e fortissimamente volli" in Alfieri's "Reply to Ranieri de' Calzabigi" prefixed to all editions of his first four tragedies. See *Tragedie* (ed. by Bruscoli), Bari, Laterza, 1946, I, 39 (*Scrittori d'Italia*, Vol. CXCIV).

[3] *Logo astratto.* This is one of the fundamental technical terms of Gentile's logic. It is the realm of the pure intellect and includes everything that in ordinary English usage is called 'science'—both the empirical and the exact

living force of the Spirit is frozen into the schematism of its opposite, Nature. Volition considered as part of experience is not an
activity but a fact; the activity withdraws completely into the act
of considering this fact. Viewed thus, from the outside, the will is
like a man petrified in a photograph, a face without its living soul;
or like vivid poetry congealed onto paper in the dead material form
of print or script. It is no longer a spiritual thing but a natural event,
part of a spatio-temporal manifold; indeed, it assumes a manifold
aspect itself, determined in all its many forms and hence deprived
of the liberty which is essential to it as an activity of the spirit. What
'character' could there be in a will thus multiplied and fragmented,
each fragment conditioned by its antecedents and stripped of that
liberty that belongs only to one who is master of himself over the
whole infinite range of his existence? And if constancy or consistency can only be ascribed to a plurality of volitions, how is it that
the whole group possesses this 'character' that is not to be found in
the elements taken singly? The fact is that even when we mean to
concern ourselves only with character as revealed in ordinary experience, we actually abandon the abstract empirical point of view and
consider the apparent multiplicity of actions as a single series or
process of development, constituting a fundamental unity in which
every action is related to all the others, and apart from which the
particular actions would be valueless and unintelligible. And what
then is this unity to which we must of necessity have recourse, if it
is not the unity of the will in its unique act—a unity which is in-
escapable when one looks at the will from within, and seeks to
know what it is through actual experience of it? Even the empiricist
reunites and unifies what he has previously separated and put asunder, when he seeks to comprehend the active power of the will; behind the multiplicity of actions which form his data he hopes to
discover an agent gradually forming a personality of his own; and
his empirical synthesis is really an alien or bastard form of the

sciences. It can be typified from the logical point of view as the sphere in
which the law of contradiction holds; and from the methodological point of
view as the sphere in which all inquiry *presupposes* the truth inquired about.
Gentile seeks in his *Logic* to show that the abstract logos is a necessary moment, but only a moment, in the dialectic of creative or 'actual' thinking; and
in this way he claims to have reconciled the 'traditional' logic of Aristotle with
the 'speculative' logic of Hegel. For a full discussion of Gentile's *System of
Logic* see Roger W. Holmes, *The Idealism of Giovanni Gentile*, New York,
Macmillan, 1937.

genuine synthesis of self-consciousness in the unique spiritual act. Hence, in order to judge a man empirically it is advisable to wait till the cycle of his empirical existence is completed; and the proverb warns us to judge no man till he is dead.

The same logic underlies the division of history into periods, and also the division of natural history into cycles (days, years, cosmic years) in the naturalistic metaphysics of the ancients. But the periodic divisions in history are not, of course, brute facts like the physical death that ends the life cycle of an individual man; they are a product of the historian's judgment. For the historian does not distinguish periods and epochs from one another by accepting terminal dates from an arbitrary chronological scale; [4] he fixes the termini himself *after* he has defined a historical period as a cycle that is logically complete, or as a perfect spiritual synthesis: the development of an initial principle to the stage of fulfillment in such a way that the character and significance of the epoch arise from this whole process of development. The guiding maxim in every case is *respice finem;* for at the end the initial principle becomes clear—the conclusion completes the cycle and illumines the whole process of development. Just as in a book that is a work of art the last page casts light upon the first; but though the unity of inspiration, the so-called 'logic' of the argument or the plot, the unity that makes the various parts echo and clarify each other, may be carefully cultivated, it is the actual motive of the work that becomes the keynote from beginning to end, and its presence can be felt in every section, even in every word. The accent of a soul is breathed into the body of a work of art and gives it character. So that even in a fragment of some ancient poet the accent of the lost work still rings true; and the scholar who studies it sympathetically can catch the echo.

3. Critique of the idea that a single will performs many actions

There is no manifold of volitions, therefore, that is not by its very nature unified into a single focus. There is the will of a day which leads us in the evening to reflection, recapitulation, and examination of conscience; the will of a whole life for which the survivors must cast the balance; the will of a people over many generations; yet always it is the will of an instant, the actual living will of the eternal

---

[4] *Con termini* (*a quo e ante quem*) *offertigli dalla cronologia bruta.*

present. 'Character' properly belongs to this will, and refers to its organic unity and completeness.[5] This is all the more easily appreciated and understood in cases where will power is lacking or is so feeble that it appears nonexistent. The agent then is no more than the shadow of a man, since his whole existence as an agent must depend on what he does, and he does not know what to do; he feels lost and bewildered, or he lives in dreams, careless of himself and his duty and forgetful of the world around him which urgently requires his decision. Because he has no character he does not count; he is not a man, and hence he is found wanting when weighed in the balance of experience.[6] Whether we observe him at the moment of action or consider the whole range of his past conduct it is impossible to discover what he wills, or even whether he wills anything at all. If for a moment we imagine that he has made up his mind on an action, we are quickly undeceived by the way that he vacillates in its performance and weakly gives up halfway. Since the aim of all volition is the creation of a self, and he lacks the conception of a self to aim at, which only decision and steadiness of will could provide, he gazes on a void. Unconscious of himself and lost in a dream, he is not a man; for to be a man is to be conscious of oneself. Humanity is self-consciousness; and human character derives from the successful achievement of self-awareness. The stronger a man's self-awareness is, the bolder his character will be.

4. Character as present and as nontemporal

When one is looking for the manifestation of character in experience there is a dangerous tendency to fix on the present as the moment of time in which it is most fully revealed; for the past is dead and gone and all of its evidence might be set at nought by actual present failure; and since the future is still in the lap of the gods, it is quite impossible to prophesy about a man's character. But when we reflect that the present is born of the past, that the past lives and survives in it, and moreover that, as Leibniz said, it is *gros de l'avenir*, we are bound to abandon this distinction of different moments of time, and recognize that character is essentially nontemporal, that it exists at the origin of all human experience and ac-

---

[5] *Come unità della sintesi in cui si conchiude l'atto dello spirito.*
[6] *Non vale come uno degli uomini che l'esperienza ad uno ad uno registra.*

tion [7] outside of time and the indications and demonstrations of character that the various moments of time may afford.

5. Character as transcendental

We are not properly concerned, therefore, with character as exhibited in time, or in a will that is temporally circumscribed and determined. When we consider the will in its temporal aspect it does not, cannot, appear to be endowed with character. Character belongs rather to the will that is not contained in time but contains it; in Kant's terms it belongs not to the empirical ego that we encounter in experience, but to the transcendental Ego that knows everything that can be a content of experience. This 'transcendental' character is what we actually discover when we are striving to find it within experience. For of course the transcendental condition of experience is immanent in it—but it is the form of experience and not its content. It is not, as was once claimed, something that can be known through sense perception; not one of the facts that become presupposed objects of knowledge when we adopt the realistic point of view appropriate to the logic of the abstract.[8] The 'form' of experience means here the principle that is active and constructive a priori, the principle that makes experience possible and so cannot be a product of experience.

6. Civil courage

At this point some remarks about the attitude of mind known as *civil courage* should not come amiss; for this attitude is one of the corollaries of character that is most highly valued—and rightly so. It consists in a steady loyalty to the dictates of one's own conscience in speech and action, and in the acceptance of complete responsibility for one's conduct in one's relations with others. It is a quality that is essential for citizenship, for if a man does not guard his own personal dignity fearlessly and bear witness in public to the truth that he recognizes in his own mind, he is not just betraying a truth that may perhaps have no need of his testimony and neither gains anything by it nor loses anything by the lack of it; he is betraying himself, for that truth is the source of his life and its value. He is

---

[7] *Tutti i fatti e gli atti della vita di un uomo.*
[8] Cf. n3 on pp. 91–92 herein.

made cheap in his own eyes, because he is defacing and destroying in his social life the personal ideal that he has created in his own thought; he is letting it go to waste by abandoning the post in the community to which his duty calls him.

But if, as we have seen, character is essentially a transcendental property that belongs to the will quite apart from any empirical relations that it may enter into in the course of social life, can we still treat civil courage as an attribute of character without passing from the transcendental to the empirical plane and so turning away from the essence of character to consider one of its accidental marks? For if he is to have an opportunity of exhibiting civil courage the individual must give up his isolation and enter into relations with others. Or is there perhaps a social link between the individual and other individuals even within the transcendental act of the will?

It will be enough here, surely, to point out that the civil courage which a man may display 'away from home,' so to speak, in his relations with others, can never be more than he already possessed at home before he left his house. In the social contacts and agreements that we make in the course of ordinary life, we may find occasion to exhibit an ability that we already possess, but we cannot acquire a completely new one; our character is certainly put to the proof by the ever-changing circumstances in which we find ourselves, but we can only give proof of qualities that we possess in ourselves as individuals.

7. Original sociality

We speak in empirical terms of meeting 'others' in society; but the truth is that these others do not fall from heaven at the feet of the individual who has to deal with them; they do not form an absolutely new realm of experience which makes a revolution in his life. Perhaps within himself he is already acquainted with a certain 'other' as well as himself; and it may be that pure will in its transcendental aspect already involves a transcendental sociality which is the fundamental ground and source of every society that can ever be established in the outer world; and thus, even at the transcendental level, character may assume the form of civil courage. This will be the subject of our inquiry in the next chapter. If we could discover this kind of original sociality we should be able to understand how within the character of a solitary man who is compelled to 'make himself a party of one,' [9] the arms are forged that will make it possible for him to face, as an individual with a view, a conscience, and a faith of his own, every blow and every struggle against others that comes his way in the task of keeping faith with himself.

[9] Gentile here makes a transparent reference both to his own situation—for when he retired to write this book he was the object of attacks by both Fascists and anti-Fascists alike—and to the approval and encouragement that Dante received in Paradise for refusing to surrender in a similar situation (see *Paradiso*, XVII, 69).

IV

TRANSCENDENTAL SOCIETY OR SOCIETY *IN INTERIORE HOMINE*

1. *Alter* and *socius*

The human individual is not an atom. Immanent in the concept of an individual is the concept of society. For there is no ego, no real individual, who does not have with*in* him (rather than just with him) an *alter* who is his essential *socius*—that is to say, an object that is not a mere 'thing' opposed to him as subject, but a subject like himself. The canceling of the pure objectivity of the object coincides with the transcending of the pure subjectivity of the subject; for 'subject' and 'object' considered simply in themselves [1] are both abstractions whose concrete reality is to be found in their synthesis, the self-constitutive act of the Ego.[2]

2. The dialectic of the Ego

The Ego is not simply Ego, nor yet simply non-Ego; for taken simply in themselves Ego and non-Ego are mutually equivalent—they are precisely *nothing*. Anyone who looks for a mediated synthesis to emerge from unmediated concepts may equally well begin from the subject or the object. Empiricists and abstract rational-

---

[1] *Nella loro immediatezza.*
[2] *Nell'atto costitutivo dell'Io.* (I take the genitive to be *both* subjective and objective.)

ists [3] have this much in common: both parties hold that it is possible to begin from something immediately given. But the immediately given is a mere abstraction; concreteness lies in the mediation of the synthesis through which both subject and object are what they are because each of them is a unity of the two terms. The subject posits the object, yes; but the subject is the synthetic unity, not an abstract something-in-itself. The unity of the synthesis is prior to both subject and object, not consequent to them. The act, the synthetic unity a priori comes first.

So that when we say that the Ego posits the non-Ego, this 'Ego' that can do so much is not the pure empty subject, but the act that distinguishes and posits both subject and object.[a]

If we distinguish and separate Ego from non-Ego in the synthesis, what we get is not the real Ego (and therefore it does not really posit the non-Ego) nor yet the real non-Ego. The Ego *becomes* Ego through the synthesis within which it posits and so becomes the non-Ego also, since 'to posit the non-Ego' means 'to posit itself as non-Ego.' And on the other hand, through its real opposition to the Ego within the synthesis the non-Ego becomes Ego; for the synthesis involves opposition, but it involves also the *identity* of the opposites. Only this identity can account for the necessary and intrinsic relation between the two terms of the synthesis which requires that the concept of one term must involve the concept of the other.

If it were not for the identity [b] of Ego and non-Ego (subject and object) the object would be a mere *thing*, impenetrable to consciousness and therefore unknowable; and the subject, confined within itself, would be limited by the thing that faced it; the opposition between them would be mechanical and the subject itself would become a thing. In order to rise above this mechanical world of

---

[3] *Aprioristi.*

[a] This Ego-in-itself [*Io immediato*] which is not Ego is the abstract subject against which ontologists, objectivists, realists, and anti-idealists of every sort and kind unceasingly do battle. And this *half-concept* of the Ego is the origin of all the various antinomies between intellectualism and voluntarism, idealism and realism, liberty and authority, tradition and genius, etc.

[b] I say identity because the Ego is *sensus sui*, both the object and subject of feeling. For if when the immediate quality of the object was canceled the Ego did not find itself in the process of mediation, then this mediation would not be the revelation of the immediate, and hence the ground of its actual existence [*e così la sua posizione o fondazione*] but rather its destruction. It would not be the canceling that preserves, but the canceling that annihilates.

things to the level of conscious freedom [4] we must hold fast to this concept of the creative synthesis that posits the opposed terms and resolves the opposition in a fundamental identity. The Ego becomes Ego inasmuch as it becomes non-Ego; and the non-Ego is truly non-Ego inasmuch as it is not merely opposed to the Ego but also identical with it.

3. Nullity

Before and beyond the synthesis there is only nullity: without us the world is void, as we are without it. This void is nothing but the nullity of the spirit, which transcends it just by being aware of it; and the awareness comes every time that the spirit's actual achievement falls short of its essential possibilities [5] so that it lacks that sense of exuberance and living force of which it is itself the only fountain. At such times it is assailed by what has been called the anguish of its own non-being, which consists just as much in a weakening of the sense of self as it does in the world's appearing colorless and alien to the mind. But through the paradoxical nature and power of the spirit this anguish defeats itself: for even anguish, though it may be heavy and opaque, is still a kind of consciousness, an act which frees the Ego and the world from non-being.

Thus even anguish, like all pain, is salutary; for to be aware of it is to be struggling toward the shore of existence, toward a life that is truly human.[6]

4. From thing to partner

Because the identity of Ego and non-Ego is necessary, the object which ideally begins as a mere *thing* opposed to the spiritual freedom of the Ego cannot remain in that status. The little child stands beside it and caresses it, and seeks to evoke some response from it. The poet addresses his solemn prayer to the moon: "Why art thou in the sky? Tell me why?" etc.; [7] and in the naive imaginings of the

---

[4] *La realtà spirituale.*

[5] *Ogni volta che non attua con tutta la sua possibile energia la propria essenza spirituale.*

[6] In this section, which is only an aside in the development of his argument in the chapter, Gentile's concern with the rising tide of existentialism is very apparent. He tries to do justice to the whole trend of thought by showing that *Angst* is a moment of the dialectic of consciousness. But his view of it is entirely positive and even rather naively optimistic. In fact he simply reiterates the theory of pain put forward originally in his *Summary of Educational Theory* in 1913.

[7] *Che fai tu luna in ciel? dimmi, che fai.* This is the first line of Leopardi's

man who is lacking in or completely careless of our ordinary experience everything comes alive and acquires human feelings. Why is this?

The reason is that through the synthesis of the spiritual act the object tends to become assimilated to the subject, and takes on a spiritual quality because of its relation to the subject. The subject speaks, so the object must speak too; and likewise it must feel and think and will. The object which the subject finds present within itself must ultimately be another self, an alter ego capable of enjoying liberty and even of living a spiritual life like that which the subject possesses and pours out in its actual existence. In order to be itself the subject has no choice but to renounce its solitude; it has to have and it does have an 'other.'

This 'other' may for a moment remain impenetrable, mute, hostile; but only for a moment. Just as in experience things remain mere things for a moment, so long as they resist the spiritualizing power of the subject. The logic of the act of consciousness requires that the mere 'thing' should become an 'alter ego,' and that this alter ego should draw near to the subject, conversing and collaborating with him in a common spiritual life.

5. The internal or transcendental dialogue

This passage from mere thinghood to membership of an ideal internal society on the part of the non-Ego happens in every instant of experience. Our experience may involve the company of others who are, to begin with, just physical bodies distinct from our own; or it may not. But in any case, whether we are with others or by ourselves, our experience consists of thoughts, and our thoughts are always expressed in a language that we might use to communicate them to others. They can be communicated to others, however, only because through linguistic expression our thoughts become intelligible to ourselves. This is not a matter of mere assumption: it can be observed and verified in an experience to which we pay little heed, but which is essential and unfailing.

We talk to others because in the first place we talk to ourselves. The first ears to hear us, so to speak, are not those of others but our own. Even when we talk to ourselves silently, without uttering one

"Canto notturno di un pastore errante dell'Asia" (*Canti*, XXIII). The whole poem can be found in the *Oxford Book of Italian Verse*, 2nd ed., no. 325, pp. 423 ff.

word aloud, it is impossible to think without using words; and the words do not disappear unnoticed and unexamined (if that happened our words and our thoughts would lose their value)—we hear them ourselves. Or again, when we write something and give the words a visible form, we read what we are writing as we go along before anyone else sees it—there is within us both writer and reader. Similarly, even in our most secret thoughts there is one who speaks and another who listens—there is the self and its interlocutor.[c] The interlocutor is invisible, but he is as present and real as the man who is thinking. In exceptional circumstances it may happen that a man 'speaks without thinking,' or again he may 'think too much.' But here too the exceptions prove the rule, for what is meant is that one man pays too little heed to his words and the other too much—and this would hardly be remarked on if everyone did not normally pay attention to what he himself says. We pay attention both to the words we say and to the tone in which we say them, listening critically and approving or correcting.

A man speaks and he hears himself speaking; hearer and speaker are the same man and yet not the same. They are two and they are one; a single personality doubles itself from within and is actually present and active in the internal dialogue which constitutes the unique act of thought. It is written: "Woe to him that is alone!" [8]

---

[c] Precisely as in a dream; for everyone realizes that in a dream a single individual is divided and multiplied into all the characters of a drama in which he alone does all the talking and all the acting. And everyone knows that the artist—the great dreamer—creates his characters within his mind and then stands back to watch and listen and obey them (to follow their inner logic) as if they were persons whose lives were independent of his own.

[8] Eccles. 4:10. Gentile cites the same text in his *Prolegomena to the Study of the Child* (1921). His comments there are as follows: "When the Bible says 'Woe to him that is alone' we ought not to think of the man who cannot establish social contact with other individuals empirically determined, but of the one who does not know how to establish bonds of community and of unity with the 'friend' and the 'judge' who lodges within him.

"A man may withdraw from any bond of external society, or from any of those definite spheres which radiate, as we have said, from the very center of his volitional activity. In this sense he can refuse to be a son, a father, a citizen, but he cannot refuse to recognize the 'other' who is within him, for such refusal would be a refusal to think or to develop his own consciousness. From this point of view the 'Woe' with which the Bible threatens 'him who is alone,' the man who does not recognize his 'other,' is spiritual death" (7th ed., Florence, Sansoni, 1940, pp. 73–74). This passage should be compared with his remarks about death in Chapter 13, sec. 7, herein.

But true solitude would be the solitude of one who spoke when there were absolutely *no* ears to hear him: a man so 'simple' as to be only half a man and hence really nothing at all. If we take the standpoint of the listener within us then there is some other who speaks, an interlocutor who is inseparable from ourselves. And this alter ego joins us in a dialogue, speaking and listening as our partner in the drama of life.

The drama in which this interlocutor takes part is the transcendental society, which is what makes man a 'political animal' in an absolute sense, from the moment when he is reflectively aware of himself [9] and becomes a real individual, a synthetic unity of self and other as opposites which are therefore identical; or even from the moment when he is an individual *implicitly,* when he has still only a *feeling* of self. From this time his solitude is ended, there is the first gleam of the dawn of his social life. All the more determinate and complex types of society are only derivatives of this primitive form and differ from it simply because of the different content that comes to maturity in experience.

Regarded simply as an existing thing [10] man is an animal; and only in the way we have described can an animal enter into humanity and be not just a thing but a comrade. Accidental physical coexistence with its mechanical encounters could never give rise to the mutual interaction and conscious community that is the dialectical essence of society. A flock of sheep does not form a society, unless we suppose that each of its members has an obscure and rudimentary sense of self, any more than a heap of stones to which no one would attribute such a capacity. The true object of the subject, our true object, is a partner; for in order to be *ours* the object must cease to be a thing and become another self; or, more exactly, *the* other self, our own alter ego, the partner within us who joins with us in the society that is innate in the transcendental Ego, and which may therefore be fairly styled *transcendental society.*

6. The moment of otherness

I hope that the importance of this concept will escape no one, for in my judgment it is the keystone of the great edifice of human

---

[9] *Dicendo Io si riflette su sé stesso.*
[10] *Nel immediatezza del suo essere.*

society. And it is to be hoped also that no one will come around to the view, which has hitherto been commonly received, that the fact to which we have drawn attention has only a metaphorical significance, on the ground that the word 'dialogue' (which implies listening and answering) can only properly be used in contexts where the persons involved are really different. There are two things to be said on this point: first, that *real difference* is maintained within the act of consciousness—the synthesis of Ego and non-Ego is bound to become a synthesis of Ego and Ego since even within consciousness the Ego that speaks is one person while the Ego that listens is another; and the distinction is clear and absolute. Second, that this otherness which has to be transcended in the synthesis through the establishment of a society is not, as one might be tempted to think, less difficult to overcome than the empirical otherness of Tom, Dick, and Harry. Experience shows that sometimes a single glance enables two people meeting for the first time to understand one another and become good friends. The eyes are such eloquent witnesses of the heart that a single look is enough to kindle love (which is the most perfect society that can exist between the two sexes). Normally, of course, a single glance is not enough. We get to know the other person gradually; and the knowledge costs us an effort of study that is made willingly enough in the hope of overcoming the limitation that his otherness imposes on us, and arriving at that stage of reciprocal comprehension which is called sympathy, a mutual interpenetration and unification of hearts which enjoy the perfect trust that the spirit naturally has in itself. While on the other hand it is a commonplace that even in one man's mind there are often most bitter tensions which are very difficult to resolve; 'tragic' conflicts as they are called, that must sometimes wait long for a solution. In such situations there is within us an 'other' who contradicts us and is hostile; someone who besieges and torments us without truce, yet we cannot understand his motives in setting himself against us. There are thoughts that torture us, and we cannot get rid of them; there are desires that seem absurd, and passions that weaken us and threaten to bring us to disaster in the end. But 'thoughts,' 'desires,' and 'passions' are abstractions; in actual experience there is someone who thinks, desires, loves, or hates; it is this someone who is hostile to us and torments us, and because this someone is ourself we seek to be justified in his eyes. At times he, this 'other' hidden within us, cannot even be said to set himself against us; he simply does not care, but remains an idle guest in the house, a mute, impenetrable enigma; but even in this role he tantalizes us, driving us to try anything in order to understand him, to break the shell in which he is enclosed and make a boon companion of him.[11]

This concrete otherness is a necessary moment in the passage of the object from 'thing' to 'spirit.' In ordinary experience it may be more or less noticeable but it is never absent; it is the matter which the spirit eternally dissolves in the process of its own formation. What a distance there is between the law *contra hostes aeterna auctoritas esto* [12] and the Christian love of one's neighbor! The *auctoritas* knows nothing of the man behind the enemy; while our neighbor on the other hand is wholly at one with us. But the *hostis* is always with us; and no love is more firmly and solidly based than that which is achieved through an apprenticeship in which the bond of conquest passes over into the bond of brotherhood.[13]

7. The dialectic of practice

The true origin of society, then, is an ideal one: it is the synthesis of subject and object that arises from the immanent dialectic of the spiritual act. The subject and object in the synthesis are real, and if they are to be identified with one another they must first be opposed; yet the opposition must be such as to lead to their identification. Their unity is found in self-consciousness which, so far as it is concretely logical, is self-concept; but this self-concept is not purely intellectual knowledge, a theoretical contemplation that proceeds on a plane above the real formation of the Ego. The forming of the Ego is precisely the actual process of self-consciousness: any distinction between them is purely verbal. The establishing of transcendental society *is* the dialectic by which self-consciousness is constituted. We are not dealing here with a dialectic of the abstract intellect, but with the real dialectic of the spirit in its practical activity.

---

[11] *Rendercelo familiare nostro, tutt'uno con noi.*

[12] "Against enemies let there be always authority" (a maxim of the Twelve Tables cited by Cicero, *De officiis,* I, 12, 37).

[13] *Quello che si conquista attraverso un tirocinio di conquista e di affratellamento dell'altro con noi.*

This dialectic is not something private, confined to the purely transcendental aspect of action, and destined in due course to attain explicit development in experience with all its rich variety of determinate forms. Every action in experience that can be marked out as establishing a social link is just this dialectic. Every object that has to become a subject and a member of society is just this internal object in which the thinking subject strives continually to find himself, seeking to see himself mirrored in it, as an identity of opposites which the dialectic of his thought eternally tends to realize. There is not one object that comes from outside and another that arises within consciousness. The object, if it is a real object, can only exist within the synthesis of subject and object through which the Ego expresses itself.

Even the man whom we meet on the sidewalk, who catches our attention because of some trivial incident, is an object within the synthesis, who required a conscious act of 'attention' on our part before he could become part of our experience. And if we had not attended he might have passed by under our nose and yet remained in the shadowy penumbra of the subconscious, where nothing is determinate.

Just as a word spoken is identical with the unspoken word that we hear inwardly though it remains unuttered; just as a word spoken by someone else, if we hear it and understand it, is identical with this inward speech and comes to our ears as if we had said it ourselves, for indeed, we may understand it even before we know who did say it; so, from the point of view of the dialectic of practice, the 'empirical other,' as we may call the person who is in the first place a physical object distinct from ourselves, is no more and no less than that internal 'other' who is present from the very beginning on the transcendental plane. For through the dialectic he enters into relation with us and becomes our own other.

There are not two 'others,' the first transcendental and the second empirical. The empirical other *is* the transcendental other, with some additional determinations gained in the process of experience. For in experience the subject takes on a particular aspect; and it is obvious that the object must do likewise. All this means is that the spirit, which is essentially the transcendental act, has a history in which at different times it takes different forms.[d]

---

[d] Cf. Chapter 5, "Experience and the Ethical Category."

All the infinite forms of social life are to be found here, in the dialectical linking of *alter* with *ipse*.

8. The crisis of the universe

But is there anything that exists prior to this society that contains all civilization and all of human history? Does the natural world exist, and in it the primitive savage who will eventually produce society? The imagination, with its naturalistic tendencies, continually returns to this myth of a prehuman nature, and a man in it who is not yet a man; and even people who know that all history is human make fantasies about a natural history that is prehistoric. The truth is that prior to the establishment of this transcendental society man is not conceivable except as a simple abstract datum, an element in the manifold that thought envisages from the point of view of pure naturalism. Once we recognize that this point of view is an abstraction we can give it full scope in the limitless realm of abstract logic, where there is a place for all of the sciences; but we must point out that the effective reality of abstract logic is to be found on the plane of concrete logic, where the one fundamental principle is the self-concept and hence self-consciousness. It is not possible to go back to anything prior to self-consciousness, unless we recognize that we are thinking about pure abstractions that depend for their existence on the actual present activity of self-consciousness.[14]

What was there then, before the act of thought whose dialectic is the root of social life? Everything and nothing. There was the universe as it would be if we could cleave the iron knot of the synthesis of which it is either subject or object, as you please— subject-in-itself or object-in-itself, something that can have no place outside of the synthesis or prior to it, because the synthesis comes first and the existence of the object as well as of the subject depends on it. If we want to imagine a natural universe prior to the synthesis, this universe can only be pictured as an amorphous potentiality which must enter into crisis, rouse itself and awaken to a sense of itself. The great sleeper, as long as he does not wake, is not merely unaware of himself; he does not exist. In order to exist he must awaken; and when he is awake he begins to reflect: "But then, before I woke, I existed but I was asleep?" This is what

---

[14] Cf. n3 on pp. 91–92 herein.

he asks himself and so he comes to believe. But in reality every-thing comes into existence just at that instant when he wakes to become the only reality that is possible: the sense of self, creative self-consciousness.

Consciousness is creative because the dialectic of self-awareness, or of this awakening of the universe, is not an abstract logical dia-lectic that is applied *to* reality and presupposes it: it is the process through which reality becomes real. It is not the dialectic of ab-stract logic but the dialectic of concrete logic.

V

EXPERIENCE AND THE ETHICAL CATEGORY

1. The uniqueness of the logical category

In my *Logic* I have shown [a] that there is one single absolute
category in actual thought: the self-concept. In a moral doctrine
that unifies theory and practice no categorical imperative or moral
law can be admitted that is not wholly identical with this self-
concept, the supreme act in which the life of the whole universe
is resolved in the spirit. For everything is spirit, certainly, but only
because nothing is spirit taken as it stands; whatever *is* is nothing;
it only becomes something by becoming spirit, self-consciousness
and hence self-concept. The whole creation of the universe is here
in the self-creation of the spirit.

2. The law of human existence: *Think!*

In seeking to define the moral law on a former occasion [b] I expressed it as strictly as possible in the admonition: *Be man.* But
for clarity's sake it is better to say like Campanella: *Think.*[1] For

---

[a] See my *Sistema di logica come teoria del conoscere*, Vol. II [3rd ed.,
Florence, Sansoni, 1942. See especially Part III, Chapter 7—Tr.].

[b] See my *Sommario di pedagogia*, Vol. II [4th ed., Florence, Sansoni, 1937.
The reference is to Part I, Chapter 1, sec. 18, p. 51—Tr.].

[1] *Pensa, uomo, pensa*, in the hymn, "Della possanza dell'uomo," ll. 72, 73.
See Campanella, *Poesie* (ed. by Gentile), Bari, Laterza, 1955, p. 172 (*Scrittori
d'Italia*, Vol. LXX).

to think is to form a self-concept, to attain human consciousness. To think means to understand oneself, and hence to understand the world around us, partly different from us and partly similar, so as to grasp what distinguishes us from mere things and from other people. Ultimately it means understanding the absolute foundation of things and of men, the foundation of ourselves, the power that maintains all in harmony: God. To understand all this is what every man does, though he may not have a clear conception of his own immanent activity, when he gives a personal accent to all his thinking and so makes it real thought. But if he is to achieve anything better than the kind of understanding that might come naturally without his deliberately thinking about it, he must want to understand with all his heart and soul; only then will he acquire a real and profound understanding, comprehending the identity and substantial unity of himself with all the rest, and so transcending the opposition between himself and all the rest, and no longer seeking his own good apart from the rest, or watching what happens to everything else with indifference, as if it were no concern of his but a mere side issue. True understanding means the extension of man's concern for himself, which is the bond of the synthesis that constitutes his being, the flame of self-love that is primitive, fundamental, and indestructible, into a concern for all things and all men, a concern for God. To understand in this sense is to love; and that not in any abstract or theoretical way, but concretely and in action, through the realization of that identity of the rest with oneself, which is what real understanding is.[2]

3. Understanding and loving

"Love thy neighbor as thyself," says the Christian commandment. This implies that we can find our neighbors around us, among the other people who are distinct from us; so that it can be understood roughly, in the common-sense fashion that is usually good enough for us, by considering other men as our brothers, sons of our common father, having at the root of their existence the same power as we have. But a neighbor in this sense is not so near a

---

[2] The echoing of Spinoza in this section is too plain to need pointing out. But we should notice how Gentile in this last sentence contrasts his theory of love, and so implicitly his whole theory of understanding with the *amor Dei intellectualis* of Spinoza. The contrast becomes ever more explicit in what follows.

neighbor as he might be. For brothers are close to us in that they have something in common with us; but they would be closer if they had everything in common with us, if their otherness were completely resolved into our own personality so that they were no longer separate from ourselves, and we could not in practice continue to distinguish between their joy and our joy, their pain and our pain. Not that every distinction could be canceled, for that would mean the renunciation of existence; but the external otherness could be reduced to an otherness which is internal to ourselves. For we have need of an 'other,' but an internal other suffices for us, because by means of it we can generate the inner dialectic of our lives and exist as individuals with a personal continuity and identity, sufficient unto ourselves within the closed circle of our own creative and unresting minds.[3] This reduction of external otherness to internal is true understanding, the unbreakable chain of love by which our neighbor is bound to us.

4. Practical understanding

By now it is clear that this kind of understanding is not merely the theoretical understanding of a man who *says* he comprehends but does not pay attention and does not even believe that he needs to comprehend. It is not the superficial understanding that scarcely touches us and leaves us uncommitted and indifferent, merely looking on at things and their relations from a safe distance. This is never true understanding in any case. For that would involve adherence, commitment, the pledging of oneself in an affirmation, drawing consequences from the truth that we recognize and seeing that we have a stake in the world contained in it, that we must confirm or falsify it in our conduct, by standing firm in the post that belongs to us in that world or by deserting it. Our own Rosmini was deeply aware of this difference between purely abstract understanding and concrete understanding or practical assent.[c] If other men are really identical with me, then I can never really understand myself without understanding them; nor can I use my own lively understanding to advance my development and gradually shape my own character, without at the same time advancing the

---

[3] *Esistere essendo sempre noi stessi, stretti a noi e chiusi nel circolo dell' operosa sintesi della nostra inquieta spiritualità.*

[c] See my *Logica*, Part I [3rd ed., Florence, Sansoni, 1940. The reference is to Part I, Chapter 2, sec. 8, pp. 76–79—Tr.].

development of others and making them ever more nearly adequate to my ideal; in short, I cannot advance without creating that kingdom of the spirit in which my redemption, and the redemption of all other men, lies. How can we come to love our neighbors except by fastening our eyes upon them and looking full in their faces, searching ever deeper into their inner selves? And what else is it that arouses and maintains in us the love of ourselves but keen attention, intelligent and penetrating awareness of what we are and what we will to be? Love is not the consequence but the crowning perfection of knowledge. One who does not love does not comprehend; his attention is diverted and he turns away from the person whom he cannot, will not, comprehend further. And who loves anything if he has not studied it? Even things that have little life or value, things that are remote from our interest and even repugnant to our feelings, gradually, as we study them, become first objects of interest and in the end objects of love, things that we cannot give up because they are somehow an essential part of us, especially if the aims and methods of our study are those of scientific research. There was an eminent malaria specialist in Rome who is famous for having used his own armpits as breeding places for the micro-organisms which he devoted his life to studying.

And what of God? The theologian requires a "journey of the mind to God," [4] but the end of the journey is in its beginning, where the mind is immersed in its own light. And though the mystic is led to prefer the darkness of immediate mystical union to the gradual enlightenment of research, yet in this union he seeks al-

----

[4] *Itinerarium mentis in Deum*—the title of a famous treatise by St. Bonaventure. There are seven stages in the 'journey' and Bonaventure compares them to the seven days of creation in a way that bears out what Gentile says: "As if, once again, during the first six days in which the mind has to be exercised that it may finally arrive at the Sabbath of rest after it has beheld God *outside* itself *through* His traces and *in* His traces, *within* itself *by* His Image and *in* His Image, *above* itself *by* the likeness of the divine light shining down upon us and *in* that light, insofar as it is possible in this life and the exercise of our mind—when, finally, on the sixth level we have come to the point of beholding in the first and highest principle and the Mediator of God and men, Jesus Christ, those things of which the likeness cannot in any wise be found in creatures and which exceed all the insight of the human intellect, there remains that looking upon these things it (the mind) rise on high and pass beyond not only this sensible world, but itself also. In this passage Christ is the way and the door, Christ is the stairway and the vehicle . . ." (Chapter 7, sec. 1, tr. by Boas, New York, Liberal Arts Press, 1955, p. 43).

ways for a kind of vision, an intellectual experience; and he does not hope to attain it without reflecting on and criticizing the lower levels of his consciousness.

In short it is absolutely true that one must love in order to understand, but we should add that it is equally necessary to understand in order to love. The correct conclusion is that loving and understanding form a circle which necessarily implies the identity of the two terms.

5. The ethical category

As we have seen, the basic principle of moral life, the supreme law to be instilled into man in ethical experience, can be stated in one word: *Think!*

As for all the men who show themselves to be cruel, wicked, insensible to the pain that they sow around them, ignorant of the internal devastation of which they are alike authors and victims, we can only suppose that they are dull-witted, distracted, unconscious, inattentive, unable to discern the light that shines in the moral world before the more skillful eyes of a sane man endowed with moral sensibility.

It is true enough that words alone have little or no value in any kind of education and that example is worth more than precept. But even the example is not worth much if the man who sets it is not regarded with respect and esteem by the one who is meant to profit from it so that he watches carefully and is anxious to understand. And on the other hand, if we cannot deny that sermons leave us cold, the reason is that we are more apt to hear them with our ears than to heed them with our minds. In the rare cases where the preacher is eagerly sought after, and applauded as an eloquent interpreter of the feelings that are stirring in the hearts of his hearers and demanding expression, his sermons move men's hearts and cause miracles of conversion, since those who heed him go through the preliminary stages in a blaze of enthusiasm and arrive very quickly at the goal of complete understanding.

6. The nonactuality of the moral sense

In the ordinary way the thinking that is the center of ethical life appears to us as a kind of feeling, something of which we are immediately aware, a 'moral sense,' or a demonic voice that says yes or no within us, when we are making up our minds to act. Immediacy is a quality that properly belongs both to feeling as such and to the subject to whom the command "Think!" is addressed. But if it were simply an immediate feeling the category of ethical action would remain *nonactual,* so it is not really correct to speak of a 'moral sense.' The 'thinking' that constitutes the ethical category is more than mere feeling; it is self-conception, the concrete Ego, a synthesis of Ego and non-Ego. It is self-synthesis. We speak of moral feelings and a moral sense only because the root of this self-conception is in the immediate awareness called 'feeling.'

This root is what gives thought its life and universal value; from it the development of self-consciousness must necessarily begin; and in it lies the spontaneity that is the starting point of liberty.[5]

7. Duty and duties

With this qualification in mind we may call the immediate feeling from which all moral experience springs 'moral sense.' Life is forever setting us new moral problems, requiring new solutions, new imperatives, from our conscience. So we must distinguish between the multitude of duties all new and all different, that crowd upon us in experience, and the duty to do one's duty which is always the same. Any word that is not a mere sound is always uniquely determinate; and the same is true of duties. Yet each single duty is duty pure and simple. When we reflect about the multiplicity of duties we overlook that unique duty which is *ours;* this duty is not something one thinks about in an abstract intellectual way,[6] but something one feels. The bond of duty is not a matter for further reflection; it is a categorical, ineluctable imperative.

It is only for purposes of reflective analysis and classification that we can talk of a plurality of duties. Duties that are not commands are not duties for the person speaking of them, though from time to time and one at a time they might become his duties; just as all the affections and passions that Spinoza discusses are nothing but thought for him—pure *intelligere,* the way of escaping from the servitude of sensing into the liberty of understanding. From the

---

[5] This section is evidence of the 'change of aspect'—as Gentile himself called it—brought about in actual idealism by the theory of *feeling* expounded in his *Philosophy of Art* (1931); cf. n12 on p. 88 herein.

[6] *Come logo astratto* (see n3 on pp. 91–92 herein).

ethical point of view the multiplicity of duties is resolved into one unique duty, and this unique duty is always quite particular and definite; just as a man is always Man with a capital letter—not one among many but *the* unique individual.

Duties do not coexist; they are successive. The multiplicity is not something given; it is a process in which the many elements are stages in the development of one whole. This process, moreover, does not take place in time in the sense that there is not first one duty and then another, one after another and each one separate. There is always just one duty; and it is always new, unique, like the words that a man says or the soul that keeps him alive. A determinate duty may seem to continue unchanged, but it does not. The 'honor' that we owe to our parents, for example, is continually changing because our attitude of mind changes from infancy to old age, and as a result our very image of our parents changes. For this reason it may happen that what is called 'the same duty' is one day a power that governs and guides our behavior, and the next day we feel it no longer. It is not still 'the same duty,' because in the first place we are not the same ourselves.

And then, too, what are we to say about the variation in 'the same duty' as it applies to different persons (because of differences in age and experience, etc.)? Duty in the abstract, the duty that is valid for all men, is *only* an abstraction. It lacks the imperative, normative quality that makes *our* duty not just something we ought to know about, but something that *belongs* to us, and concerns us in such a way that because of it we are necessarily committed to be what we are bound to be.

8. A mistake of method in ethics

The mistake that is usually made in ethical theory lies in treating it as a matter of pure theoretical knowledge, a presupposition belonging to the domain of abstract logic. As a result duty loses its specific value. Of course, there is talk of its value; but it is discussed from the point of view of 'man in general' (a creature who does not exist) and not from that of the man who is at a given moment the unique individual, the man who is talking about the value of duty and trying to explain what it really is. One who talks about it can never know it for what it is, unless he feels it, and only so far as he feels it. Rosmini was vividly aware of this subjective character of ethical values and indeed of truth itself.

But any philosophy that does not adopt this strictly *actual* point of view lets slip the essence of moral value, and of genuine moral life; and the same is true in dealing with art or with any other aspect of spiritual life.

9. The necessity to think more about 'duty' than about 'duties'

For this reason moral philosophy and all moral reflection should be concerned not with the multiplicity of duties (the external side of the problem), but with the one duty (the internal reality). But of course we must not deny or undervalue the multiplicity which is the concrete, determinate aspect of duty.[7]

10. Good and evil

Our duty is to will the good; but here we must not think of the good as the object of a particular and distinct form of spiritual activity, as people do when they distinguish between three clearly differentiated ideals in the life of the Spirit, the Beautiful, the Good, and the True—or when they add the cruder and less noble name of the Useful to this most illustrious company.[8] Truth is the moral law of cognitive thinking; it shines before the inquiring intelligence as the ideal to be attained through our own free efforts, or as a reality to be established by our own creative activity, a duty, a good to be realized; though when we pass from one plane of our ethical experience to another, and Truth appears as something abstract, objectively subsistent and not involving our own subjective personality, its full ethical value may no longer be apparent. The same might be said of the beauty of a work of art, which, like every

---

[7] To reconcile these two requirements in the light of the preceding paragraph is not easy; it almost seems as if the only way to "adopt the strictly *actual* point of view" would be to stop *talking* about 'duty' altogether, and get on with doing *our* duty. But then there is no place for 'ethical theory' at all; and this conclusion is an example of the 'mistake' that Gentile is castigating. If, instead of discussing ethical theory abstractly we seek to discover *our* duty as ethical theorists, we shall perceive that our *one* task is to offer a program of action for *our* time ("the multiplicity which is the concrete determinate aspect of duty") not for *all* time (the multiplicity of abstract ethical theory). We should emulate Fichte in his *Addresses to the German Nation* rather than Kant in the *Metaphysic of Ethics*.

[8] The reference is, of course, to the four 'grades' or 'forms' in Croce's *Philosophy of the Spirit*, and the whole section can be read as a criticism of Croce.

other duty, dictates to the artist the law that governs his creative work: *Think!* Or in other words it commands him not to spare his efforts, not to hesitate or give way to the temptations of laziness, vanity, or any other base impulse; to put his whole heart into the struggle to subdue his material so that at the last the beauty of his work may be manifest. The Good is value in general, not simply the value peculiar to one form of spiritual activity that is supposed to be different from the others. In short the Good is the activity of the spirit.

And since value always involves free choice, a conscious act of freely choosing between being and non-being, truth and falsity, good and evil, beauty and ugliness, any mention of value or spiritual actuality, implies a reference to disvalue, the contrary or negation of this actuality; and it is clear that we cannot discuss good without discussing evil as well. The search for good takes the form of a flight from evil, and the discovery of truth appears almost as a war against error.

But if value is defined as the actuality of the spirit, then the negation of value in error and evil, which like truth and goodness are only two aspects of the same thing, must be sought for where this actuality is lacking; in other words they can only be conceived as absolute negation, as nullity. In reality, evil—sin, guilt, or any kind of error—is *Angst,* the root from which all the manifestations of life spring: the nullity that spreads havoc in the depths of a man's heart every time that he hesitates and comes to a full stop, uncertain what course he ought to pursue. To use an apt phrase, he loses heart, he feels the spirit die and ebb away within him. His own real life ebbs away with it and he longs to escape from this nullity, and once again take hold of reality.

Evil is nullity. We might even say that it is *nature,* if by 'nature' we mean that being-in-itself which is negated by the dialectic of the spirit at the dawn of human life. For this reason I formerly identified evil and error with the past of the spirit—the ideal past, that is.[d] By this I meant the past that has been transcended, the past

---

[d] The facile critics who object to this view by pointing out the many truths that belong to the past do not consider the ideal significance that I attach to the word. *They do not realize* (1) that a truth belongs neither to past, nor present, nor future, because it is eternal. *They do not realize* (2) that properly speaking these true thoughts that have survived down to our own day, unmoved amid the scurry of time, do not exist, for if they did they would be abstractions belonging to the domain of abstract logic; whereas every doctrine

that is dead and can never be brought to life; the past that exists only as the content of the spiritual act which transcends and cancels it, by substituting good for evil. The sin for which we have repented has no reality outside of the act of repentance. It is nonexistent because it is nonactual.

Those who rebel against the identification of evil with the nonactuality of the spirit hold that this doctrine must lead one to deny the substantial existence of the evil present in the world, against which we ought to fight; since the claim that evil is nonactual implies that whatever is actual is good. But objections of this kind are always derived from an incorrect analysis of experience. If we have recourse to analysis we must never neglect the conditions of the fact that we wish to explain; and in this case it would never do to forget that the only phenomenology to which we can refer is that of the individual spirit. For an individual's experience provides us with an empirical model of the operation of spirit in its infinite individuality. When the actual existence of evil is established, the person who establishes the fact is not considering his own present moral status but that of other people; he takes his stand on the plane where there is a plurality of individuals each one of whom becomes a machine, an enigma endowed with a liberty that is no liberty (like the monad of the worthy Varisco).[9] When once the indaquacy and the provisional character of this point of view are corrected we can see that it is not at all the case that the evil deeds of others belong only to them and not to us as well. Cardinal Federigo feels responsible for the terrible transgressions

---

gains its life (that is to say, its truth) through a process of continual rebirth in the mind that reflects upon it and sets it in a new light—and from this new point of view the previous point of view is an error. And finally *they do not realize* (3) that the past which we are talking about is past *de jure* and not past *de facto*. An idea may remain fixed; but then it is not a real idea, not a moment of actual thought. *Present* thought is the thought that counts, the only true thought. And in relation to present thought, the past is absolutely past.

"But do you want to deny the heroism of Socrates, then," asks the objector, "because it belongs to the past?" I do not want to deny it at all, because *it does not belong to the past*. We have only to read the *Phaedo* in order to see it before our eyes, and feel it present and alive in our hearts. It is past for the pure scholar, but not for the historian or the ordinary reader. Mark you, if the latter makes a distinction between Plato, who depicted the greatness of Socrates, master of his soul in the face of death, and himself, the present reader of the *Phaedo*, he can no longer recognize this greatness; he will only recognize it if and insofar as he manages to re-create for himself the Platonic picture of Socrates and so brings the heroism of Socrates to life in his actual experience.

    [9] See n25 on p. 191 herein.

of the Unnamed; [10] and Gandhi was brought up by his father to take on himself the task of expiating the sins of his sons and his pupils.[11] Other people are not absolutely 'other' than ourselves: they are our neighbors, our own real selves. And on this plane the evil deeds of others, the evil that can be condemned, is that which is revealed in our own contrition and our anxious desire to expiate it. Similar considerations apply to the evil that has its place in the pattern of past history, which must certainly be recognized as evil deserving censure and condemnation. But no historian worthy of the name stops short at this preliminary condemnation which expresses the repugnance of the moral conscience in the face of its own negative or opposite. He must go further; he must comprehend the evil, discover its sources, the reasons for its actual existence, and the consequences that followed from it even when they were "beyond the providence of human sense." [12] He must construct the pattern of his period as an apt illustration of the rationality of history and thus see how the evil was a necessary moment in the development of the human spirit, a link in the chain on which the good of that particular period depended. And so, since the true subject of history is not particular but universal, the evil is again driven back out of existence into the realm of the nonactual. For, in the final analysis, the actuality of history lies in the consciousness of the historian, who cannot discover evil without canceling it by means of his own purifying judgment.

And not only is all evil past, or nonactual, but the converse is true also: everything that man turns his back on (everything that is transcended, past, nonactual) is evil. It matters not whether his decision is right or wrong. The universal spirit of man is always right. If man does wrong he will sooner or later set it right and put things in order. For no one ever turns his back on the good when he recognizes it.

What he does and must turn his back on is his sinful nature,

---

[10] Manzoni, *Promessi sposi*, Chapters 22–23.

[11] Gandhi does say that he felt obliged to do this (in the complete edition of his *Autobiography*, Part IV, Chapter 36, Washington, D.C., Public Affairs Press, 1948, pp. 418 ff.). But he does not say that his father taught him to do it. Gentile's Introduction to the abridged version (*Autobiografia, a cura di C. F. Andrews*, Florence, Sansoni, 1931) makes it clear that he is thinking of the *example* set by Gandhi's father in weeping when his son confessed to deceit (*His Own Story*, New York, Macmillan, 1931, pp. 64–65).

[12] *Oltre la difension di senni umani* (Dante, *Inferno*, VII, 81).

the original sin from which only the Grace of God can free us, the nullity which is the eternal antecedent of the eternal life of the Spirit—and which is not merely moral but absolute nullity: the impenetrable chaos of brute nature, mechanism, spiritual darkness, ugliness, falsehood and evil, all the things that man is forever fighting against. Every man weeps at his birth for the world in which he finds himself; he feels the dragging burden of matter that is laid upon his shoulders and his whole life becomes one long struggle to get free from it.

If we wish to call the good by a name that will shine in splendor before the eyes of mankind, let us call it *liberty*. For liberty is in truth the essence of the spirit which labors perpetually to attain it. And let us define evil as *slavery:* the slavery of matter which stands as the direct opposite of the spirit. For evil is just the burden of all the material things that drag us down and clip our wings against the flight to the heavens for which the spirit yearns.[13]

---

[13] Cf. Plato, *Phaedrus*, 247 ff.

VI

THE STATE

1. Definition of the State

In order to understand the true essence of the *State* we must not stop short and rest content with any of its empirical features. The State is the universal common aspect of the will.

2. The State and the Nation

A nation is not to be defined in terms of common soil or common life, and the consequent community of traditions and customs, language or religion, etc. All this is only the matter of the nation, not its form; for the nation can only exist where men are conscious of this matter, and accept it in their hearts as the substantial content of the national personality [1] and the proper object of the national will, the will which gains concrete and actual expression in the State. It makes no difference here whether the State is an established fact or an ideal aim; indeed it is always an ideal aim, for it is an act of will, and even the maintenance of an existing constitution is the continual creation of a new one.

The claim that 'nationality' carries with it the right to autonomous statehood rests on an error. For it is not nationality that creates the State, but the State which creates nationality, by setting the seal of actual existence on it. It is through the *conquest* of unity

---

[1] *Essenza spirituale.*

and independence that the nation gives proof of its political will, and establishes its existence as a State.

3. Law

The will of the State is *law*—'public' or 'private' law, accordingly as it regulates the relations between the State and the citizen, or between one citizen and another. In any case the will of the State is actually expressed in the will of the citizen so far as the citizen's will possesses universal validity. There is no such thing as right or law apart from the State, and any individual who 'asserts his rights' must always appeal to a universal will to which all private inclinations [2] must submit just because they are only inclinations.

But are we speaking here of *positive law?* Law is not worth anything unless it is positive, for only positive law has the effective authority of universal will over private inclination. But this positivity is by no means peculiar to the strictly juridical activity of the State. Even the moral law is positive, in that one's duty is always some definite, particular, concrete *act of will.*

There is a sense, however, in which legal right is positive while moral right is not—as will become apparent if we consider the etymology of the word 'State.' A 'State' is not something that is even now coming into existence; it exists already, it is *static*—and so it must remain. Its authority must be respected, its laws must be fixed, and its power strong enough to carry them out and prevent their violation—all the better therefore if it is God-given, hereditary, absolute.[3] The State is already there (or so it seems). Indeed, its existence produces a great web of consequences, in the shape of public order and the rule of law; and at the head of it all there is the 'government,' the motive force of a machine that is all complete and in working order.

The State exists; and so does its will—the law. From birth till death the citizen finds here his *limit,* the presupposition of his existence and condition of his liberty. The will of the State with which he has to deal is not a decision in the making, but a decision already made [4] and already promulgated in a clear, explicit, and definite

---

[2] *Arbitrio.*

[3] *Immediato* (cf. pp. 125–26, herein). A State which exists 'immediately' would be one that is taken for granted as part of the natural inevitable order of things—as in the case of the proverbial 'laws of the Medes and Persians.'

[4] *Volontà non in atto, ma già posta, già voluta.*

formula. And the promulgation of the State's will must *precede* the cases which it regulates.

So that the subject for whom the law is intended cannot obey it unless it is there before him as something which is already decided and is in *this* sense of the word 'positive.' From this point of view the moral law is a present voluntary decision, whereas positive law is a decision already made. (Something that has been decided and is therefore now accepted: a *de facto* law, like the laws of nature which operate quite independently before we become aware of them and begin to come to terms with them.)

But this positive law and the State that makes it are only abstract moments in ethical life. They belong to abstract logic, and correspond to an ideal position of the will. For once a voluntary decision is made it ceases to be voluntary: [5] it is an object which the will cannot accept as it stands. The real synthesis is a unity of present act and past decision in which the present act is embodied in the past decision, while the past decision gains spiritual value from the present act.

Thus the *positive* character of law is transcended in the concrete act of will, which cancels it and obeys the moral law of absolute *liberty*. The limit is canceled only so far as it is preserved: it is recognized, that is posited, and hence it is a self-limitation which in no way diminishes the freedom of the act but rather proves it.

When once the positivity of law is transcended, the whole of law is resolved into morality.

4. Government and the governed

This same positivity reappears in the opposition between government and governed, which is wrongly but generally confused with the duality of State and citizens. The government (whether absolute or representative) makes the law and sees to its observance; and those subject to it must take its activity for granted if they are to be governed. And in the abstract that is how it is. But just as positive law is canceled in actual ethical action, so all opposition between government and governed vanishes in the consent of the latter, without which the government cannot stand.

This consent may be spontaneous or it may be procured by coercion. The moral ideal of the State, within which the govern-

---

[5] *Volendosi si fa voluto.*

ment exercises its authority, requires that spontaneity be increased to a maximum and coercion reduced to a minimum; but it is impossible that either element should ever stand alone, unaccompanied by its opposite. The nations swing restlessly between the two poles of a minimum of coercion with a maximum of spontaneity, and a maximum of coercion with a minimum of spontaneity: between democracy and absolutism, for it is very hard to attain that mutual tempering of the opposed principles which is their dialectical synthesis.[6]

5. Authority and liberty

There is much talk nowadays of authoritarian governments and liberal governments, which is all based on the abstract opposition of authority and liberty, the government and the individuals governed. The individuals are conceived as atoms, each one standing on his own and possessing in himself all the rights and duties that have any meaning for him; and the government is thought of as a purely limiting power which coordinates the free activities of the individuals. People are unwilling to recognize that the choice of suitable machinery for the tempering of the two opposed prin-

---

[6] There is a contradiction in this section. For Gentile first admits that the moral ideal is a maximum of spontaneity with a minimum of coercion and then goes on to characterize this ideal as 'democracy,' one of the two extremes between which a mean must be found. Surely the dialectical synthesis would be for him the true ideal aim? Yet he has just come to the conclusion in the previous chapter that *liberty* is the essence of morality, so that his first statement follows logically from his ethical theory.

The problem here seems to me to arise from a confusion of terms caused by the apologetic undercurrents present in this chapter. The opposed principles that have to be synthesized are not 'spontaneity' and 'coercion' but 'liberty' and 'authority' (cf. the next section). It is obviously impossible to have a genuine synthesis of spontaneity and coercion: the synthesis occurs precisely at the point where liberty *ceases* to be *mere* spontaneity (caprice, *arbitrio, Willkür*) and authority *ceases* to be regarded as coercion—or in other words the point where free action gains moral value through willing subjection to a universal law. All talk of 'synthesizing spontaneity and coercion' is as crudely empirical as anything in the liberal doctrines that Gentile opposes. The confusion between empirical and speculative issues is one of which he himself is guilty, and the reason for it lies in his desire to justify his adhesion to Fascism. The assertion that the moral ideal of the State requires that coercion be reduced to a minimum makes a curious contrast with his much more notorious claim that all force, even the blackjack, is moral force. It is the memory of the latter that causes him to emphasize the empirical aspect of the problem until one almost forgets the ideal aims altogether. Only complete forgetfulness could make us accept the blackjack as a proper instrument of political action.

ciples is not a problem to be solved by reference to *eternal principles*, but in accordance with historical criteria founded on considerations of expediency appropriate to different historical situations. These are matters of degree in which the intuition of a statesman is worth more than the theorems of a political scientist.

What the philosopher ought always to emphasize is that authority must not destroy liberty, nor should liberty pretend to do without authority. For neither of the two terms can stand alone; and the necessity of their synthesis is a consequence of the essentially dialectical character of the spiritual act.

6. Liberalism

Anyone who is acquainted with the history of liberalism will be aware that it had its origin in a particular historical situation at the end of the seventeenth century, and that its development has run parallel with that of the bourgeois industrial society of Europe. In other words, it is not really a philosophical doctrine in the true sense—for philosophy always deals with man *sub specie aeterni*—but the solution of a particular historical problem; and this problem is now solved. It is over and done with. It coincided with the formation of what we call the 'modern State,' which assumed two different forms that have been illustrated with varying degrees of clarity and emphasis in the various countries of Europe, but are so closely connected that the second form cannot be understood in isolation, since it is the logical development of the first.

These two forms are rooted in a reaction against the feudal State of the Middle Ages; and any present-day upholder of the liberal parliamentary system who looks for its earliest antecedents in the medieval parliaments is only showing that he has no clear conception of the historical ground and essence of the liberal State. For authority in the feudal State was founded on 'Divine Right,' it was granted by the Grace of God as an immediate gift like a natural property.[7] The fact that the feudal system was organized in a variety of parliaments did not affect the essential nature of this authority which was the core of the State's power and value. Only in the Seigniories, a product of Italian humanism, was this authority denied; for here the State was a historical creation, the result of human power (or *virtù* as they called it) operating in ac-

---

[7] *Come qualche cosa di natura, un che di immediato* (cf. n3 on p. 122 herein).

cordance with the fixed principles of political dominion. It was
no longer established by Popes or emperors; no authority transcending the human will brought it into being; it had its origin in a voluntary act, or rather it *was* a voluntary act.

The Seigniory, in its turn, was a transformation of the Commune,
which was thus the real cradle of the liberal State. But it had one
vital advantage over the Commune: it established a central power
and resolved the atomism of individuals and classes in the personality of the State which was striving to achieve complete self-consciousness. The Seigniories were the source of that principle of
absolutism represented by the national monarchs who conquered,
controlled, and defended their realms and at last could say: *L'État
c'est moi.* Philosophers and political theorists then bowed down
before the 'enlightened monarch,' who represented in their eyes
the real interest and intelligence of the citizens, all sharing equally
in rights and duties under the supreme power, the self-conscious
personality of the State. And if it were really possible for all citizens
to be equal and undifferentiated—as they took it for granted that
it was—then an enlightened absolutism would be the true ideal
of the State. It actually lasted for just so long as within the sphere
of civil society which the monarch directed and governed there was
no noticeable breach in this indifferent equality of all citizens,
caused by the establishment of individual or group interests which
through work, initiative, talent, industry, etc. gradually acquired
so much social prominence that their great worth and importance
could no longer be overlooked. The bourgeoisie emerged: a new
class that would eventually undermine the old privileged classes
of nobility and clergy, natural allies of the despotism which, although it was a product of history, appeared to the ordinary citizen
as a natural entity,[8] a purely mechanical limit. A class that laid
claim to everything, men without a past, without titles, without
ancestors, relying on their own strength, and indeed giving proof
of it through their work and through every kind of personal initiative, creating by their industry the goods that all men need for
daily life. This is the class that contains all the men who are really
worthy of the name in the modern State, in which man (the Prince)
is valued for his knowledge and ability alone, that is for his capacity
to make a contribution of his own to the world.

The bourgeoisie with its productive power could not be absorbed

---

[8] *Un immediato* (cf. n3 on p. 122 herein).

into the system of absolute government, but as it gradually became externally differentiated from the other classes and internally differentiated owing to the inevitable variety of the tasks and the interests that it created, so it came to share with the existing governing class, in various ways and in an ever-increasing degree, in the creation of those interests which the State contains and guards. Bit by bit as industry was developed through the division of labor (the development of thought) the importance of the bourgeoisie continually increased. The French Revolution, like the English and American Revolutions before it, was a declaration of independence on the part of the third estate, the bourgeoisie, which at a certain stage in its development awoke to the fact that the Prince's will in opposition to its own was only subjective inclination, and rose against him in order to reduce him to an executive organ of its will. From that time forward it has been assumed that this will can be expressed through national representation: and so we get liberalism.[9]

But do we need reminding that the development of great industries in the last century necessarily brought a fourth estate into existence behind the third, since industry created capitalism, and the labor of the capitalists would have been a mere abstraction apart from the labor of the working classes? Once again the have-nots arose against the haves. Socialism and communism were born; and the liberal State, the State of the bourgeoisie, began to be attacked as incapable of safeguarding the liberty of the laboring masses who constitute a majority of the citizens. The liberal State entered a crisis when it began to part company with the socio-economic realities for which it was originally intended to provide a political structure. The representatives no longer expressed the real will of the citizens and the State was left devoid of its proper

---

[9] In the preceding two paragraphs there seems to be an attempt to combine the analysis given by Hegel in the *Phenomenology* (in which the rise of absolutism reduces class distinctions to meaninglessness and so makes way for the democratic ideals of the revolution) with the later Marxist analysis (in which a new governing class takes the place of the old one). The two analyses are really distinct and both are essential to Gentile's argument. Perhaps the proper way in which to harness them together would be to regard Hegel's analysis as 'formal' (or 'ideal') and Marx's analysis as 'material' (or 'real'). But this would mean that we must accord to 'liberalism' an 'ideal' status which Gentile hardly seems willing to do. He emphasizes the Marxist 'reality' as if the liberal ideal were only an epiphenomenon. Thus partisan prejudice leads him to adopt for the moment a materialist point of view. One need hardly point out that this is at variance with his own basic philosophy.

content. The effective will of the citizens of the State was alienated and began to destroy the fake structure of the State in two ways: first by joining in the game of representation, treating it as a hollow sham that was bound to break down, and by sheer force of numbers twisting parliamentary forms to the betrayal of their original functions—a negative method of attack which has corrupted the parliamentary system in the various States, and dissipated the vital forces which the original liberals thought they had safeguarded and strengthened through parliamentary liberty; and second, by forming a separate system of syndicates,[10] thereby creating their own true State, the genuine expression and hence the efficient guardian of their own interests.

The problem of the State today is no longer to secure the political recognition of the third estate—which was the task of liberalism— but to secure for the worker and his syndicates the political significance [11] which they claim but which they can never possess until the pluralism of the syndicates is reconciled in the unity of the State. For man considered as a political animal *is* the State; and he is one State or he is nothing. Whereas the syndicates, being groups of individuals arranged according to the economic categories of production in which they are employed, are like a crowd of individuals, each different from all the rest and therefore solitary, not disposed to recognize any but his own private interest. This is both the strength and the weakness of the syndicate; in it the individual rediscovers that quality of immediacy that he finds initially in himself. It contains nothing external to his own interest, nothing 'generic' that could appear to him as imposed from above or from the outside. It is like the family for a man who regards his family as the concrete fulfillment of his own personality in a narrow circle where everything is domestic and intimately known to him, every pain and every joy is his, and the life which forms the general topic and concern is his own. And in fact the syndicate

---

[10] *Sindacati*. Gentile is clearly referring to the 'syndicalist' movement in Europe, which was predominantly revolutionary in character and hostile to existing parliamentary institutions. His commentary will hardly apply to the relations between trade unions and the American Congress or the British Parliament. The most important document of the movement he has in mind is Georges Sorel's *Reflections on Violence* (1908; tr. by T. E. Hulme in 1914; latest edition Glencoe, Ill., Free Press, 1950).

[11] *Valore*.

like the family has been extolled as the most effective school for the worker, a school that draws him naturally beyond the bounds of his primitive egoism, and teaches him to appreciate and feel a common interest as his own and thus to find the norm for his own conduct in an ideal higher than mere natural instinct.

But a syndicate is just one syndicate and the homogeneity of its structure, along with the *division of labor,* implies the existence of other syndicates. They exist, and they are bound to exist. And once the workers have formed syndicates against the employers of labor they are bound to be faced by unions of the employers. This social atomism is in flagrant contrast with the necessary interrelations that exist between every syndicate and all the others. Thus the syndicate is an atom from the point of view of its unit members; yet it is not an atom because its independence is transcended by its natural connection with the other atoms. It transcends and must transcend the particularism that arises from its socially abstract universality.[12] A syndicate is a faction of humanity; but humanity cannot exist in fractions. So the State is not a syndicate, but the reconciliation and resolution of the syndicates in the fundamental unity of humanity which is articulated in and through all of the syndical categories; and this unity is not a result, but rather the basic principle that makes the pluralism of the syndicates possible.

So that really the State *is* the syndicate in the same sense that it *is* the individual: for the effective will of the individual who is conscious of his own real complex individuality is the State; and similarly the syndicate is the State when it rises above its narrow limits as a social category, and becomes fully conscious of the one universal will that animates and maintains all the categories.

Both syndicalism and the old-fashioned liberalism, which forever returns to parade about the world in a new disguise as the last

---

[12] In case the meaning of this outrageous piece of Hegelian jargon is not clear from what follows, a word of explanation may not come amiss. The 'universality' consists in the fact that a 'syndicate' includes *all* those who fulfill a given function in society: and it is 'socially abstract' because of course the function can only really exist in the context of society as a whole. 'Particularism' here means group selfishness, refusal by the group to recognize its dependence on the total social context. 'Transcending particularism' means recognizing dependence on the social organism as a whole which would be the 'socially concrete universal,' or in Gentile's terminology 'the State.'

word in political philosophy, involve the same blunder: the atomic conception of society as an accidental gathering and heaping together of individuals who are only abstractions, or of syndicates which cannot legitimately claim or pretend to exist because they are equally abstract. This view is only possible if we accept the standpoint of materialism and regard society as a multitude living together and obliged to accept a unity to which they are in themselves absolutely opposed; a group of mutually alien individuals engaged in a 'war of all against all,' or of syndicates, equally alien and hence unable to achieve a unity which is contrary to their nature.

The answer to abstract syndicalism, therefore, is not to be found in the equally abstract liberalism of the individualists. Their liberalism is a kind of deep-rooted materialism that was always opposed by one liberal who knew what liberty was—Mazzini. Mazzini desired liberty, as every man does who is aware of his own nature; but he knew that it does not belong to an individual in the abstract, but to the People, the concrete substance of every individual. An Italian can only be free insofar as the Italian people is free; if his people is enslaved he can only be a slave. Hence the first essential was a free and independent Italy; the Italian people could not exist as long as they were divided and ignorant, unable to rise to the consciousness of their own unity, nor could they exist as long as they were subject to a foreign yoke. The individual can only be free in a free State. Or, more precisely, the free individual is the free State, since the State is not really a relationship between individuals; it lies within the individual, in that unity of particular and universal which constitutes his individuality.[a]

7. Ethics and politics

The distinction between ethics and politics is one on which recent Italian philosophy has harped most insistently, only to dis-

---

[a] The liberty of the citizen is the liberty of the State. There can be no liberty within the State unless it is independent in external relations. But external independence involves war and hence a limitation of internal liberty; and without this limit liberty is impossible because independence is impossible.

Generally speaking, where the authority and autonomy of the State is shaken, the foundation of liberty is compromised and undermined.

In fact, those who threaten the State's authority do not mean to abolish it altogether, but only to destroy one State in order to build another. So that revolutions occur, yes, but they are *transitory*.

regard it in order to make room for the application of ethical criteria in politics.[13]

The distinction is always based on the abstract consideration of the different moments that can in fact be distinguished in the life of the spirit. 'Economic' action (simple volition or pure force) and moral action, for example. But the force of the will, when it claims to have the 'force of law' (*dura lex sed lex*), is the past decision that stands as a present limitation of liberty, a limitation that is necessary and cannot be dispensed with. It is the moment of law, the moment of State authority, the mighty will to which all private inclinations must yield.

The State is the universal aspect of the individual. Hence it is bound to possess the same morality as the individual, since it is not a presupposition of his existence—a limit to his liberty—but the concrete actuality of his will. Whenever we distinguish and oppose the two terms 'State' and 'individual' the distinction is simply empirical. Of course we can imagine an individual whose morality is not consistent with the law of the State. But still, the State is a will with a universal law, a categorical imperative, which is bound to be moral. And any inconsistencies can only arise from the diversity of the problems to be solved, problems which are always diverse even within the sphere of what is called individual morality.

8. The Ethical State

It follows from this that the State has an immanent ethical character. Who would want to deny it unless he had some reason for opposing the State? People in opposition, for whom the State is a target of attack, naturally begin by treating it as a *res*, a thing without value and unworthy of any kind of respect. But those who

---

[13] This is a reference to Croce's rather complex and, in Gentile's opinion, inconsistent views on the subject. 'Politics' and 'Law,' according to Croce, were sharply distinct from 'ethics,' and the State was simply a focus of pure force. Hence his extreme aversion for Gentile's theory of the 'ethical State.' But at the same time he held that the whole realm of political action must be guided and governed by the moral conscience; and apart from this conviction his resolute opposition to Fascism would have been absurd. English readers should consult *Politics and Morals* (tr. by Castiglione), New York, Philosophical Library, 1945; London, Allen and Unwin, 1946. Also *History as the Story of Liberty*, London, Allen and Unwin, 1941; New York, W. W. Norton, 1941; or Meridian Books, 1955.

deny the ethical character of the State make haste to restore to it
with the left hand what they have taken away with the right. For
it is only the State created by other men that they refuse to recognize as ethical, and they want to replace it by another one, which,
when rightly understood and rightly organized, can once more be
credited with the value that a moral and religious conception of
life confers on it, by making it an instrument of higher ends. They
do not seem to realize that a *thing* (or instrument) can never acquire any value, so that the only possible end to this road is *theocracy*—which brings us back again to the disputed concept of the
'ethical State,' since it postulates a State that coincides with the
divine will.

But if *theocracy* is not just an empty word there is no reason
to fight shy of it. For whether we consider it simply as an existing
authority,[14] or accept its full significance as the concrete actuality
of our will, there is no doubt that the will of the State is a divine
will. God is always there; the God of the Old Testament and the
God of the New.[15]

The moral rebellion which the 'ethical' State provokes is itself a
confirmation of its ethical character. For a nonmoral force would
never be liable to moral judgment. The rebellion occurs whenever we
feel the power of the State but do not recognize its positive value.
We still attribute a value to it even in this case—but a negative
one as in the case of a sinner. We want the sinner to perceive his
error, to repent and be redeemed; and this implies that we believe
him capable of redemption.

The most striking proof of all that the State is an ethical institution is to be found in the conscience of the statesman.

All the familiar problems about divergences between morals and
politics belong to the division of ethics known as *casuistry*.[16]

---

[14] *Nella immediatezza della sua autorità.*

[15] I.e. 'Law' and 'Morality'; cf. also Chapter 8, secs. 1–2, herein.

[16] These two concluding sentences are somewhat oracular. One can see that
for Gentile the conscience of the statesman who has to make political decisions
would be of crucial importance since the statesman is quite conscious that he
is acting for the State, and also at the same time would claim to be doing his
duty. Thus in his action the 'ethical' State is fully self-conscious. But the
statesman himself may well be aware, as Cavour was, of a gulf between his
behavior as a private individual and his behavior as a statesman: from this
root spring all the difficulties that Gentile dismisses as *casuistry* in the last sentence. Both he and Croce held that casuistry depended on an abstract and
erroneous view of ethics. The last sentence is thus the unkindest cut of all at
Croce, and the next section provides a commentary on it.

9. Moralism

There is no more effective proof of the State's ethical character than the moralism, whether genuine or hypocritical, naive or rhetorical, with which the adversaries of this doctrine try so industriously to discover and to heal the moral sores of ordinary political life. Having logically despoiled the State and the world of politics in which it actually exists of every moral attribute, they are horrified at the picture of humanity which they have concocted in their own minds; a humanity that is not human, since morality is certainly the most essential characteristic of the human spirit.

A state that was by nature nonethical would not be immoral; it would be something worse. I should say that it would be inhuman, if it is true, as we have argued, that there is no conceivable form of human activity that is not *ipso facto* subject to the moral law. It would be worse than immoral because an immoral thing is destined to be redeemed and refashioned by morality; whereas an amoral thing is excluded by definition from all possibility of becoming moral.

How can man allow anything within the orbit of his activity to be withdrawn from the authority of that moral law which is the only thing that makes truly human existence possible? [17] Man subjects even the domestic animals that he is induced to admit into the circle of his daily life to a rudimentary discipline of behavior, involving the distinction of what is permitted and what is not, a distinction which he tries to inculcate in every way, until he can be certain that they have grasped it and will abide by it. And in the face of the "fierce might" that "claims unto itself the name of right," [18] sheer brute force ignorant and unmindful of any standard of justice, the Briareus of a hundred arms that lays hands on everything, doing and undoing the work of the individuals who constitute the real moral world,[19] there arises the natural need of the human soul to proclaim and defend the moral law, the salvation of the spirit. In the end this force must be respected and conserved, but only because it can serve spiritual ends of which it knows nothing and which therefore transcend it.

---

[17] *Creatrice della sola vita possible all'uomo.*

[18] Manzoni, *Adelchi,* Act V, Scene viii, ll. 355–57: *Una feroce/Forza il mondo possiede, e fa nomarsi/Dritto* (traced for me at the *Fondazione Gentile* through the courtesy of Professor Spirito).

[19] *Sono in concreto la realtà morale.*

The spirit is morality; it is liberty. Well then, the State, although of itself it knows nothing of this higher liberty, which transcends it and is quite incommensurable with it, ought still to encourage and promote the exercise of this liberty, by means of its institutions. It 'ought'? But does the State, then, have a moral duty? Is it also an ethical subject, like every single individual that we can distinguish within it, who has his duties to the ideal of liberty? In that case it would be like an animal that needs domesticating; for as we have already remarked, the process of domestication is nothing but the admission of an animal into our society, even into our family; it is a practical contradiction of that subhuman and therefore antisocial nature that we attribute to animals without thinking too much about it.

So that if we begin by making the State deaf to the moral law, we must end by seeking to subject it to a higher guidance, a kind of artificial moralization or humanization. And out of the arbitrariness of the initial assumption there springs a sort of impatient zeal, a violent eagerness to do more than enough. Because of this it is no longer the clear and eloquent simplicity of true morality that we find in the political philosophers who make this assumption, but a passionate and rhetorical moralism that pours out over the whole of history, and submerges it in an indistinct play of light and shade which obscures the real historical process that gives life to the State, and the result is that the great problem of the State, the problem of universal history, is reduced to a petty bourgeois problem of dragging or summoning this State or that, this or that dominant party or statesman, into the court of the moral ideal. The more firmly morality is excluded from its proper place, the more violent this moral anxiety becomes. The anxiety, the yearning . . . and even the rhetoric, are all motivated by a despair of ever again coming to grips with the flesh and blood of moral life.

VII

THE STATE AND ECONOMICS

1. The economic nature of man and hence of the State

Nihil humani a me alienum puto.[1] And since we can also say that
the State is man, it follows that nothing human can be alien to the
essential nature of the State. For the State includes, unifies, and
fulfills every human activity, every form or element of human nature; so that every concept of the State that omits some element of
human nature is inadequate. And no one would want to deny that
'useful' action, action that serves as a means to an end and constitutes a special form of human activity which is the subject matter
of economics, is such an element. No one who pays attention to the
most obvious experience can possibly deny that man is guided by
the criterion of utility in the search for pleasure, or, more correctly,
in fulfilling the hedonistic purpose that is immanent in his nature.
Difficulties only arise when we wish to determine the relation between this utilitarian aspect of human action and the ethical character that is universally regarded as the essential property of all
genuinely human behavior.

The recent solution of this problem [2] in which economic action
is treated as a primitive stage of volition, from which the will is
destined to advance to its complete fulfillment in ethical action, to-

---

[1] "I count nothing human alien to me" (Terence, *Heauton timorumenos*,
I, 1:25).
[2] By Croce; see especially his *Philosophy of the Practical* (tr. by Ainslie),
London, Macmillan, 1912.

135

gether with the related doctrines of law and of the State as mere
force, or purely economic activity, is very persuasive, like all theories
that appear simple and clear because they are framed in a system
of concepts which are sharply distinct from a formal point of view.
Nevertheless, it has caused much perplexity; and even its author
has been constrained by a kind of obscure presentiment that the
truth lies elsewhere to postulate an 'ethico-political' form of activity
which tends to unite what he at first violently put asunder, in order
to picture the life of the State as an essentially ethical process.[3]

2. The humanity of economic behavior

First of all, it is important to notice that from an external point
of view the criterion of economic efficiency can be applied to the
lower animals as well as to man, though the former are generally
thought of as lacking the essential human attribute of liberty. Even
the behavior of the lower animals is purposive and therefore 'useful'; indeed, it is more strictly utilitarian than human action, because it is more immediately hedonistic. For this reason too it is
infallible, unlike human action, which not infrequently fails to
achieve its aim. This infallibility is connected with the fundamental
characteristic of the utilitarian behavior of animals: their behavior is
not free but mechanical, and in that sense necessary—which is what
we mean by calling it *instinctive*. 'Instinct' is rational behavior, behavior which is always exactly appropriate to its end, but the rationality is unconscious and transcends the agent. The rationality of nature? Or of God? Certainly, it does not belong to the single animal
which pursues the prey that will satisfy its hunger or flies from the
danger by which it is threatened. To some degree it does resemble the
functioning of the different parts of a living organism; for such
functioning is always rational, considered simply as a means to the
fulfillment of the general purpose of the entire organism, and of the
special purpose of that particular organ. The rationality arises from
unconscious obedience to a law and is therefore completely lacking
in liberty.

And the analogy between the instinctive behavior of brutes and
the utilitarian activity of man does not break down because intelligence is involved in the latter. For intelligence is not absent even
in the action of the lower animals, as is shown by the complexity

---

[3] Cf. *Politics and Morals*, Chapter 3.

of certain courses of behavior consisting of many coordinated actions all directed toward one definite end, and by the subtle cunning and even the farsighted slyness that animals display in activity schemes of this kind.

A distinction can, of course, be made within intelligence itself, between that of man and that of the brutes, the latter debased into a sort of unconscious mechanism, and the former elevated into a conscious activity directed by free reason, and controlled by a free judgment of its value. It makes no difference. For intelligence can never be anything but an antecedent of economic action; it can only serve to establish the precise terms of the particular economic problem that is to be resolved. The economic activity itself, even on this higher plane which human intelligence opens up for it through more exact definition of the problem or more perfect knowledge of the means appropriate to its solution, will always be a kind of instinctive behavior, necessary, mechanical, without liberty. Whether the economic behavior occurs on a higher or a lower plane does not matter; considerations of that sort are relevant when we are seeking to establish the conditions of economic behavior by abstract analysis, but they do not affect its essential nature.

3. 'Utilitarian' behavior or 'useful' behavior?

We must, in fact, be very careful in distinguishing the sense in which 'useful' behavior is human. If we may use Ockham's Razor as a criterion, then it is correct to describe behavior as 'useful' rather than as 'utilitarian.' It is true that we ordinarily use the latter expression in distinguishing between behavior and its result: the result is called 'useful' and the behavior 'utilitarian.' But really the 'result' of an economic action, like the 'result' of an ethical action, should not be regarded as something external to the action, for they are one and the same. Water is not in itself 'useful' to quench thirst; for it would never possess this utility if we were not first of all thirsty; and once this relation between the subject and the thing is granted, the utility no longer belongs to the thing alone prior to its entry into relation with the subject, or considered apart from that relation; it belongs to the thing so far as it is enjoyed, or in other words absorbed into its relation with the subject who profits by it. So that it is really the quenching of thirst that is useful, or in other words the action that changes the relation between man and his environment, in such a way that the environment participates in his life; the action that creates a new man in the place of the old, a man whose thirst is quenched. Everyone knows that there is something ridiculous and absurd about the miser's treasure hidden away and so withdrawn from all use. It is obvious that money has an economic value only when it is spent, and employed as a means for the acquisition of goods that are actually enjoyed, goods which man procures by means of money, for the satisfaction of his needs and hence the transformation of his own mode of being and the fulfillment of his pleasure-seeking self.[4] This transformation and fulfillment are not the consequence of useful behavior; they *are* useful behavior. Such behavior 'produces' pleasure certainly, but only while the activity lasts, and maintains by its own actuality the sense of satisfaction which is what is pleasant. When the activity stops, there follows satiety, dislike, nausea—*surgit de medio fonte leporum amari aliquid.*[5] In order to enjoy drinking one must be thirsty; the enjoyment disappears once the thirst is quenched—and then one can drink no more. Similarly the joy or happiness of life is in us, not in things; when once the inner life is spent, the life that makes us love things and people and enjoy living among them, the external reality kindled into flame by this inward fervor, falls to ashes as the fervor dies; the world turns gray because the light that illuminated it from within our hearts has gone out.

It is not the natural objects located all around us in space that are useful, not even when they are the finished products of our manufacture, but only the actions by which we succeed in creating a mode of existence for ourselves that would never have been possible apart from our own efforts. In this transformation of our personality 'things' play a part, but our own efforts are much more important. This is the kind of utility that is specifically human: a utility that is *causa sui.*

4. Body and soul [6]

But does this 'self-caused' utility which man senses at the very basis of his existence constitute an *actual* part of his spiritual life?

---

[4] *Perfezionamento edonistico della sua persona.*

[5] Lucretius, *De rerum natura,* IV, 1133–34: *Medio de fonte leporum/Surgit amari aliquid* ("From the very fount of delights there rises something bitter").

[6] In the Italian text this section is entitled "The human and the subhuman" and the next "Body and soul." But the reader will speedily perceive that this is a slip. The two headings need to be transposed. The distinction between 'human' and 'subhuman' is not actually mentioned until the end of section 5.

Man is both soul and body. This much everyone is agreed on; the disagreements and errors only begin when we seek to clarify the relation between the two terms. There are those who have been called 'the philosophers of the indifferent copula (*and*)' [7] because they are so entangled in the dualism of two autonomous substances that they cannot account for the unity, which is the certain datum of our constant and incontestable experience. If there are really two substances then each is infinite, and it is absolutely impossible to pass from one to the other. The mind can never get outside of itself; to use a phrase of Spinoza's, the body can only be *objectum mentis,* so that we can have no reason for positing a corporeal substance distinct from the thinking substance, except an ignorant and arbitrary dogmatism. All the difficulties arise from the fact that men have sought to understand the idea of the body without first discovering how it originated. We speak of the body as the foundation of our conscious life. Everyone can see and touch it, and so they think that nothing could be better known to them; indeed, it is commonly regarded as the standard of comparison for evidence and certainty in our knowledge. Yet in reality, none of us could say offhand what this 'body' is that we are all so sure we know better than any other part of the world that is present to consciousness.

5. The 'human' and the 'subhuman'

To begin with it would be well to remember that the 'body' to which everyone refers is precisely his own body, the body that he calls his 'own' because it is present in his consciousness as the immediate object of the primary fundamental awareness [8] apart from which he would never be aware of anything. This primary and elementary awareness, the original consciousness that every man finds at the root of himself when he abstracts from all the determinate contents of his experience and leaves only the principle from which that experience, in all the rich variety of its actual determinations, must have initially developed, this is the soul, the source of man's conscious life and existence. But even in its most rudimentary form this soul-feeling is not just a matter of being alive,

---

[7] I believe the reference is to Hegel, *Encyclopaedia*, para. 389; the context seems to indicate that the Cartesians and Occasionalists are meant.
[8] *Sentire.*

or more precisely, being 'lived through' by some force that transcends our individuality; for we find it at the root of *our* being, *our* personality, precisely at the point where we begin to be selves, possessing a unique and indestructible individuality of our own. This soul-feeling is thus a *sense of self:* an obscure self-awareness in which already the activity of sensing and the thing sensed are opposed. They are identical yet different—so far different that they are opposites, each the negation of the other; and yet they have the same being, for only their identity gives meaning to their opposition.

And thus the soul is inwardly double: it is itself (soul) and its own opposite, the contrary of that which is aware—the body, which is felt but can never feel because it is the *internal object of the soul-feeling.*[9] There in the depths, at the very origin of his psychic development, man first encounters his body and begins to have knowledge of it. He must come to know himself, for his whole destiny is to be self-conscious; and the first time that he takes a look at himself, so to speak, he is presented with his body, the body through which all other bodies, the whole of nature, the whole physical universe, will eventually present themselves. We can now see how the body is at the basis of the life of the spirit. Our body is unique and therefore infinite; initially it is quite indistinct and indeterminate,[10] but through the progressive development and enrichment of the psychic life it will gradually become determinate. The determinations are not imposed on the soul from outside— granting that both the soul and its original content, the body, are infinite, such a thing would be impossible. They arise from its own rhythm of alienation from self (dialectical opposition) and return to self (the unity of the synthesis). Subsequently everyone constructs for himself in thought a physical body with ever more detailed anatomy and physiology; but this later embodiment of the soul is always a development or transformation of the primitive immanent body, which remains the nucleus of all the more differentiated forms. It is not, mark you, a development or transformation of the *idea* of the body, but of the body itself, which exists for the soul and through the soul, and lives out its life in virtue of the crea-

---

[9] *Il termine interno al sentire dell'anima.*

[10] Cf. the famous phrase used by William James to describe how the world appears at the dawn of conscious life: "one great blooming, buzzing confusion" (*Principles of Psychology*, New York, H. Holt, 1890, I, 488).

tive power that is the *vis interna* of the soul. The whole life of man
is nothing but an assiduous and incessant care for his own body, in
an effort to educate and spiritualize it, to make it a more docile instrument, a swifter vehicle for the purposes of the spirit, in the perpetual process of self-formation whereby it produces itself from its
own opposite—where it had hitherto lain submerged in darkness.
The spirit was not there before, but only its negation: not liberty
but mechanism; not the becoming of the spirit, but the immediate
being of nature. Body, nature, mechanism are all quite opposed to
liberty, which is the essential attribute of consciousness. But how
can the spirit come forth from its own negation?

An emergence of this kind, such as positivists and naturalists find
themselves obliged to postulate, has the superficial appearance of
something impossible and absurd. The apparent contradiction arises
because they see the opposition but cannot see the underlying unity
of the opposed terms—and they misguidedly set to work to whittle
away the opposition, which is really absolute, in an attempt to make
the impossible possible.

It is not from the body that the soul emerges, but from the soul
itself, the original sense of self which contains the antithesis of body
and soul because it produces it; and it only produces the antithesis
in order to resolve it again in its own productive unity. This unity
involves the body, and it involves a strict opposition between body
and soul, since the soul is the negation of the body; but it involves
also the negation of this opposition, and thus the negation of the
body considered as the abstract negation of the soul.

The body, therefore, is a negative that negates itself; and if it
did not negate itself it would not even have the negative significance
that belongs to it. Analysis, which distinguishes the opposites within
the synthesis and so establishes the abstract existence of the body,
does refer to something that really exists, something that has a place
in the concrete being of the synthesis; but it is something that
demonstrates its own existence negatively, as the abstract content
that enters into concrete experience by negating (transcending) its
own abstractness. To descend below the synthesis, to dismount from
it, so to speak, in order to separate the moments of which it is the
logical result, is quite possible and permissible; but only on condition that we keep it well in mind that these moments have their
concrete existence within the synthesis that unifies them, or rather
posits them as a unity in their mutual distinction and opposition.

The moments considered in their analytical abstractness are not humanity but the *subhuman* (which presupposes humanity); man finds the subhuman within himself but he is already beyond and above it, and through his superior energy he posits its being and gives it the right to share in the formation of existence.

Such is the position of the body and of nature in general. It is not human but subhuman, something that is there on the threshold which we have already crossed. At the threshold it still sticks, and cries "No" to everything that is on this side and can only exist on this side. It is spatiality and therefore time; it is mechanical because it is manifold; and it is immediate being, whereas on this side there is mediation, unity, and liberty.

6. The 'natural' character of utility

The realm of utility, of means to an end, belongs to this subhuman sphere; here we are dealing with the will as a mechanical—or even instinctive—coordination and adaptation to ends. A will that man can observe in himself, just as the soul is aware of the body; or in other words as his own opposite, the negation of his true and proper will; a sort of natural will that stands in his way as pure force, possessing no rationality except its appropriateness to its end. This will would remain a mere abstraction if it were not absorbed into a true and proper will, a will that is self-conscious and free. But in its abstractness it has its legitimacy as the negative of liberty; it is the non-being from whose negation liberty can spring.

There is no soul without a body, and hence there is no conscious will without this immediate will, strong and steady like a force released by nature; or like nature itself which the will can only conquer by absorbing it and in this way governing it. This is how the economic will of which we spoke in section 3 exists and takes shape within the body, which is par excellence the *instrument* of the soul, or in other words the instrument of the true and proper will. All the actual and potential pleasure of any useful thing [11] is kindled for the soul within the body which, considered in its abstract opposition to the soul, is a mechanism obeying necessary laws and knowing nothing of liberty.

This abstract will of the body—which in concrete experience is

---

[11] *Il piacere e tutto l'edonismo di ogni utile.*

already found resolved in the conscious will—is not properly will at all, because, like everything belonging to the body or to nature, it is immediate, and therefore it suggests the notion of 'instinct' or unconscious natural will. But it presents itself to consciousness as the double fountain of the will, divided into pure volition or force, apart from which there is no action either good or evil, and ethical volition which raises this immediate will to the plane of spiritual universality and so attains to real moral activity. The abstract science of economics, the science of man's pursuit of pleasure,[12] is concerned with this double fountain.[a]

7. Abstract logic and the abstract sciences

There is a certain logic—common-sense logic, the logic of identity—that treats these abstractions, these shadows of thought, as solid realities. This is what I have called 'abstract logic,'[13] which exchanges real thought (reality) for the thought that is merely an object of actual thinking, and labors over this object as something that exists in itself, whereas concretely it does not exist except as an element in actual thought.

The earliest and most naive philosophers took the essence that is manifested in this abstract thought as the real nature of things.[14] But since the time of Socrates we have been conscious of the ideal character of this thought and have drawn a distinction between the concept of reality and reality-in-itself.

But whether we call this abstract thought 'reality' or 'concept of reality'—whether we call it *nature* or, like Plato and the long line of metaphysicians who have followed in his footsteps, *idea*—the fact remains that once the link between the thinking subject and his thought is broken, and his thought is regarded as an objective being, something that actual thinking must always presuppose, the logic

---

[12] *La vita edonistica dello spirito.*

[a] The interpretation of Machiavelli's *virtù* as pure force is erroneous. It is already a moral force, like that of the State. [The reference is probably to Croce again; cf. *Politics and Morals,* Chapter 2, sec. 1—Tr.]

[13] *La logica del logo astratto.*

[14] Full explanation of this sentence must await publication of the *History of Greek Philosophy* (down to Plato) which Gentile left in manuscript at the time of his death. But he seems to be taking Parmenides' dictum, "To be thought is the same as to be," as the logical conclusion of pre-Socratic philosophy.

of this view leads inevitably to the annihilation of the spirit as a subject who takes possession of reality in freedom; [b] the whole of reality stiffens into a schema which negates the very essence of consciousness and leaves only an eternally ignored spectator.

8. The schema of naturalism in abstract logic

In this scheme of pure Being as opposed to the mind that thinks it, everything that the mind introduces in thinking of it must be cast out at the beginning. And so we find Democritus distinguishing between primary and secondary qualities; once the latter are discounted, nature, the totality of real existence, is found to be a mechanical manifold of real elements, all separate and distinct, moving in a void, where movement is communicated from one element to another and every movement is both cause and effect of other movements. The result is a universal determinism, an iron law binding everything to itself and to every other thing in a system ordered "in number, measure, and weight," a system that can be exactly expressed in mathematical terms. *Incipis numerare*, said St. Augustine, *incipis errare*.[15] But he was speaking of the Trinity, the God who is Spirit. The contrary is true about that which is by definition the contrary of the spirit. Galileo was right: the book of Nature is written in mathematical characters.[16] That is the reason why all the sciences concerned with abstract nature and governed by abstract logic tend to employ mathematical forms of expression. And even Plato, a great idealist but one who was ignorant of the logic of the concrete, played with geometry, and ended by believing that it was the most appropriate introduction to philosophical knowledge. 'Nature' means mechanism; and 'mechanism' means mathematics.

9. The mathematical form of economics

There is no clearer proof of the naturalistic character of economics, therefore, than the perfectly legitimate and quite unde-

---

[b] We have only to think of the theory of innate ideas that Plato invented, and which his followers have continually appealed to in order to preserve an appearance of spiritual value in the face of the Ideas and of objective reality in general. For instead of doing this it confirms the nullity of the spirit that is implicit in metaphysical realism. With innate ideas we get a spirit that is not spirit, because it exists immediately: it lacks liberty and is therefore valueless.

[15] I have not succeeded in locating this.

[16] See *Il saggiatore. Opere complete* (*edizione nazionale*), Florence, Barbera, 1890–1909, VI, 232.

niable need to deal with the subject in mathematical terms. This is a sure sign of the mechanical character, the strict causal determinism of its laws. Economic theory is subhuman; the truly human will has a perpetual tendency to interfere with this mechanism, bending the rigid formulas of mathematics into conformity with the changing requirements of a political life governed by liberty. Political life mirrors the constant becoming of the spirit, which is forever renewed by its own incessant activity of self-creation. The name 'political economy' is a plain contradiction in terms, unless the adjective is simply meant to mark the contrast between this more concrete form of economics and the others which are certainly more abstract (such as 'private' or 'domestic' economy). To suppose that it signifies an essential character of economics arising from its political nature, or from the requirements of political life, would be like talking of 'political mathematics' or 'political mechanics' and meaning it literally. Economics is mechanical and politics is free. The name may perhaps serve, however, as a warning to economists that they must hold their peace if statesmen sometimes fashion an unorthodox economics of their own, when the general situation of the State makes it advisable to transgress against the natural laws of that artificial creature 'economic man.'

10. Utilitarianism

The State is like the private individual, who is not infrequently faced by a conflict, which the utilitarian ethics suggested by an economic conception of life gets rid of by observing that the real interest of the individual does not conflict with honesty but coincides with it. (The real interest of the shopkeeper lies in giving fair weight, etc.) But this is a self-destructive confession: for if we must know where our duty lies before we can act in our own interest, then the principle of utility is not in itself a sufficient criterion of conduct, and only the discovery of ethical duty can provide us with a guiding light and norm. Moreover, it is a proof that even in the pursuit of that pleasure and happiness which it is in his nature to desire, man can only act as a human being when he frees himself from his immediate inclination to pleasure, and from the instinct that leads him infallibly to pursue it; when he rises above the natural desires that weigh him down into the sphere of conscious liberty. Only someone who overlooks the essential difference between expediency and duty can maintain that 'interest properly understood' would be simply the result of a utilitarian calculus that prescinds from every moral consideration. For it is this difference that confers on the agent the dignity that he must have if he is to look after his 'interest properly understood'; it consists always in the liberty that belongs to ethical action, and not to action that is merely expedient and as such necessitated like instinctive behavior. In short, the higher type of utilitarianism that is founded on liberty is no longer a system of utility; it is a system of ethics.

11. Hedonism

One might say the same about hedonism. For there is a kind of hedonism involved in the ethical conception of the spirit, where 'pleasure' means nothing but the positive element in the spiritual act—which as Plato recognized is indissolubly conjoined with its negative, pain. But there is also a naturalistic kind of hedonism in which pleasure, like utility, is viewed externally as a natural fact or datum; in this sense it is something that the spirit must transcend and negate in order to attain its proper liberty. Even the hedonism of Epicurus tended, through the ideal of ἀλυπία, to evade this naturalistic conception of pleasure, which is the limit of nonethical hedonism, and so to regain the liberty of the mind that is master of itself. But given the definition of 'usefulness' as 'capability of procuring pleasure,' there are only the two possible interpretations. If we fall into the lower kind of hedonism, then economics remains below the ethical level, and is a natural science clearly distinct from ethics; and if we rise to the higher kind, economics is resolved into ethics, as was the case with Spinoza, who was very careful to conduct his search for felicity within the bounds of naturalism, but who aspires to liberty and even deludes himself into thinking that he achieves it.

12. Morality and eudaemonism

Kant's polemic against eudaemonism in morals is directed against this abstract hedonism or naturalism; it falls to the ground when we consider the higher identity of morality and happiness, toward which Kant himself tends, though he travels by roads that cannot lead him to this goal, since even in their final unity he always conceives the two terms abstractly, as mutually contradictory and exclusive. If true pleasure is really the positive moment of the spiritual act, then no pleasure that is sought for outside of the virtuous act, as its just reward, can be true pleasure; it would be an empty accidental pleasure, the fruit of a particular inclination that is alien to the spirit and in conflict with its nature. Any such outside interference is repugnant, since it destroys the immanent liberty of consciousness and in the last analysis it means depriving virtue of the reward that belongs to it, in order to impose an improper one upon it by force.

Hence it has often been recognized that "virtue is its own reward" [*praemium virtutis ipsamet virtus*], just as the joy of artistic creation is the reward of art. For the artist there is no higher joy— nor even a lesser one. For his joy is his own, the only joy, the joy that makes him brother to the gods. True pleasure is the divine rejoicing of the spirit, the being of the spiritual act, when it opposes and conquers its own non-being.

13. Nature and Spirit

All these explanations will perhaps suffice to enable us to understand the relation that exists between the State and economics. The State is concrete universal will, whereas economics is concerned with the subhuman life of man—the corporeal, natural, subhuman element that has its place in human consciousness, but only as an abstract moment already transcended.

It follows that there is an economic element in the will, and hence in the State; but it has been transcended, transfigured by the light of freedom, and endowed with ethical and spiritual value. In the world of freedom man is no longer a slave of nature; not because he can escape from natural laws and cease to obey them, but because he uses them for his own purposes, or rather he uses the increasingly accurate knowledge of them that he gradually acquires, modifying the data of nature, to produce a nature of his own.

The history of mankind is all contained in this progressive subjugation of his natural environment, and this progressive re-creation of his own human nature. And though he will never gain the victory that the poet sighs for, wresting the shaft of death from the hand of Fate,[17] this is because death comes to him on the plane of nature, and not on the human plane; he pitches his camp in the field of the spirit, and here on his own ground he disarms Fate and conquers life immortal. As man advances, the nature that limits and

---

[17] I have not succeeded in identifying the allusion here.

destroys his humanity retreats; it becomes subject to the human will and part of the kingdom of the spirit. The mountains and oceans that nature has set between the peoples to divide and separate them one from another are pierced and crossed by locomotives, and sailed over by ships; through the genius of mankind they have become means of communication and fraternization. Pestilent swamps are drained, and become fertile fields irrigated and cultivated by human labor, inexhaustible fountains of riches and life where previously there were only misery and death. Man toils busily in the bowels of the earth which yield to him metals and various kinds of fuel; all the earth and the air, like the waters of the sea, come under his control and he makes them serve his will in the gradual building of civilization, which is the task of the spirit through the centuries.

14. Economics and politics

The laws of economics considered as a natural or mathematical science belong to the realm of abstract logic; they are the laws of a science conceived abstractly as existing in itself quite independent of man, who studies and apprehends it theoretically, without any subjective contributions of his own. And when he has understood it or constructed it, man makes use of it in the subsequent development of his conscious life, turning it to the ends of the spirit, ends which are quite unknown to abstract economics, since they only arise when we pass from the plane of abstract logic to that of concrete logic, where the thinking subject breaks in with his problems. His problems do not even make sense in terms of abstract logic, or as we say, in scientific terms; and they require solutions which abstract economics cannot supply. To expect an economist to solve them would be like asking a student of acoustics to solve a problem in music.

The claim of pure economics to interfere in politics and to dictate laws to the State without taking into account the special historical problems that arise in the total context of actual social life [18] is a perpetual source of irreconconcilable conflicts between the theoretical economists, secure in the mathematical stronghold that keeps them safe from any unpleasant encounter with reality, and the politicians, who are all too conscious of the heavy burden of their responsibility to society.

---

[18] *La vita sociale nella sintesi concreta dei suoi momenti.*

VIII

THE STATE AND RELIGION

1. The essential connection between the two terms

There is no State that does not concern itself in one way or another, positively or negatively, with religion, oscillating between theocracy and a State religion on the one hand, and complete separation of Church and State in an agnostic pseudo-liberal democracy on the other. Even this latter attitude is polemical in a way that is inconsistent with its pretended agnosticism. No State can ignore the religion of its people, any more than it can be indifferent about their customs, or their moral attitudes, or anything else so closely connected with their political life. The reason for this necessary connection between the State and religion must be sought in the very nature of the former. The purpose of the State is to achieve peace, and the rule of law which is its outward manifestation; or in other words, it seeks to achieve *unity* in the popular consciousness because of its immanent tendency to realize the will of the people. But the will of the people is the universal will of man; and the universal will of man is religion, or more precisely it contains religion. The will is self-concept; and as such it is religion both in the moment of subjective immediacy (the divine spark that we all feel within us) and again in the moment of objective immediacy (when reality seems complete and leaves no place for man, who therefore bows the knee before it and adores it).

So that the State could not be the fulfillment of man's humanity

149

if it did not contain religion. A completely secular consciousness, or a completely secular State, is a figment of the imagination.

In the dialectic of the will, God is the moment of law, the moment of past decision. The rigidity of the law has something of the ineluctable necessity of the divine nature. Think for instance of what Pindar says about "Law that is sovereign alike over mortals and immortals." [a] Religion is the moment of immediacy. Hence the alliance between throne and altar is natural; and when the Emperor set himself up against the Pope, it was because the Empire itself claimed a divine origin. The King is 'King by the Grace of God'; and the law is only law if it is rigorous, unimpeachable, fixed —the will of God. Such is the character of the State as a legal institution.[1]

As an ethical institution in the full sense, the State returns again from objective divinity to the infinite divine spark in the heart of the subject, the point at which the universe has its center.

2. Secularism

We must distinguish between negative and positive secularism: on the one hand the secularism that ignores religion or renounces it; on the other the secularism that recognizes and accepts religion, but transcends it. This last is the higher kind of secularism typical of the individual (or the State) who knows that religion is an essential element of his (or its) own personality, and is therefore concerned about its development, promotes religious education, supports the national religion, etc.; but strives to resolve the immediacy of religious dogma through the critical mediation of the self-concept (reflective thought). The other lower kind of secularism is typical of the ignorant and the weak. But God, even when He is unrecognized or ignored, is always present in the depths of our hearts; He goads and torments and disturbs us as long as He remains undiscovered or unconfessed. And He exists immediately, always there before our eyes, in the iron logic of the system of nature with all its necessary laws.

3. Religio instrumentum regni

Religion, then, is not a cunning invention of politicians; it is not an instrument of government. Campanella was right in his op-

---

[a] Νόμος ὁ πάντων βασιλεὺς θνατῶν τε καὶ ἀθανάτων (fr. 169, Schroeder).

[1] La posizione dello Stato come diritto.

position to Machiavellism considered as a work of the devil, or as Achitophelism.[2] The religion of the State is not something external to its ethical will, but rather the constitutive element of it. And if, in order to represent successfully the perfect antinomy of the State, we pretend to recognize a Church that is subservient to its 'earthly' ends, we can indeed make use of the fiction as a trap for the credulous,[3] but only up to a point. Then, when our deceit is discovered, this art of political trickery becomes worthless. For a religion that is merely a useful tool for purposes quite extrinsic to its nature is no religion. And anyone who wishes to obtain from religion the power that it can in fact bestow must above all else respect it as religion; he must hold it in high honor, believe in it himself, and in short take it seriously for what it is—just as when one wants to cure a disease by using a drug, one must begin by getting hold of the right drug. Neither religion nor any other form of spiritual life can ever have a merely instrumental value, since this would be inconsistent with its character as an end in itself, and with the freedom and infinity of all spiritual activity.

4. The immanence of religion in the State

An instrument is something external to the action in which it is used, and to the subject who performs the action. When any instrument comes to be viewed as essential to an action, and when the action itself is recognized as the determinate expression of the agent's personality, the instrument ceases to be something arbitrary or accidental like any other instrument, and becomes a constitutive attribute of the subject's essential nature. Consider for example the sculptor's chisel, the painter's brush, or the writer's pen: in every case the instrument is a complement of the agent's personality on a par with his own body. In the actual process of creation (while he is carving or painting or writing) it is internal to his spirit; he does not feel that it is an extraneous thing that must be bent to his will and used as a means to his own ends, except where it offers resistance to his free activity, and becomes an embarrassment and a nuisance, something that has to be dealt with as a limit or an impediment rather than as an instrument.

---

[2] Campanella's polemic against Machiavellism was continuous and omnipresent. But see especially *Atheismus triumphatus* (Rome, 1631), which he himself describes as *Antimachiavellismus.*

[3] Literally "as a mirror for larks" (*uno specchietto per le allodole*). No comparable English idiom occurs to me.

The truth is that consciousness is always an organic whole.[4] And religion, like art and morality, is never completely absent from it, whatever form it takes. If politics were deprived of all religious import it would become an artificial, brute mechanical activity lacking all spiritual inspiration; there are signs of this in the political career of any person or group dominated by a spirit that is poorly endowed with religious feeling. For whenever the human spirit is not whole and healthy, whenever its nature is not clearly expressed in the fullness of its life, it is infected by this sort of impotence. This impotence is apparent for example in the words of an insincere man, a pedant of any kind, who does not say what he feels and feels something that he cannot say, because, as a result of his education and his artificial way of life, he no longer knows how to express the feelings that he shares with all other men; or in the actions of a man who has no sure aims but only daydreams.[5] A daydream is a failure of will caused by weakness of character; strength of character involves wholehearted commitment [6] to action.

But what then is the religious element that is immanent in serious political action? It is the religion of a man who in one way or another believes in God, and at every moment feels the presence of God in his own conscience as a judge who calls him to account for every thought and feeling; a judge of whatever he does as a free and responsible agent, so that his every word or thought or feeling is a voluntary act for which he must answer. He cannot escape judgment in this court without hurling himself into the abyss of nullity. For even this human justice presents itself to him as something that transcends his mortal human nature, as a supreme authority that he cannot rebel against without becoming a brute and completely blacking out his own moral consciousness.[7]

---

[4] *Lo spirito è sempre tutto lo spirito.*

[5] *Velleità* (cf. Chapter 3, sec. 1, herein).

[6] *Unità di tutto lo spirito.*

[7] On 9 February 1943 Gentile delivered a lecture entitled "My Religion," in which he claimed to be, 'after his own fashion,' a Catholic. On 28 May Antonio Bruers responded in a lecture on "Catholicism and Giovanni Gentile" by declaring that no one could seriously claim to be a Christian, or even to have any religion at all, unless he believed in survival and divine judgment after death. Without posthumous sanctions he argued, "Justice does not exist, and so God is not just, and if He is not just He is not God, and so God does not exist" (*Il cattolicismo e Giovanni Gentile,* Rome, Edizioni Stella, 1943, p. 14). He therefore asked Gentile to state plainly whether he believed in an afterlife with penal sanctions. Gentile gives his answer in Chapter 13; but he clearly intends first in this passage to overthrow the fundamental premise of Bruers'

It is this same religious sense that constitutes the moral earnestness of every man, even if by abstraction we consider him merely as a private citizen; and it has its place in every aspect of his activity (scientific, artistic, etc.). It gives to all moral obligation an absolute character that sets a limit to liberty. The absoluteness is at first an immediate element in the dialectic of consciousness which must be canceled and transcended in the mediation of the synthesis; but it is essential to the synthesis precisely as a limit to be canceled and transcended—an eternal limit that forever inhibits the force of selfish inclination in the subject's free activity of self-positing. An eternal object, which, considered in itself, coincides with the subject in itself, setting the bounds of past and future for the spiritual act which is the concrete expression of human individuality. In thus marking the boundary of the Ego, it has always the form of a pure infinite object which annihilates the subjectivity of the Ego by positing an Absolute which is not the Ego itself.

This religious sense is a moment of the self-concept, an element of the will and therefore of morality. Thus religion is not properly something to be added to morality; it is immanent in it and without it there could be no morality. Nor could there be any State.

---

argument. The word *coscienza*, which is here translated 'moral consciousness,' is used broadly enough in Italian to be translatable sometimes by 'conscience' and sometimes by 'consciousness.' But in Gentile, especially in a passage like the present, the two usages are brought together.

IX

SCIENCE AND THE STATE

1. Science and philosophy; and the relation between philosophy and the State

We speak of 'science' in two senses. Sometimes it means science in the wide sense,[1] in which it is synonymous with knowledge in general, or with any organized body of knowledge that is methodically arrived at and historically controlled in its development. But it also means the criticism of science in this first sense, and the formation of a systematic concept of the whole of knowledge and of the subject of knowledge, man himself. 'Science' in the first sense certainly involves thought, but it is provisional in character, and hence it is abstract and dogmatic; whereas in the other case thought claims to have transcended this provisional character, to have conquered its abstractness, and to be free of the dogmatic character of ordinary, particular knowledge. Of course, it is philosophy that makes this distinction, and draws attention to the provisory character, the particularity and the dogmatism of empirical science. And it is clear that science as such cannot escape from this particularity and abstractness without taking up a philosophical position; and so, no matter how emphatically the scientist may refuse to be sub-

---

[1] Gentile says *stricto sensu*. But this 'strict' sense is only an interloper in English usage made necessary by translations like the present one. The reader will observe that neither of the senses recognized by Gentile coincides with what we should call the 'strict' sense.

jected to the higher criticism of philosophy, it is also clear that every science, being unable to avoid the dogmatic character which is a necessary consequence of its particularity, presupposes a form of thought that is conscious of this dogmatism, and *ipso facto* has already begun upon the philosophical criticism of science—regardless of any attitude the scientist himself may adopt toward philosophy.

In any case, quite apart from the pronouncements of philosophers and scientists who are always busily defending their own positions, the ordinary man lives his life in terms of a more or less clear or obscure personal conception of the world and of his own potentialities. So that philosophy is in the air he breathes. It may be good or bad, confused and undigested, or illumined by a powerful intellect that subjects it to continual criticism; but it always provides the substantial frame of reference [2] in terms of which all men, whether individually or in groups, formulate and criticize their programs for life, nourish their practical faith, and fight for it and the institutions to which it is bound or in which it is incarnated. In public opinion, in the newspapers, and in discussions, every individual is forever occupied with his own ideas or the ideas of others —though naturally more often with the latter than with the former. Everyone philosophizes; and philosophy runs about the streets in the guise of 'common sense,' the awareness that every man must have of himself and of the world to which he belongs.

Philosophy therefore (whether it be the true and genuine article or only a faked copy) is bound to come into contact with, indeed to coincide with, the State, the absolute form of the self-consciousness that is the essence of humanity. Thus there arises the possibility that they may be empirically in accord or at odds with one another. There could be no question of their being in accord or at odds, if politicians and philosophers were concerned with different subjects, and their interests were directed along different paths. But instead we find such agreement or disagreement in every age, even when philosophers, jealous for their own status, have disdained any contact with the government, and have lived as private citizens completely withdrawn from public life. Philosophy is a conscious aspiration toward absolute knowledge, and therefore it requires above all else an unqualified freedom—remember for instance how Spinoza refused a professorship offered him by a prince.

---

[2] *La sostanza del pensiero.*

But even in such cases as this, the withdrawal of the philosopher is a kind of aversion, and has in fact always aroused suspicion and excited reactions and persecutions. Consider the case of the Stoics at Rome in the first century of the Empire: as citizens of the world they offered no opposition to the government, yet their negative attitude had a certain weight, since it constituted a continual protest with implications that were by no means politically negligible or even tolerable in a regime of imperial absolutism. Which of us does not know that in certain situations silence is more irritating than any insult or injury? But since philosophers, unfortunately for them, are bound to be representatives of philosophy, the popular pretense that they always set up to be superior to common opinions and to those who are governed by them, and likewise superior to the ideals that are actually operative in a political system, is natural enough. For philosophy criticizes, controls, and passes judgment on all thought. It follows obviously that philosophy is always in conflict, and never in agreement, with political ideologies; and whenever one finds agreement rather than conflict one must obviously suspect connivance. The last hypothesis that popular opinion is ever likely to adopt is a belief in good faith; as if a philosopher—who is a man like other men and not a personification of philosophy—could never have the practical satisfaction of finding an actual political system inspired by a philosophy in harmony with his own; as if he could serve truth better by combating in other people—because they happen to be at the head of the State—the truth that they find in themselves, so that they are logically bound to strive for its triumph in society. Are we seriously meant to believe that Plato was moved by private interest in writing his letters to the King of Syracuse? [3]

2. The necessity of this relation

In view of the critical function of philosophy the accord between philosophers and politicians can never be quite without a rift; it is bound to be accompanied by a certain mutual distrust. But whether we like it or not, a meeting between philosophy and the State is necessitated by the ethical nature of the State, which could

---

[3] We must remember that while he was writing this book Gentile was being accused by many critics of adhering to Fascism, and prostituting his intellect in the service of the Party, for the sake of power and position (see my *Social Philosophy of Giovanni Gentile*, Chapter 8, pp. 249–51).

not be a form of the human will if it were not self-conscious and therefore reflective. It is all very well to distinguish the temporal from the eternal, the sacred from the profane, and to set both philosophy and religion on high in the heavens, in the kingdom of the spirit, leaving the State to care for the things of this world. But it has always turned out, and it always will, that sooner or later the State feels compelled to include among its earthly cares the education of the people. For good or ill, but with the purpose of continual self-improvement, it makes provision for education and shows itself sensible of the interests of culture.

3. Culture

Culture is knowledge; but it is not particular, dogmatic, factual knowledge; it is critical of any positive knowledge that settles in man's mind without proving itself useful and necessary in the building of his life and personality. In short it is critical of all knowledge that is not genuinely human—all knowledge that man does not need for the actual realization of his human nature and for the growth and health of his moral character. There is a certain kind of instrumental knowledge which man can acquire and make his own or which he can neglect. Or at least this seems to be the case; and if we consider knowledge in the abstract it undoubtedly is the case. But in concrete experience there is no instruction, however dull, useless, and mechanical it may be, that does not affect the path of conscious development, and prove somehow or other to have implications for the future. By remaining at the abstract level a man may become learned without becoming cultured; but then the learning is not part of real life, and he does not comprehend it any more than an ignoramus.

Culture is the knowledge that molds a man's personality, by clarifying and enriching the consciousness that every man should have of himself, and by reflective criticism of his mind and character, of what he can and ought to do in order to attain his true destiny.

This is the culture with which the State is concerned, for the State itself is the consciousness that man has of himself and of the way in which his consciousness develops. Culture in this sense embraces all knowledge and rejects nothing as long as it is informed by man's self-consciousness, which is the heart and center of the whole sphere of knowledge.

4. The natural sciences

Even the natural sciences, every science that is useful in the conquest of nature (mathematics, economics), and of all the various kinds of forces and principles that can only be conceived naturalistically, have their place in that consciousness of the world which is the complement of *self*-consciousness, the proper concern of philosophy. As long as we keep this complementary character in mind we can say that science is culture and belongs to the subject matter of philosophy.

We can say then, in conclusion, that philosophy constitutes the self-consciousness that the State will achieve, if it does not confine itself to a static intuition of its own nature or mode of existence, but has a program, a conception of its own mission; just as every man is human because in addition to remembering his own past he in some measure keeps his future in mind, and knows that it is in his own hands.

In fact there is no statesman who has not, at least *in nuce*, a philosophy of his own.

5. The critical obligation of philosophy

It is commonly held that philosophy should not let itself be put to use as 'State philosophy'; and this is not altogether surprising—("Oh shame! Philosophers for hire!"). Of course no one can reasonably pretend that the philosopher should oppose merely for the sake of opposing. Or that, when he has to choose between the government and those who oppose it, he is duty bound to join the opposition in order to perform his own part properly, even if it seems to him that really they are in the wrong. But still, a statesman, being a physical individual, always represents in his positive aspect something static and abstract as well as a political aim, a regime, or a determinate political organization. This moment of static self-identity is the system of past decisions, the legal system; it is something that must be canceled and transcended in the moral life by the actual synthesis of self-consciousness—that is to say by philosophical reflection. For this reason philosophy properly appears to be endowed with a critical function; it cannot be allied with, or worse still in the service of, the government, for it must attack the static system of what is and work for progress toward an ideal. The philosopher must always be the apostle of an ideal, never the guardian and defender of the status quo.

But in the first place, there is criticism and there is *self*-criticism. True criticism, the criticism that is positive and effective, is not external and abstract but internal and concrete, since it arises from the same source as the thought that is criticized—in other words it is self-criticism. So that serious political criticism should have a point of contact with the static system that is criticized. If we are adopting the strictly philosophical point of view, we must not forget that the government or regime itself performs this self-criticism in some measure; and it can do so because it too has a philosophy of its own.

In the second place, we must remember that the function of the self-synthesis of actual moral will in relation to the system of past decision is not *merely* [4] negative; it is both negative and conservative, as the synthetic moment of any dialectic naturally is. The system of past decision has to be negated insofar as it is itself negative of present decision; but leaving aside this negative relation to present volition, past decision itself makes its contribution to the positive power of present volition; and anyone who rejects past decision completely is refusing to make a decision at all. His action becomes purely negative, sterile, and vain, as is obvious even from the point of view of common sense.

Hence even the essentially critical activity of philosophy involves an essential and indispensable recognition of the positive element or content of every regime or specific organization of the State in its historical actuality.

In short, it would be well to keep in mind that when we talk of the relation between the State and philosophy, it is arbitrary and dangerous to personify the two terms, one in the statesman and the other in the philosopher, since the conflicts that arise from distinctions of this kind need to be brought back to the concrete experience of actual consciousness, where 'philosophy' means for every individual the philosophy that he himself grasps and holds to be true. So that the philosophy that exists for the statesman is not the philosophy of academies and schools; it does not come from somewhere else; it is his own philosophy, and it may be better or worse than that of the professional philosophers opposed to him, but in

---

[4] *Astrattamente.*

any case it is the only philosophy that he can, should, and indeed must take into account.

And on the other hand the only State in which he can apply his philosophy is the State that is within him, the State as he sees it and wills it; it is not an abstract entity, objectively definable, and historically situated in a fixed place and time. Apart from this inner world of actual experience, there are only phantasms among which the imagination vainly strives to conceive conflicts and harmonies. And as for those "philosophers for hire" in the France of Louis Philippe—the fable invented by Ferrari whose mind was as full of shadows and fancies as it was acute and lively—all sensible men realize, even when they are not fully informed, that they are dealing with a fable and no more. For anyone can see that these poor philosophers for hire must either have been philosophers, in which case (as Plato teaches) they were not for hire, or they were hired, and then they were not truly philosophers. But we must not exclude the possibility that they were neither hired nor philosophers—which was perhaps the case when Ferrari took up the cudgels so vehemently.[5]

6. The immanence of philosophy in political life

But in any case, whether we conceive of philosophy as inside or outside of the State, it remains essential to the State because it is essential to human life. Without it there could be no State, no religion, no art, science, or morality. For the spirit in any of its forms must not be conceived abstractly; and as a concrete living reality, an actual process, it is that dialectic of self-consciousness which is the root of philosophy. It is a dynamic thing which shuns stillness as a living thing shuns death; every man possessed of any spiritual sensibility regards the stagnation of consciousness as the negation of life and the destruction of the value that belongs to it alone. It is phi-

---

[5] The reference is to Giuseppe Ferrari (1812–76), Les philosophes salariés (Paris, 1849), a book to which Croce had drawn attention in his polemics against Fascist idealism; for Plato's views see Republic, 346–47.

It should perhaps be noted at this point that Gentile never accepted any stipend for the many offices and positions that he held as a Fascist. This was revealed by his deputy in the Istituto nazionale fascista di cultura, when Gentile was accused by Fascist opponents of taking advantage of his position in various ways. Gentile himself was away in Germany at the time. Had he been present to defend himself this fact would not have been made known (see "Parole chiare" in Educazione fascista, October 1931, pp. 963–64).

losophy that is the leaven, the very soul of life; for the concrete realization of the self-concept is the fulfillment of self-consciousness. Philosophy is continual vigilance and reflection over what we are, and what we make of ourselves; a burning restlessness, a dissatisfaction that never accepts us as we are or the things we do as they stand.

X

THE STATE AND OTHER STATES

1. The liberty and infinity of the State

The State, being identical with the self-concept or the will, is free and therefore infinite. Hence the conception of the State as existing among other States which set limits to it involves a contradiction. And it is no use making the distinction that is often made between absolute liberty and relative liberty, attributing absolute liberty to the State in respect to internal affairs, but only relative liberty in respect to external affairs.

For in the first place the State would cease to be infinite as soon as it entered into relation with other States; and in the second place if the State were not free in external affairs it could not be free in internal affairs either,[a] since the real world in which its internal liberty would have to be effective is the same as that in which its external life effectively occurs.

2. The plurality of States, and the unity of the State

The problem of the multiplicity of States is analogous to, or rather identical with, that of the multiplicity of individuals. It is only when we adopt an external point of view that there is a plurality of individuals. Within the self-consciousness of an individual, the other individuals are freely posited by that self-consciousness, and

---

[a] Cf. the note to Chapter 6, sec. 6 [p. 130].

are unified with it because they are internal to it; and it is only within self-consciousness that the individual can be known because it is only there that he is made [and "truth is what is made"].[1]

So that the real individual is unique, and therefore infinite and free.

3. Critique of intellectualism

A plurality of States exists in the mind of a man who regards them all indifferently and theoretically; for in his eyes all are alike. But when he distinguishes from among them one that is *his own*, what does the possessive pronoun mean? Between him and 'his' State there is a relation that is not to be compared to the relation existing between other separate states and their respective citizens, although it is analogous. And the peculiarity or even uniqueness of this relation consists in the fact that, unlike other states, 'his' State is not for him merely an object of theoretical knowledge (something whose existence or nonexistence does not affect him, and which is what it is regardless of whether he exists or not); it belongs to him as a kind of essential property, so that his existence is connected with the existence of his State. This relation makes 'his' State the only one that exists for any and every 'separate' individual.

4. The concrete practical point of view

In order to understand the ethical character of other States we must prescind from this relation and put ourselves, so to speak, first in the shoes of one foreigner and then of another, and so on. We can do this by abstraction; but sooner or later we are inevitably recalled to concrete experience, where every man has but one fatherland, just as he has but one mother: one sole State, because he is himself a unique individual.

The other States exist only if they are recognized. And this recognition is always a free action, a self-limitation; so that all limits are internal, not external, to what is limited.

---

[1] *Verum et factum . . . convertuntur* (Vico, *De antiquissima Italorum sapientia,* Book I, Chapter 1). All that is actually given here in Gentile's text is the phrase *verum-factum* in parentheses. But that is because he had already made the quotation a commonplace for his Italian readers. It is given in full in the *Theory of Mind as Pure Act* (English translation by H. Wildon Carr, London, Macmillan, 1922, pp. 15–17), with some account of what Vico meant by it and of how Gentile thinks it ought to be interpreted.

5. The recognition of other States and international law

Recognition implies that the will of the other is resolved into our own as a past decision. We will the same thing; there is only one will, only one State. Hence the immanent tendency of international law, which is the unification of states by use of *treaties*. But if this tendency were completely fulfilled (in a confederation, a centralized empire, a society of nations, or what not), the result would not be the absolute realization of the State but its death. For the State, despite its name, is not something static. It is a *process*. Its will is a synthesis that resolves all immediate being. If the State presented itself to us all fine and finished, if its uniqueness were simply an immediate datum, a matter of fact, and there were no further *otherness* to conquer, since the dream of *perpetual peace*, the eternal heart's desire of humanity fleeing from the horrors of war, had come true, then the movement which constitutes the life of the State, the life of the spirit itself, would cease. And instead of the very best of States we should have the death of all States.[2]

6. War

The moment of *otherness* is essential as the moment of pure objectivity in the dynamism of self-consciousness. The otherness is destined to be transcended; but it has to be there, and it has to be conquered. First there must be the opposition, and then the conciliation and the unity. This is the eternal rhythm of human social life, the rhythm of moral development. Master and pupil, parent and child, teacher and learner, lord and slave, dominant peoples and dominated peoples (where superior civilization may be the index of superior power or vice versa), these are all original and inevitable oppositions which spiritual activity transcends and reconciles. And among the methods of transcending opposition is war. The phi-

---

[2] The argument in this section is, of course, quite fallacious. There is a *quaternio terminorum,* since the 'complete fulfillment of the immanent tendency of international law,' even if it means a single center of political power, is not necessarily the same as 'the State all fine and finished with no otherness to conquer.' In fact, Gentile's argument here is contrary to the whole doctrine of this book; he ought logically to argue that the State does not depend on other States any more than the individual depends on other individuals for society. And by the same token, we may add that physical conflict between nations is no more essential to his theory of the State than it is essential to his theory of education that the pupil should be caned. This remark will, I trust, throw a glaring light on the ambiguities of the remainder of this chapter.

losopher must recognize that there are a thousand forms of war and that these forms are multiplying with the multiplication of the ways in which human thought is expressed, and the human will made effective. There is war with pin pricks and war with cannon balls. The pin pricks are only words; but the words are used in pursuit of aims substantially similar to those for which cannon balls are employed—the annihilation of the enemy. War properly so-called, however, is conflict between States waged with all the most murderous weapons, in order to establish their rights when one of them hinders another in the attaining of ends that are essential to its existence; and the resolution of the struggle does not really consist in the annihilation of one of the contestants, but in the destruction of that antagonism of the will which is what sustains the contest. The enemy must be placed in a position in which he can no more offend; and he must recognize our will as his own. He must therefore survive to set the seal on our victory by his recognition.

Thus war does not derive from an inhuman desire for solitude. The other people, with whom we disagree, are our collaborators; they play their part in the formation of that spiritual organization or patrimony which is our world. The cause of war is only dissent, and its end therefore is nothing but the conquest of this dissent.

7. Peace and human collaboration

So what usually happens after a war is quite natural: the need for fraternity and human solidarity is more strongly and more widely felt. Our hearts are open wider. We feel that our neighbor is a part of the rhythm of our own mind, and through him we seek to enrich our own spiritual life.

8. Empire and new order

The ideal of nations at war who seek to extend their own territory so far as to unify all interests and conciliate all future disagreements without further recourse to war is a natural illusion, but it is an illusion and no more. Unity is a fine thing, but it must be a unity amid variety, including all the differences that eternally arise from its own process of realization. The great empires decline and break up precisely for this reason. Sooner or later they fall in ruins. From the very heart of unity there arise again differences, and the greater the violence employed in suppressing the elements to be unified, the quicker is this resurgence.

XI

HISTORY

1. History as the story of the State

As the concrete activity of the spirit, the State is a developing process—it is history. All other histories (histories of art, religion, economics, science, etc.) are abstract, because they are the histories of ideal or abstract moments and forms of spiritual life; and the spirit is only concretely expressed in the State. Philosophy alone is as concrete as the State; but the determinacy through which philosophy attains its effective concreteness is not to be found outside the history of the State. So that the history of philosophy marches together with the history of the State, as long as we do not picture it as a development of pure theory, which has then to be brought down into the historical process of the State, in order to become the real concrete logic of the self-concept.

2. The story of man

The history of the State is the story of humanity as a real individual, the unique universal subject; it is the process of development of the unique reality. For of course reality is not a substance that sets itself in motion, but exists in itself as the condition of this motion. Its essence lies in its motion. We can never say of it that it exists in itself immediately. The moment of immediate being is indeed an ideal element in the life of the State; but if it were more than an ideal element the State would lose its spiritual value and degenerate into a blind mechanism, and as a result it would be swept away by revolution. In its spiritual essence the State exists always and yet it never exists. And hence it is not fully revealed in pure immanence; or at least not in an immanence which is the simple antithesis of transcendence. Its ideal is always in advance of its present mode of existence; like every spiritual value, it has life because it is sensible of its own true self above and beyond its present self, as an ideal to be reached, a transcendent reality. This transcendence is the reason why it belongs to the world of liberty.

3. State worship

Inasmuch as it is the unique reality, the State is beyond doubt divine. But the people who shudder at the idea of *worshiping the State* are quite right if the State is conceived as pure immanence, though they are wrong if the State is conceived as the unity of being and non-being so that it always implies a transcendent element. For in this transcendent State, this higher ideal that operates as an end in the actual life of the State, the theists have all the room they can desire to make a distinction between the divine and the human aspects of the State, and set the higher norm to which they would have the State subordinated above and beyond the *perpetuum mobile* that is its history.

Worship of a State that exists *de facto* is idolatry; but the religion of the spirit conceives the State as an ideal. Not an abstract ideal set apart from historical reality, but the concrete ideal of this reality; the only ideal that is really conceivable, the ideal that is itself real inasmuch as it is at work in a reality, which from the ideal point of view always and yet never exists.

4. The self-criticism of the State

This distinction of being and non-being which is the negative moment within the spiritual reality of the State explains the instability of every political structure, the inevitability of change, not as an external fatal law of decadence that seals the doom of every empire in all its might, but as the free and spontaneous law of development that is rooted in the nature of consciousness. For man cannot be conscious of himself without being dissatisfied at his own mode of existence, and finding that pleasure degenerates into pain, certainty changes into doubt, his solutions turn into problems; so that he is driven by his own nature into a perpetual quest for himself. States do not fall nor are they transformed because of criticism leveled against them by others (opponents, other states, or forces different from those represented by their own governments). The criticism that destroys or transforms them is always *self-criticism*, as is obvious when we remember that in reality the State, like the individual, is both itself and the others, since it is what it is in relation to these others; they appear to be extraneous to its essence, but in reality they help to constitute its mode of being.[1]

5. Revolution

If the State is an eternal process of self-criticism, then revolution is not death for it but life. As a particular catastrophic happening, a revolution is a matter for relative judgment, and does not allow of exact definition; but in general the word covers any *change in the constitution of a State*. Now every constitution remains immutably fixed in its written formulas; but in practice, even without any express changes or explicit declarations, it is continually changing in its interpretation and application. Hence the suggestion by conservatives in all countries that the slow development of the State's fundamental institutions be left to time and usage, without any explicit deliberation about reform, which, by clearly establishing the possibility of change in the minds of the citizens, undermines their salutary faith in the perpetual untouchability of the charter that is the juridical foundation and the perennial guarantee of the State. In short the State charter can be a useful myth in the consolidation of the ideal *static* moment which is essential to the life of the State. But in spite of the myth constitutions change from day to day, with the changing of the minds in which they live; written words remain, but they are read, understood, and brought to life

---

[1] There is at least a very dangerous ambiguity in this section. For in the sense in which the State is 'both itself and the others' it is obviously not identical with the government. So it does *not* follow that 'States do not fall because of criticism by forces different from those represented by the government.' Gentile might, indeed I think he probably would, try to wriggle out of this difficulty by arguing that the 'forces represented' by government and opposition are not really different. This will not do, however. For the government and the opposition may stand for different *ideals* (which is presumably what Gentile means by 'representing a force'), as was clearly the case, for example, in Croce's opposition to Fascism. It is plain that Gentile wishes us to infer that his own attitude toward the Fascist State was the one that most fully accords with his philosophy as here set forth. But as soon as we cease to identify the State with the government this is obviously false.

in the political consciousness of the people, which is continually renewing itself.

Political life therefore is an eternal self-criticism, an eternal revolution. And this revolution is not to be taken as a delusion or, if you prefer, a source of anxiety for the lovers of a quiet life, the people who hate all revolutions and abhor the word itself, so often besmirched by the blood of civil wars. Like the character in Molière who spoke prose without knowing it, we had better get it into our heads that revolution is not something that only happens at exceptional moments, when the populace rises with unusual violence to destroy things or men who represent a government that is no longer tolerable; rather it is an everyday affair scarcely noticed and indeed unnoticeable. It is like the drop of water that hollows out the stone, the effect of which we can recognize only after a certain length of time; this reflection may lead us to stand on the alert, and take timely precautions against the processes, which, if they come to maturity, will manifest their catastrophic character. Certainly the history of the State is the story of its continual revolution, the story of the process in which the State properly consists.

6. The unique reality

The individual is unique because he is free and therefore infinite. The State is unique because it is the concrete and absolute individual. In short, the spirit is unique and free because it is infinite. The spirit is in us and we are in it. Apart from it our every value is only a false image of good. The individual who is the fulcrum of liberty in liberalism, and the absolute principle of liberty in individualism, does not exist; individualism is only a shadow that looms over the field of politics and makes it sterile. The State cannot be a product of the individual will. In order to create the State the individual must already possess it: virtually he must *already be* the State (the universal will). We are already within the State, when we go in search of it. "In it we live and move and have our being." [2]

Hence the citizen who is fully conscious [3] of this inward char-

---

[2] Acts 17:28. Gentile, of course, quotes from the Latin of the Vulgate so that no change of pronoun form is necessary in switching the reference of the text from God to the State.

[3] *Abbia consapevolezza;* I take it that this indicates a more reflective awareness than the usual *coscienza.*

acter of the State is bound to adopt a religious attitude toward it: he must feel that it belongs to him, that it is his own substance, something whose fate is his fate and whose life is strictly bound up with his own. He must feel respect for the *res publica;* and above all he must feel that it is *res sua.* This is the sense of public interest, the political sense that continually develops with civilization; it is rare among primitive or uncultured peoples, who have as yet no mature experience of the universality of their own will. Within a single nation there are cities, regions, diverse groups, all with a different historical background; and they vary in the extent to which they possess this political sense of the public interest that makes each man regard the *res publica* as his own, so that all of them become keen observers and judges of their government and its methods, and in this way collaborate in various modes and degrees in the business of governing.

Individualism in politics is just like egoism in morals; but it is egoism on a larger scale, absolute egoism so to speak. It has always been the ideal of democracy to educate the individual into a sense of political responsibility and concern for the public interest, whereas absolute governments tried to keep the people at a distance from all matters of government business. The difficulty lies in the system of political education. Parties and parliaments are abstract forms that derive their efficacy from the habit of political responsibility; they may favor the growth of this habit, but they cannot create it. And such institutions will *mis*educate the people out of all real and healthy concern for the public good, as long as they remain artificial forms corresponding to merely conventional principles, rather than to those tendencies and needs of individuals which accord with their effective interests.

This was the aim of the recent Italian political movement; and even if the provisional forms of application were vitiated by the transitory necessities of the political situation (internal and external), its constitutional experiments cannot go to waste since they answered to that need for a more organic system of representation which had already been coming into its own for half a century in the most enlightened current of conservative liberalism.

The intelligent moral cult of the unique reality is the cult of Man: the cult of the power that makes man eternally human.

It is the new *humanism* of our times.

7. The humanism of labor

To the humanism of culture, which was indeed a glorious step in the liberation of man, there succeeds today or will succeed tomorrow the humanism of labor. For the creation of great industry and the advance of the worker onto the great stage of history have profoundly modified the modern conception of culture. The word used to mean intellectual culture, and especially art and literature; it left out of account the vast segment of humanity who do not raise their eyes toward the free horizons of the higher culture, but labor at the foundations of human culture. There at the foundation man is in contact with nature, and *labors* on it; but he labors *as a man*, he is aware of what he is doing, aware of himself and of the world in which he is incorporated. His work reveals that same activity of thought which forever sets and solves the problems in which his actual existence is continually knotted and untied in the world of art, literature, scholarship, or philosophy. The peasant labors, the artisan labors, and so does the master craftsman; the artist labors and the scholar and the philosopher. Gradually the material through which man puts himself to the test in his labors grows lighter and is, as it were, dematerialized; so that the spirit is released to fly freely in its own air, outside of space and time. But matter is already conquered when the hoe bites into the earth, breaking up the ground and making it play its part in the pursuit of human ends. From the very beginning of his labors man is human; he has risen into the kingdom of the spirit, where the world is his world, the creation of his thought, or in short his own self. Every laborer is *faber fortunae suae* or rather *faber sui ipsius*.

It was necessary, therefore, that the conception of human culture appropriate to literary and philosophical humanism should be extended to embrace every form of activity in which man labors to create his humanity. It was necessary that the high dignity which man by taking thought had discovered in thought itself should be accorded to the 'worker' also. It was necessary that thinkers, scientists, and artists should join hands with the workers in this consciousness of the universal dignity of humanity.

There is no doubt that the social changes and the parallel socialist movements of the nineteenth century have created this new humanism, the actual organization of which in concrete political terms is the task and the concern of our century. The State can no longer be thought of as the State of the citizen (or of the man and the citizen) as in the days of the French Revolution; it is and it should be the State of the *workers,* separated as they are by their different interests into the natural categories that are gradually becoming established. For the citizen is not man in the abstract; nor yet the man who because he is more cultivated or wealthier is called a member of the 'ruling class'; nor even the man who knows how to read and write, and so has in his hands an instrument for unlimited spiritual communication with all other men. The real man, the man who counts, is the man who works, and whose worth is measured by his work. For it is indeed true that value is labor; and a man's worth is to be measured according to the quantity and quality of his work.

8. The family

But man cannot be weighed as an atom as he is in communist theory. Man is the family. An individual labors for himself but also for his children: "he plants trees for another generation." [4] The State has an interest in cultivating and developing the instinct (which in man becomes a vocation) toward the procreation and recognition of offspring; and hence it has an interest in the formation of the family nucleus through which the individual is led by natural impulses to break the crust of his selfish egoism and ignore the boundaries of his natural individuality. This is the root of the sense of immortality that breaks the grip of the flying instant and makes every man reach out into the future. Even the family can change, and it is in fact always different. But the love that creates it is eternal; and this love is fulfilled in offspring, through which man perfects his individuality and demonstrates his power to make a mark in the life of the cosmos. Woe to the man who is condemned to sterile solitude; woe to the State that ignores the integration of the human personality in the family, cemented by love and perpetuated by *inheritance.* For the family is the perennial moral nursery of humanity.

---

[4] Gentile here gives merely the Latin phrase *alteri saeculo,* but he seems to be referring to the tag of Statius Caecilius which is twice cited by Cicero: *serit arbores quae alteri saeculo prosint* (cf. *De senectute,* 24; *Tusculans,* I, 31).

9. Political representation and the categories of labor

No one is simply a member of the general category 'worker.' The artist's work is very different from that of the dustman, and even from that of the engineer. This is so far true that it often happens that one man is not disposed to admit the value of another's work if it does not produce goods that satisfy *his* needs.

There are different kinds of work, and through working at his own task an individual laborer comes to belong to a category that has interests peculiar to itself, different from the interests of other categories; these interests must be harmonized with the interests of all the other categories so as to constitute a system of civil society which is the raw material of the State.[5] The individual will to which the will of the State is congruent is not therefore an undifferentiated will but one that is differentiated into an organic system, in which every individual by willing himself wills the system. This is the concept of the modern State (the 'corporative' State as we have called it in Italy), which seeks to achieve popular liberty by adherence to the effective characteristics of the people to whom the liberty is to belong. If this liberty is attributed to a nonexistent abstraction and not to the people as it effectively exists, it never comes to fruition and there is some risk of its becoming a swindle. A swindle is all that liberalism of the French type is; and the English liberal tradition which arose at the end of the seventeenth century to justify the government of the landowning classes at the expense of the mere workers is even worse. The free State, the State of the man who works, must take into account the moral and economic essence of labor as it is necessarily differentiated in the system of national economy. Otherwise the State will be turning its back on the living individual in pursuit of a man of straw.

---

[5] Doubtless all readers will be reminded at the end of this chapter of Hegel's *Philosophy of Right,* in which the family and 'civil society' are the prior stages in the synthesis of the State. But it is perhaps hardly necessary to point out what a contrast there is between Gentile's conception of 'civil society' and Hegel's. In Hegel the harmonization of interests (economic cooperation and division of labor) is brought about by free competition, with the State simply looking on. Anyone who reflects on Hegel's debt to Adam Smith will know how to estimate Gentile's unjust dismissal of the English liberal tradition below.

XII

POLITICS

1. Definition of politics

Politics is the activity of the spirit as State. But it is not the activity of a spiritual substance called the State, nor of any entity that subsists independently in opposition to the human individual. Some such entity has often been invented, but it has always been a mere abstraction which only the imagination could endow with a body and some kind of active power. From our point of view the State is identical with the self-consciousness of the so-called 'separate' individual,[1] the self-consciousness of the real man. For a man is positively real so far as he is a universal will, and coincides with the State.

In order to understand the actual political experience that is essential to the very constitution of human consciousness, and hence immanent in the individual, we must declare war on all such abstract notions as hypostasized spiritual functions or, conversely, human individuals isolated from their functional context. The State conceived as an external relationship existing *inter homines,* opposed to and set over the individual person, is an abstraction. The individual who does not contain the State within himself, but must look for it or encounter it outside, is an abstraction. The law that is imposed upon the will as a past decision is an abstraction; and the will that presupposes law as a reality to be known and

---

[1] *Il così detto singolo* (cf. p. 163 herein).

174

recognized is equally abstract. A self-consciousness that is not already an act of will is an abstraction; and the will that is not the immanent essence of self-consciousness is abstract likewise. The purely juridical will which has still to be fulfilled and integrated in ethical volition is an abstraction; and the ethical will that is conceived as an integration of political action is equally abstract.[2] And finally need we repeat once more that theory as distinct from practice and practice as distinct from theory are both abstractions?

2. Ethics and politics

In concrete experience the political activity of man is identical with ethical activity since the will resolves the otherness of society ad infinitum, and thus absorbs the whole world of social relations into the infinite process of its self-realization. The process of resolution is infinite because there is no one act that can be conceived as a definitive resolution; within the unity of the eternal act, every act that can be empirically distinguished from others is negated as soon as it is fixed and confined within its empirical unity, because it is itself the negation of the act in which the essence of consciousness consists. There is thus always and yet never a resolution in time. The problem is eternal and the solution is eternal—as has already been observed apropos of one aspect of the spiritual process, namely the history of philosophy.[3]

The process of conscious life cannot be confined within any limits without transcending them; it cannot come to a halt in a world of heterogeneous atoms and not automatically deny this atomism. The most we can say is that there is a certain transcendent ideal element that can always be distinguished from the practical development that is achieved by way of the mundane relations in the midst of which political activity is carried on. The contrasts and the struggles of political life are generated and recognized—

---

[2] This assertion was at first sight so astonishing that I was inclined to emend the sentence to read "the ethical will that is *not* conceived" etc., thinking that the omission of the negative was merely a slip. But then I realized that the whole series of 'abstractions' is simply a catalog of Croce's 'errors.' Gentile here refers to Croce's view that the State is an 'economic' institution that has to be subordinated to the moral conscience. He wishes to assert that both terms in the distinction are equally abstract. Politics in his view does not need to be integrated into the ethical will—it is ethical—so that any ethical will conceived as separate from it must be an abstraction.

[3] By Hegel, but the precise reference eludes me.

and once recognized they provoke and maintain the activity that overcomes such struggles and contrasts—in pursuance of the end to which the life of the spirit is eternally directed: self-consciousness, or the identity of the self with itself and the exclusion of any opposition or otherness. So that if the identity of self-consciousness is the *ethical* form of the spirit which in this way creates the only reality that has any value, the reality of consciousness, then ethics may be regarded as the leaven of politics—the end which is immanent in it but which it never perfectly achieves. A distinction of this kind is purely ideal, since the transcendence of which we are here speaking is not such as to exclude immanence, and will not allow us to posit a merely political mode of behavior prior to ethical action.

Either there is no political mode of behavior, or if there is, it is already ethical behavior, since ethics represents the form of conscious activity which is most adequate to the nature of the spiritual act. So that politics can never provide an alibi for the moral conscience.

3. The impossibility of a nonpolitical ethics

Still less can ethics provide an alibi for avoiding political action, as if politics contained something more than moral action, and were a divergent activity. Man too often seeks this alibi for his laziness. Political life is a struggle which draws us out into society and gets us involved with people of disparate mentalities and diverse interests. We lose the peace that comes from solitude and from the mental concentration that flourishes in solitude, the peace that makes the meditation of the thinker more fruitful and more dextrous, the lyric inspiration of the poet more immediate and spontaneous, the mystic converse of the soul with God more solemn. But in solitude also the egoist takes pleasure from his natural impulses and from the natural world on which he depends for their gratification. This is the eternal temptation of the original sin, the temptation to let ourselves go, to give way to natural inclinations; it drags us down until we shrink from the effort that action involves for someone who has the courage to advance.

Λάθε βιώσας [4] is the logical conclusion of the Epicurean conception of life; and it is the temptation to which every man who

---

[4] "Live unnoticed" (Epicurus).

desires peace at slight cost is naturally subject. It is the 'doctrine of the clerks,' the intellectuals who withdraw from the world and make out that they despise the hurly-burly of politics as a deviation of the spirit from 'higher things' like philosophy or art. Obviously it would take a higher brand of courage to break free from one's moral obligations altogether—though there have been some who in the Dionysiac madness of poetic or philosophical inspiration have pretended that *they* for their part were above good and evil. There is an equivocation here; for the claim to be above the current moral standards, where it arises from reflection and the need for spiritual elevation, is and always will be itself a moral resolution directed toward the achievement of a higher type of morality and a more perfect kingdom of the spirit. In general, the 'flight from the world' is meant to be a quest for higher perfection, or at least it always presents itself in this way and with this claim.

4. 'Private' and 'public'

The logic of this avoidance of politics is founded on the familiar but fallacious distinction between the 'public' and the 'private' life of an individual. 'Private' life is supposed to include every action that touches the interests of the agent and even of other people, but does not concern the total social complex organized and fused in the personality of the State. Thus the relation of friend to friend, of husband and wife, of father and son will be 'private' since such relationships belong to the individual as a separate person.[5] But these same relations begin to have a 'public' import when the person concerned is regarded as a citizen, a member of the State. The education that a father gives his children provides a typical example, inasmuch as we agree that the State cannot simply ignore it. The moral to be drawn from this example is that an action is either 'public' or 'private,' depending on whether we think of it concretely or in the abstract. And the truth is that within the State everything that is abstractly 'private' becomes 'public' in a concrete situation; relations between particular separate individuals need to be regulated by what is called 'private' law to distinguish it from 'public' law which regulates relations between the State and its citizens—but the very existence of 'private' law proves that the

---

[5] *Nella sua singolarità.*

State has an interest to protect, by intervening in 'private' relations, and by granting them its seal of approval.

In any case, the distinction can no longer be maintained when the empirical character of all distinctions between 'individual' and 'society' or 'individual' and 'State' is recognized; for, as we have seen, the State exists already in the private individual, and every empirical State is only a development of a new form of this original transcendental [6] State. What is vital is that we should attribute to the transcendental State the absolute infinite universality that belongs to it from the beginning; then the imagination will not compel us to break open this infinity and conceive a wider State, which can never be anything but an empty fancy. For at any given time the only State that really exists is the one that expresses our own perpetually infinite and absolutely universal will.

5. The theory of the limits of the State

In reality, every time that this distinction of 'private' and 'public' is appealed to, the attempt to employ it is motivated by the desire to limit the activity of the State in practice, so as to secure and guarantee for the individual a sphere of interests outside the State's competence. *That the State's competence is limited* has been one of the classic tenets of the individualistic philosophy that liberal theory always tends to fall back on. Catholics in every country have used it as a weapon in their struggle to take the education of the young at least partially out of the hands of the State, by requiring its agreement to a 'private' school system parallel with and independent of the 'public' system.

It is not usually noticed that in demands of this kind the negation of the premise, and the consequent admission that every school even if called 'private' is really 'public,' is implicit in the demand itself. In general it is implicitly granted that the State is present even beyond the limits which the State itself establishes for its own activity. For it is impossible to admit the legitimacy of a private school without defining and regulating it—and in practice this means subjecting it to State control. The 'private' character of the school refers only to the power of initiative involved in its foundation, to its financial support, and to other details which must still, moreover, be known and hence authorized by the State, so that

---

[6] *Essenziale.*

in one way or another they fall within the sphere of its sovereign power. In any case, the tendency to limit the power of the State is surely nothing but a way of opposing a potential State will to the actual positive will of the State. It is a sort of revolutionary action establishing a new State of one's own that is to be the negation of the existing State. Obviously someone who is entirely satisfied with the way the State acts does not seek permission to act on his own account within the sphere of State action; so that in practice the request for permission always implies dissatisfaction and criticism of the State. The criticism may be legitimate but this can never mean that there is an abstract right to limit the action of the State; it represents a concrete effort toward a State that is or could be really ours, and the consequent virtual negation of the State actually in power which does not properly act for us. This negation in its turn would not make sense if it did not implicitly contain at least the virtual affirmation of a State that is really ours, a State which, as far as we are concerned, is the only genuine and effective State there is—the possibility of any other divergent yet still legitimate State being thereby excluded.

6. The authoritarian State and democracy

There is nothing really private then; and there are no limits to State action. This doctrine has two aspects; if we examine only one of them it becomes disfigured and essentially altered. It appears to make the State swallow the individual, and to absorb into authority completely the liberty that should be set against every authority that limits it. The regime corresponding to such a doctrine is called 'totalitarian' and 'authoritarian' and is set off against 'democracy,' the system of liberty. But one might say just the opposite: for in this conception the State is the will of the individual himself in its universal and absolute aspect, and thus the individual swallows the State; and since legitimate authority cannot extend beyond the actual will of the individual, authority is resolved completely in liberty. Lo and behold, absolutism is overturned and appears to have changed into its opposite; and the true absolute democracy is not that which seeks a limited State, but that which sets no limits to the State that develops in the inmost heart of the individual, conferring on his will the absolutely universal force of law.

The Greeks distinguished the middle πολιτεύεσθαι from the active πολιτεύειν, being acutely and immediately aware of the profound difference between the citizen who merely belongs to a State and the one who participates actively and consciously in its life, and so contributes to its existence. And in their democracy, which gave power to the individual but preserved a strong sense of the substantiality of the πόλις as that from which the citizen derived his political significance, they set the duty and right of membership [πολιτεύεσθαι] far above the fact of participation [πολιτεύειν].

7. Anarchism and liberalism

The antithesis of the State which establishes its authority with conscious energy and makes it effective is not represented by the liberal system but by anarchism. Anarchism pushes the theory of individualism to its ultimate logical conclusions, whereas liberals appeal to it and then strive in eclectic fashion to reconcile it with the substantiality of the community or 'people.' The anarchist courageously does without this idol called the 'people,' which cannot be anything substantial if it is just the sum of the individuals who compose it; with firm faith in his atomic conception of the individual he dismisses every political superstructure, and every limit set against the absolute autonomy of the individual, as an arbitrary and tyrannical contrivance. The individual must be the only source of legal right since he alone really exists. Nor can it be granted that a social contract cancels once and for all the unlimitedness of the individual's will. For since the contract is not derived necessarily from the nature of the individual, it cannot be more than a matter of arbitrary choice, and therefore like any other contract it can be ended in the same way as it was begun. There is nothing substantial and absolute above the individual. Far from being a negation or even a tempering of anarchy, the contract theory provides the anarchist with a confirmation of his views.

Both anarchism and liberalism alike deny that the State is something original. Liberalism strives to deduce it—an undertaking as absurd as that of certain neopositivists and Kantians in the last century who tried to derive the things which appear in individual consciousness as a priori, and hence not deducible, by appeal to the evolution of the species. The middle terms always betray uncertainty, incoherence, and very slight capacity for rigorous thinking.[7] Whereas anarchism with the brutal violence of strict logic denies that we can talk of the State at all.

8. *Bellum omnium contra omnes*

Both views begin from the hypothesis of the 'war of all against all'; and they think they advance from this starting point. But their motion is purely imaginary, like a journey made in a dream. The war may be arbitrarily suspended, but it remains the constant and necessary law of a society where death for one is life for another [*mors tua vita mea*]. Once the bond of the spiritual synthesis immanent in every human soul is broken, the bond that naturally binds the single subjects into a substantial unity as fast as they establish and distinguish themselves, war ceases to be an anomaly and becomes the norm, peace is no longer the synthesis which resolves the antithesis but an original gift to be preserved by each individual within the immediate circle of his own individuality. As soon as this circle is infringed there is only eternal warfare between individuals; and if, by contract, States are formed, then apart from the quite contingent interruptions caused by treaties, which are like contracts at the international level, there is war between the States.

This fiction of the *bellum omnium* is the most nauseating form of ignorance of man's primordially social nature, or of the fundamental unity of the human race as it issues from the spirit. Consciousness does indeed involve war and contrast, for conscious life depends on contrast; but the contrast would not be real if it did not at bottom arise from an original unity, and tend toward the renewal of harmony in a higher unity which is the true unity of the spirit. The original unity which has generated all human history was long sought for in, or relegated to, the myth of a common Father, so that in the past it has been easily overlooked or misunderstood, since it was never looked for in the depths of the individual soul viewed as a transcendental activity. That is where it is, and from there it shines with all its light; if we are not deceiving ourselves, that is where *we* have discovered it.

---

[7] Gentile says "Middle terms which betray etc.," but he has not specifically stated what the middle term in the liberal 'deduction of the State' is. What he has in mind is obviously the 'social contract.'

9. War and peace

And it is for us the key of war and peace, the clue to man's grim destiny and to the light that shines at the end of the road that he painfully travels. For the concept of the synthesis implies that war is necessary,[a] but only in order to scale the heights of peace where man will forever find satisfaction for the deepest need of his nature. Peace among the peoples, and among fellow citizens, peace between those whom "one wall and one ditch contain";[8] peace within the family and peace in the heart of man himself. This inner peace is possible only if the self a man finds when he examines his own conscience is in accordance with the ideal pattern provided by his self-consciousness; the ideal is present to him as his own actual essence and only in terms of it can he achieve actual existence.

10. Order

International peace presupposes national and civic peace, and ultimately peace within man himself. Peace takes definite and determinate form as the system of social order, the maintenance of which is the primary task of every State; and no one can pretend that the *police force* is all that is required to meet this essential and fundamental need. The police may be helpful in preserving peace, but only if order reigns in men's hearts by virtue of the political sense in which the State is rooted and from which alone it gets its vital sap. Police work is a medicine; and just as no medicine can keep alive an organism threatened by an inner failure of vitality, so no police force can restore the health of a State when the *vis medicatrix naturae* has run out.

11. Political sense

The political sense is the soil in which the tree of the State sends down its roots. Abstract conviction of the intimate connection between oneself and the life of the State is not enough. There are so many things we know and believe, but we do not feel them. They are not, as we say, 'flesh of our flesh,' things that are born naturally in our minds, so that they are always simply there with-

---

[a] Cf. Chapter 10, secs. 6–7, herein.
[8] *Un muro ed una fossa serra* (Dante, *Purgatorio*, VI, 84).

out our needing to think about them—like the love of a mother for her child, a feeling which governs her actions as an inseparable part of her nature. This is the characteristic property of feeling, which is prior to thought and at the basis of it. It is something that thought releases of its own accord as part of its vital rhythm, and finds itself faced with as a condition of its own existence; something rather like the body which the individual finds in his own consciousness as the foundation of his existence and activity.[b] The State is not simply there like one's bodily constitution. But even the body develops with consciousness; it becomes determinate and advances beyond its primitive indistinct immediacy to a status which is, relatively speaking, derived, though it always remains immediate from the point of view of the consciousness that takes it as a base for its own existence and activity. Similarly, the State comes to birth in the transcendental rhythm of self-consciousness through a process which we have accurately described; but from the point of view of the further development of consciousness, it becomes, once it is born, a primitive possession of the subject and the constitutive principle of his own essential structure. This structure must have life, such as it can have only if it is a feeling, a political sense, the secret source of every passion that the political activity of the individual brings to light. When this fountain dries up, political action loses all sincerity and warmth; it is emptied of all constructive energy and decays into a mere game for dilettanti.

12. Political genius

The more vigorous this political sense is, the more powerful and effective political action becomes; herein lies the secret of *political genius*. For the creative genius of artists, philosophers, saints, historic heroes, etc. is not, as everyone knows, a product of art, but a natural gift; it is not the result of reflection, instruction, and training, but a kind of divine inspiration, a God-in-us,[9] that quasi-nature *of* the spirit and *in* the spirit which we call 'feeling.' From it arise the intuitions, the revelations, discoveries, and exploits that are not based on careful deliberation and ordered reasoning. Reasoning and attentive observation of facts are involved; and gradually they give rise to the 'wisdom of experience,'[10] and an astuteness

---

[b] See Chapter 7, sec. 5, herein.
[9] *Deus in nobis;* cf. Ovid, *Ars amatoria*, III, 549.
[10] *Un'esperienza privilegiata.*

that presupposes a rare knowledge of human nature and the affairs of the world. But all that would amount to nothing if it were not put to profitable use by a hidden creative power, possessing the intuitive, spontaneous character natural to sense experience, which, like all other natural powers, never goes wrong, and always achieves its aims by the shortest and easiest route. Genius is Nature, or in other words it is feeling.[c]

13. The politics of childhood

Because of the immediacy of feeling, political genius, like artistic genius, is most clearly marked in childhood. The child lacks the maturity of experience and the habit of reflection through which the adult continually enlarges his sphere of political activity; but within the relatively narrow range of his limited life he already exhibits not merely a steadfast sureness of political feeling, which advancing years and the multiplying problems that adult life brings with it may tend to weaken rather than to reinforce, but also a remarkable readiness of true and genuine political intuition. In this respect his attitude and behavior within the tiny society of his brothers and his parents, his peers and all the companions with whom day by day he weaves an ever tighter web of personal relations, is well worth studying: the art that he spontaneously displays in dealing with others, drawing them into the range of his interests and his will, making use of all the means at his disposal to secure their consent to his desire. The child's desire is for him a program of universal import, the conception of a world under the dominion of a single will, with a coherent logical structure of its own, and a system of ends which appears to him as the only thing worth achieving. On this basis he founds his 'policy'; or in other words, he seeks hour by hour to achieve that unity of his world which accords with his own will—a unity which hour by hour disintegrates before his eyes, and breaks up into varying tendencies. This is the eternal, or as it once used to be called, 'innate,' politics of human consciousness, which governs man's whole life from the cradle to the grave.

---

[c] Cf. my essay on "Genius." [Probably the reference is to the essay "Poesia e genio," published in *Giornale critico della filosofia italiana*, 1934, pp. 1–12, and reprinted in *Memorie italiane*, Florence, Sansoni, 1936, pp. 245–60. But there is also a chapter entitled "Genio, gusto, critica" in the *Filosofia dell'arte* (1931), Florence, Sansoni, 1950, pp. 265–90—Tr.]

14. The political aspect of all forms of human activity

It governs man's whole life. For if, as the complex personality of every man unfolds, there is good reason to distinguish the father of a family, the citizen, the artist, the thinker, the man of faith and the statesman, there is nonetheless a kind of politics involved in all these various forms of human activity. This is as obvious in the life of a paterfamilias within the walls of his own home as it is in the life of a statesman. But even the types of activity that appear to separate the individual from all companions, and confine him to the secret labor of his own thoughts or to the concentration of mystic fervor, have in the same way a political aspect. The political problem is different in each case but it is always present and always intimately connected with the actual conscious activity concerned.[11]

15. The politics of art

When art passes from its ideal nonactual status into the actual concrete form of a work of art, the subject issues from his pure subjectivity and develops to the point of self-consciousness through the total rhythm of thought. He would never rise to this level if he did not set himself up as object against himself as subject, and then conquer the otherness by assimilating it and returning to punctual identity with himself. This is, as we know, the process through which society and hence also political personality is formed. The objects the artist deals with may appear to be in some cases dead things [12] and in others living people—people close to the heart of the artist, or even sometimes people of very different and contrasted types, as far removed and as violently opposed to him as negative from positive. In reality even the dead things have for the artist a soul of their own, they have feelings, they share *his* feelings; and there is no character, however repugnant in aspect, who is not understood by his creator, cared for and cherished as one who little by little will manifest his humanity—in short every character is in a way loved. The Unnamed, defiled by so many crimes, and viewed with so much horror, is in the end embraced by Cardinal Federigo, or in other words by Manzoni himself; and

---

[11] *L'attualità della vita spirituale.*

[12] *Natura morta* is the usual Italian phrase for a still life. The English way of putting it makes Gentile's point for him.

if Don Abbondio remains Don Abbondio to the end, nonetheless the author's moral condemnation is accompanied by a certain smile of indulgence, a smile of sympathy and understanding for the often unconquerable frailty of human nature which lies in the depths of all our hearts, even Manzoni's.[13] Thus the artist solicits his object to divest itself little by little of its otherness and rise to its own true life in the mind of the artist himself. And at the end, after the manner of God Himself, the artist can behold "all the things that he has made" and see, like Him, that they are "very good." Tragedy, as Aristotle with profound insight recognized, should lead to catharsis; and through spiritual catharsis the poet and his public take comfort in the peace of the conflicts overcome, and rejoice in the victory of the spirit.

16. The politics of science

The thinker (whether scholar, scientist,[14] or philosopher) operates with concepts, and abstracts altogether from the world of living men. But even he has objects to deal with, and he has to overcome the various degrees of resistance that they offer against assimilation into the concreteness of actual thought. Only rarely are these objects people—as in the case of the historian. They are natural events, empirical phenomena, spiritual interests; and in general they are problems to be solved. A problem that has not yet received its appropriate solution presents itself to the investigator as an object which, were it not for the transcendental dialogue, would remain so absolutely impenetrable that it could not even maintain its status as a problem. And the transcendental dialogue always involves the internalization [15] of the object, which little by little as it is understood (and does it let itself be understood, or rather *make* itself understood?) must through our efforts speak, and answer our inquiries. But if the object must answer and lead us to that mutual compenetration of subject and object in which understanding and hence the solution of the problem lies, then lo and behold we are faced with a problem that is political in

---

[13] The reference is, of course, to *I promessi sposi*. For the character of Don Abbondio see Chapter 1. For the character of the *Innominato* see Chapter 19 ff., and for his redemption, Chapter 23 (English translation pp. 1 ff., 281 ff., 303 ff).

[14] 'Scholar and scientist' are used here together to translate *scienziato*.

[15] *Spiritualizzazione*.

something more than a metaphorical sense. The same caution and prudence that is advisable in sensible political behavior must here be used to govern the effort and commitment of scientific reflection struggling, as it must, to overcome the opposition of the object—which is always really an opposition of the self to itself.[16] Every such conflict must be resolved into unity if we are to achieve the intellectual satisfaction that is perfect self-fulfillment, peace of mind, order, and freedom of action. The difficulties that arise on the path of research, the objections to the tentative and provisional solutions that an inquirer arrives at, are goads to further inquiry for someone who sincerely desires to arrive at the truth; but they could not bring themselves to his notice because they would have no voice if he did not lend them his own voice and allow them to be heard in his own mind. They are another person with whom he must come to terms if he is to complete the task he has set himself. Or rather, generally speaking, they are several other persons, existing only within his own mind certainly, but nonetheless real for all that, determined to obtain his attention, able to make themselves felt and impose their will on him. He must deal with them as reasonably as he can in the hope of persuading them to assent to his individual-universal solution of the problem, and to behave themselves accordingly. I have added the "behave themselves accordingly" because ultimately assent is an action which involves making up one's own mind,[17] a free action that creates its own reality. Even in the most intense meditation man is never alone; he is in the society through which his actual thinking expresses itself, he moves always, by way of opposition and struggle, from a nonactual unity toward the actual realization of another higher unity which is alone effective. The opposition and struggle, be it noted, are not always a matter of enmity, a conflict of adversaries each desiring to annihilate the other. Indeed, properly speaking, this desire never exists; for if the other were annihilated he would no longer be the other whom the subject needs to bear witness to his own universality, by reuniting with him in the synthesis of self-consciousness, which generates the opposition precisely in order to realize itself as a unity of opposites. The enemy, therefore, as Hegel pointed out,[18] is not really conquered when killed, but

---

[16] *Opposizione tra sè e sè.*

[17] *Una autodecisione;* the English idiom needs to be taken literally here.

[18] *Phenomenology* (tr. by Baillie), 2nd ed., London, Allen and Unwin, 1931, pp. 233–34.

only when preserved and subdued; for only in that event does he surrender to the will of the victor and acknowledge it as the only will that counts, against which his own will cannot stand. The most rational kind of struggle is that which, by force or persuasion, whichever is more appropriate and opportune, conquers the enemy's resistance, and achieves the goal of "sparing the conquered" [19] in the harmony of peace and the unity of will that is essential to the life of the spirit.

17. The politics of faith

Even religious faith has its political aspect. Needless to say we are not referring to any mere political cleverness, such as the proverbial art of 'getting round' priests, saints, and even the gods themselves. In this book the word 'politics' is used always in the highest sense, whereas the 'art of getting round' [20] someone is only a caricature invented by rogues, which like all policies of expediency brings momentary success but ends in failure. Pure religious faith, in its essential content, is that form of conscious life in which the spirit turns toward the absolute object which is the second moment of the self-synthesis. This moment, taken by itself, is abstract and nonactual like the first moment,[21] but it is nonetheless real within the concrete unity of opposites. The opposites must both be there as such if the synthesis is to be genuinely productive and not operate in a void. They exist of course within the synthesis; but they exist there as opposed, each moment the negation of the other. Religious faith is just this abstract positing of the object, set up within self-consciousness as negative of the subject; the moment when the object alone exists and the subject which would limit it does not. Hence the object is infinite; and anything that presents itself to thought as existing along with it must be derived from it and somehow brought back to it. The object here is the Absolute or God. It is easy to see that since nothing can be thought of except as an object, there is always an ineffable spark of divinity

---

[19] *Parcere subjectis*, a tag taken from the famous line in which Virgil describes the policy of Rome toward her enemies as *parcere subjectis et debellare superbos* (*Aeneid*, VI, 854), "To spare the conquered and war down the proud" (Pope).

[20] *La politichetta;* cf. the colloquial American use of 'politicking.'

[21] I.e. pure feeling; see Chapter 5, sec. 6 and n5, herein; also secs. 11–12 of the present chapter.

in the objective aspect of anything at all: an infinite and absolute quality because of which every object that we really want to *think* about requires our full attention and involves concentrating our whole mind on that one point, so that there is nothing outside it that in any way distracts our thoughts.

Of course, if faith stopped short at this abstract moment of objectivity, it is clear that it would always remain nonactual. But in fact it is no secret that every mystic, even while he is asserting and reiterating his own annihilation and immersion in the dazzling light of the Divine, is himself standing forth to proclaim his own ecstasy, if nothing else, and to analyze the thoughts and states of mind that have brought him to it. He makes poetry of his mystic joy, and builds temples and altars, thereby celebrating the triumphant creative power of his own subjectivity even while he denies it. Religion, like art, is a nonactual, ideal tendency which becomes actual in the self-synthesis of concrete conscious experience, where there is neither abstract subject nor abstract object, but the two together, facing each other and remaining opposed to each other as they are in their nonactuality. Subject and object are inseparably bound together in the primitive and necessary nexus of self-consciousness or thought. In religion, man—being aware of the value of his faith, or of the logical necessity, which invests his whole spiritual being, that there be an object which is the absolute negative of all subjectivism—turns toward this object, yearning to break down the opposition, to restore peace, to escape from the nullity to which he would be eternally condemned by separation from the object, and, in short, to redeem himself from sin. He turns to it precisely as the subject always does even with particular determinate objects, to abolish the distance that separates it from him, and draw it into the fire of the 'intellectual love of God.' Thinking of God, *really* thinking of Him, means constant perseverance in the effort to penetrate His essence, to understand Him and make Him a concept (*the* concept) of our own minds, and so to make the concept one with our minds.[22] And He, the object, comes alive,

---

[22] Note how Gentile approaches Spinozism in the process of relating this section to the last. The extreme simplicity of his dialectic makes some connection necessary since both religion and scientific knowledge belong to the objective moment. But clearly Gentile finds no hardship in this. His sympathy with Spinoza makes the transition easy for him. But, on the other hand, his 'intellectual' love is very clearly a form of *practical* reason (cf. Chapter 5, secs. 2–3, herein).

He becomes a person; He becomes man, pays heed to man and answers him. He answers him, of course, from within, with the voice that speaks to every man from his own heart. He is our Master, our friend and benefactor, to whom we can turn with absolute trust in time of need and therefore He is the Power to whom we can pray for His consent to our desires, the Power that must above all else be loved and adored. Here too is a society requiring its own law and order and its own politics. All the particular problems that have arisen in history for members of a single church community, or for one community in its relations to the others existing at the same time and place, depend on this transcendental society; and above all the problem of relations between Church and State, for religious feeling has a special regulative power over the conduct of the Church toward the State—or over the conduct of the individual as a believer and member of a Church toward that universal element in his own consciousness which is the State.

18. The Church and proselytism

But the special problem of politics with respect to religious faith is the one that concerns the church community itself. The very establishment of such a community would be inconceivable if religious feeling really succeeded, as it is so often believed to do, in isolating the individual in a supramundane relationship of man with God. The solitude of the pious anchorite is a longing of the soul which real experience of conscious life proves to be absurd. For the anchorite himself carries a society within him in the transcendental dialectic of consciousness, and he cannot turn his back on it. This society is reborn from moment to moment in the meditations of his desert solitude, through the very dialogue that is continually renewed between himself and the Eternal God.[23]

It follows likewise that the Protestant theory of *private judgment*

---

[23] This argument is most unsatisfactory. The anchorite does not desire to be alone, but to be alone *with God;* and this is exactly what the transcendental society makes possible, as this paragraph and the whole of the preceding section seek to prove. The doctrine of the transcendental society does *not* prove that religion is not "a supramundane relationship of man with God." What it does is to show how such a relationship does not preclude the possibility of a religious community. A transcendental relation is a 'supramundane' relation that makes *possible* a mundane one; but it is a serious error of logic to suppose that it makes it *necessary*. There is nothing demonstrably absurd about withdrawing from the earthly city in order to increase one's awareness of membership in the Heavenly City.

in matters of faith is absurd; all of our Italian thinkers, Catholic and non-Catholic alike, from Bruno and Campanella down to Gioberti, have condemned this religious individualism as a kind of skeptical subjectivism. Here truly it is the case that "one witness is no witness" [*unus testis, nullus testis*]; the testimony that the religious conscience bears to religious truth, like the spirit's witness to all truth, can only be universal. Hence the proselytism of the faiths, and their tendency toward propaganda and universalization.[24] It is not just because, as our friend Varisco [25] was so fond of repeating, community life is a useful adjunct to the initiative of the individual in the search for and discovery of truth; thought is universal by nature and no one can think without doing so for everyone, in spite of all the delusions brought on him by his experience. For that matter, experience may indeed inflict wounds, but, as we say of liberty, it also heals the wounds it inflicts. For although differences of opinion and conflicts of thought arise in experience, it is there also that differences and conflicts are gradually and continually composed, and the way to the *consensus gentium* is opened.

19. The doctrine of toleration

This is the root of the intolerance that arises from religious dogmatism. One who is certain of the truth cannot allow it to go

---

[24] It is clear also that Gentile's interpretation of the Protestant theory of 'private judgment' is extremely prejudiced. His theory would never allow him to dissent from the fundamental Protestant tenet that a man must follow the dictates of his own conscience rather than any other authority. He himself said that he had "preached this all my life." While, on the other hand, no Protestant sect known to me ever denied that the truth to which we must all bear witness as best we can is in itself unique and universal. As far as proselytizing is concerned, the doctrine of 'private judgment' was never intended to do more than make certain kinds of pressure illegitimate. One might add that the sects that come closest to what Gentile calls 'religious individualism'—the Quakers for instance—are, to say the least, extremely chary of proselytism. This is not because they are skeptical about the 'light' but because they have a mystical trust in it. Gentile's philosophy gives him every right to disapprove of such quietism, but no right to accuse quietists of inconsistency. Indeed, his philosophy of religion is far better adapted to explain Protestant attitudes and assumptions than those of Catholics—a fact which in view of its Hegelian origins need cause us no surprise. But Gentile, being an Italian, prefers to see the good side of individualism in the Renaissance and only the bad side of it in the Reformation; Hegel, of course, fell into the converse error.

[25] Bernardino Varisco (1850–1928) was for some years Gentile's colleague at the University of Rome, and his immediate predecessor in the chair of theoretical philosophy. At least two of his books, *The Great Problems* and *Know Thyself*, have been translated into English (London, Allen and Unwin, 1914 and 1915 respectively). His philosophy was a kind of monadology.

unrecognized by others. The distinction of what is 'certain' from what is a 'matter of opinion,' so as to leave a generous margin for freedom of thought and belief in 'matters of opinion,' is here a useless remedy; it is a distinction affirmed in theory but rarely employed in practice, since every 'opinion' easily acquires for the man who holds it the force of a theorem or at least of a necessary postulate. And intolerance is all the more difficult to avoid when the 'certainty' of the truth one possesses is not the result of reasoning, but an immediate gift of grace, the fruit of an unlooked-for illumination. For then truth and error become simple exclusive alternatives and humanity is sharply divided into the 'elect' and the 'damned.' Everyone must come in or stay out; and if one cannot bring it about that the unbeliever's heart is touched by grace, there is nothing more to be done—the unbeliever is beyond the pale of humanity, he cannot be saved, therefore he has no right to exist. His death then becomes the only possible solution of the desperate problem of his existence as a man.

But one cannot fight intolerance with skepticism, for dogmatism will always make a good case against *that*. The 'matter of opinion' doctrine is Protagorean subjectivism, skepticism after the manner of Pontius Pilate left perplexed by the question without an answer: "What is truth?" Intolerance is not immoral because it is beyond the power of human intelligence to answer this great question. Indeed, man answers it all the time; his whole life is an incessant response. But this does not mean that the truth can be formulated in a dogma and defined once and for all with the right of 'forced currency.' [26] Truth is to be found in human thought; but it must conform to the nature of that thought or it could not be contained in it. And thought is movement, development, process —never anything immediate. If we want a child to understand something—and the love we bear him makes us want it—we must have patience. He understands little at first, and one might say strictly that he does not understand at all. We must have patience as the farmer does when he sows his seed in the soil, well knowing

---

[26] *Corso forzoso.* This phrase, which is placed in quotes by Gentile himself, "refers to State bank notes which must be accepted as a means of payment, as opposed to the *corso legale* which implies the right of exchange for metallic money. (It was instituted once only in Italy after the war of 1866)" (Panzini, *Dizionario moderno,* Milan, Hoepli, 1931, s.v.). Gentile is comparing the right to receive 'real' money for one's paper with the right to rethink a dogmatic formula for oneself.

that he cannot harvest it the same day. He waits and trusts to time. Our human world is full of children; the man who has no patience, and is disgusted by the nonsense he hears talked all round him, yet will not stop his ears against it, can swing his mace—but to what purpose? One cannot teach or spread the truth like that. The kingdom of the spirit that we would like to build remains simply a disappointed desire.[27]

When Manzoni declared that truth and error are not separated by a clear line, and that two litigants who maintain contrary positions may both have right on their side,[28] he certainly was not intending to profess himself a skeptic; he was alluding, albeit somewhat obscurely, to the 'graduality' of truth, which is not simply given, but has to be conquered progressively, so that every stage or moment is inadequate and may appear false. But it is not so really, since we reach the truth by passing through it and it does itself contain truth, though in a form that is still inadequate and immature. The children are not yet grownups, but they will be; and therefore Jesus called them around him to give them credit when he said, "Suffer little children to come unto me."

20. Politics as a right and a duty

At all ages, in all conditions, in all the forms of conscious life that can be distinguished, politics is an immanent activity of the human spirit. And anyone who, sincerely and with full understanding of his own words, proposed to stay out of all politics would have to give up living. Political action, therefore, is a right, insofar as it is necessarily involved in a complete existence. For it is the right of every man to exist as only he can, not simply preserving his life like an animal,[29] but continually achieving the humanity that is his only if he freely chooses it. But he has the right to exist in freedom simply because it is his duty to do so; for my *right* is something which others have a *duty* to respect. And though this

---

[27] One wonders whether Gentile was conscious that this comment applied to his own case. In a speech for the Fascist party in 1924 he made the notorious claim that even the blackjack was really a 'moral force' (*Che cosa è il fascismo*, Florence, Vallecchi, 1925, p. 50). Of course there is this difference between the mace and the blackjack; the former kills where the latter merely leaves a nasty bruise. But the educational results of the blackjack were not much more than a "disappointed desire."

[28] Manzoni, *Promessi sposi*, Chapter 1 (English translation, p. 12).

[29] *Non conservando il proprio essere naturale.*

reciprocity of 'right' and 'duty' implies existence in society and the relation of 'self' to 'other,' we ought always to remember that 'existence in society' means essentially membership in the transcendental society that the individual has within him.

This point is worth clarifying. My right to exist is the duty of others to secure my existence. To say that a son has the right to be educated is the same as saying that his father ought to educate him. But where does this duty come from? It arises from the relation between them, and where this relation is progressively realized, the 'other' ceases to be an 'other' and the two become identified. This identical self receives, in virtue of the internalized relation, only what he also gives. He has a right which is also his duty. The duty that every man has of being human, thinking, willing, and, in short, creating his own self-consciousness, is at the same time his right to human existence, inasmuch as the 'other' whose duty it is to recognize this right is within him. Indeed this 'other' is himself—even though it may assume the semblance of a materially distinct person, or of the total complex of all persons with whom he has relations. The man who has a 'right' to exist is *always* the one whose existence *we* have a duty to secure.

Participation in politics, therefore, may well present itself as a right which no one can be denied; but only because political life is a duty which no one can evade. The rights must certainly be recognized; but the first person with a duty to recognize them is the subject himself whose rights are being talked about. Others can recognize his rights only if he first sets them a good example. This is what is forgotten because of the habitual slackness of the ordinary moral conscience. Men are very ready to claim their 'rights,' oblivious of the fact that they are dealing with their duties at the same time. In reality, as Mazzini was so profoundly aware, life is neither a pleasure nor a right, but a duty.

XIII

TRANSCENDENTAL SOCIETY, DEATH AND IMMORTALITY

1. The motive for faith in immortality

One of the articles of faith to which Christians hold most strongly is the dogma of the immortality of the soul. The scholastic philosophers sought, in travail as long and bitter as it was obscure, to establish a rational proof for it, on a foundation secure against the difficulties of a wavering and inadequate speculative tradition. Modern philosophy with its denials, critiques, and doubts has aroused grave perplexities about it. But the less the article of faith seemed to be guaranteed by unimpeachable rational arguments, the more precious it became to the believer. When the Averroists of the Latin schools made the controversy about the meaning of the unique intellect in Aristotle fashionable, and began to undermine the foundations of the concept of an immortal soul, it was the theme of most passionate discussions, not only in the schoolroom but in public meetings and in the market place. From that time forward men's minds clung all the more closely to religion, as they became less able to put their trust in rational speculation on this question of supreme concern. Today, indeed, religion is more sought after and more highly appreciated by most people as the sure promise of a port in which every man's ship of life can anchor at the end of its earthly voyage full of risk and pain, than for the other comforts it offers against the present and unfailing sorrows of life. And thus religion, instead of being a treasure house of truth enough to satisfy every deepest need of human intelligence, is commonly thought of as the science from which we can obtain the certainty of a future life, or as the satisfaction of the most tormenting anxiety that troubles man in this life. It is not a case of religion being the principle from which the dogma of immortality follows as a corollary; it is rather the need to be able to count on immortal life that makes us seek religion as the pillow on which we can lay our weary heads at the end of the day's labor.

Nor is immortality desired, as some philosophical theories would have us believe, in order to solve a problem in theodicy, because it allows us to postpone to another life the solution of the problem about the rewarding of virtue and the punishment of vice, which does not seem to be settled in this life.[1] These old-fashioned problems of theodicy have been transcended by the modern mind, which is more concerned with the problems of experience and history, scarcely noticing that it is precisely here that all the problems of theology lie hidden for anyone who wants to think rigorously.[2] The most vital interest that moves modern man to look beyond the grave is his desire for happiness. Man loves to anticipate future pleasure and embitters every present enjoyment with his fear and suspicion that it must after a time come to an end. So that the man who is happy and clings to his happiness in fear for its future, yearns for it to last 'even to the end and then beyond' [usque ad finem et ultra]. In short, he wishes his happiness were not destined to finish; and above all that his life, the source of all his joys, might last indefinitely. Oh, if only youth could last! If only old age would delay coming and not cut short every pleasure of this life so sweet for one who can still drink deep from the cup of youthful reveling. And then, would that everything did not have to finish. A strand of the energy that makes us savor the sweetness of existence is reinforced and strengthened by the moderation and careful governance of the tired years. It ceases to be dependent on the aid of the body and its pristine vigor, and gradually becomes thinned out and refined into the delicate fruit of the pure exercise of the soul, which in the vigil at the end prepares itself for a life wholly spiritual,

---

[1] Gentile has in mind the thesis of Antonio Bruers cited in n7 on p. 152 herein.
[2] This is Gentile's retort to Croce's condemnation of actual idealism as 'theologizing philosophy'—that Croce's historicism is only half awake.

but still desirable and dear, such as it will be able to live beyond the grave, dependent solely on its own powers. But how could the continuance of a single individual's life appear desirable to him if it were emptied of the content which from day to day fills and enriches it? Our life is the life of this world, where our parents, our brothers, and our children are, the people with whom we spend our lives and share our every joy, multiplying it in the sharing; so that without these others the fount of all our joys would be dried up. The continuance of our lives as individuals is only possible on condition that the lives of our dear ones continue also; so the death of a loved one is excluded from the list of events which the future as a man loves to imagine it holds in store for him; it comes on him unexpected and unlooked for, like a thunderbolt that falls upon the tallest tree and threatens to uproot it. But then he is led to hope that beyond this life the companionship of his loved ones will once more be renewed, so that the course of his happiness shall not be broken off in a moment without a reason. How could a man continue to work without seeing beyond today a tomorrow that will belong to him particularly, to him and to the persons he most dearly loves, those whose lives are completely bound up with his own? The logic of happiness may allow of interruption as long as it is only temporary, like those many intervals which suspend our joys in this life only to compensate for the break by renewing the sweetness of the first taste when we take them up again.

The father will die before his children, but being a good father, he has looked ahead from the moment when he begot them to their life after his death; and his spirit will continue therefore to hover over them present and provident as long as they need him in any way—that is to say as long as they live. And after that? Then they will find themselves once more with him and he will have them again as boon companions in that happy life that is never to end. And if one of the sons should die before the father, what else can the remainder of his life be for him but a period of waiting for the life that will bring back everything as it once was, a waiting accompanied by an unsleeping memory continually refreshed by a tenderness forever reborn? [3]

This is the eudaemonist logic of everyday life. It may come up against a mysterious 'block' when, to use the Platonic image, we are boarding the raft to make the journey after death to the world be-

---

[3] It should be noted that Gentile had recently lost a son.

yond;[4] but in the ordinary course of life our thoughts pass surely over the years from the present to the future near and far. There is a necessity in this logic against which no doubt can offer an insurmountable obstacle. For man lives in tomorrow, he lives by expectation, by faith in the future—and not merely, as the poet makes us feel so vividly in *The Village Sabbath*,[5] when the future promises us a festival, but every day, no matter what tomorrow brings. The past interests us no longer: it is a whirlpool into which the life we have lived has fallen and vanished so that it can no longer be taken up again and relived. The present moment is all, and even the future would not be life but the negation of life; it would be Hell itself, if it did not draw nigh instant by instant and become present before our eyes like the brooks of Casentino before the eyes of Master Adam.[6] But the present moment is quickly gone, and the joy of a bright dawn would not comfort the eye of the beholder if it were a light that is extinguished the very moment it is lit. Dawn is a promise of day; the present is only life if it is the beginning of a period extending to the future. No man lives in the present without asking himself what is to come. *Après moi la déluge?* It may be so; but if I were not borne up by a secret hope, however timid, that the deluge may not come, how could I bring myself to act?

This hope, which is the law of life in our world, leads us to cast our eyes beyond the end of our earthly lives and, in order not to despair of the happiness which is life's substance, we conceive a life after this one which is nonetheless a continuation of it.

There is, of course, the pessimist who fills our ears with his complaints about the impossibility of being happy. But does he despair of his own happiness? Or of every satisfaction that could make life dear to him? He plays at being a philosopher and his philosophy brings him, while he is actually engaged in it, a certain bitter taste that is for him the "origin and cause of every joy,"[7] to use a pregnant phrase of Dante's. It is his *raison d'être*, not merely for the moment, but for his whole life as he pictures it to himself, today, tomorrow, and always—or at least for as long as it lasts. And apart from the joy of discovering and demonstrating the truth, as he believes and

---

[4] Possibly there is here a confusion of *Phaedo*, 85d and 113d.

[5] Leopardi, "Il sabato del villaggio" (see the *Oxford Book of Italian Verse*, no. 326).

[6] Dante, *Inferno*, XXX, 61 ff.

[7] *Principio e cagion di tutta gioia* (*Inferno*, I, 78).

proudly boasts that he is doing, how many others are not peeping out of the shadows of his mind from behind this basic and essential satisfaction. He, the philosopher of inevitable defeat, reasons against his foes real or imaginary; he writes and publishes his thoughts and savors in advance the joy of victory, victory over his adversaries, or better still over all men—for they must all surrender their exploded illusions, accept his arguments, become his pupils, and honor him as a master of wisdom and of life, etc. One might say that the consistent pessimist is the suicide. But even suicide is susceptible of moral judgment; and this is the case because it is a free action, a decision that is the result of deliberation. It is not total despair but is sustained by a hope, like that of Brutus, who by rebelling and standing out against Fate does not despair of gaining the victory even over Fate itself.[8] The suicide looks forward to a dark future, but even his eyes are turned toward it and he foresees it the way he wants it.

So it is truly said that the last of the gods is Hope. If science with its concern for all things mortal does not comfort us with the hope of another life beyond this life, if philosophy, being unable resolutely to transcend the point of view of science, does not come to the aid of our unconquerable hope, well then, let religion come to assure us by faith of this future, indefinitely prolonged existence, that our minds cannot do without. And if religion offered us a God unwilling to guarantee it for us, it would lose its greatest value and leave the heart of man indifferent.

2. Immortality and religion

But what is the relation between religion and the faith in immortality? At first sight it is rather the denial of immortal life that seems to follow from the conception of religion. For man is exalted by the certainty of a life without end; whereas when he begins to feel himself in the presence of God, he falls into a passion of such profound humility as to feel that he is nothing. And truly, if God is, He is all that is; there is nothing outside of Him and therefore the man who conceives himself as in the presence of God is nothing. But in the next phase, man, having negated himself as opposed to God, is immersed in Him, and becomes identified with Him; he

---

[8] See Leopardi's "Bruto minore" (*Canti*, VI). My thanks are again due to Professor Spirito and the *Fondazione Gentile*.

becomes divine or sanctified, and participates in the divine being and feeling, thinking and willing. Mysticism, which is the identification of man with God, may abase the consciousness of man, but it must also exalt it; and God Himself must be human so that the identification can take place—or in other words He must be spirit as man is spirit. The Mysteries were in fact the cradle of faith in immortality in Greece. Man became convinced that by his estrangement from and opposition to God he was courting destruction and death; that life or a rebirth into life could only mean for him union with God and sharing immortality with Him.

Death is the consequence of the sin that separates and alienates man from God; salvation and eternal life are the effect of the redemption through which man, by God's help, returns to Him. Hence religious practice, with its rites and ceremonies, aims at the salvation of man through reconciliation with God. Ancient Orphism, like modern Christianity, is founded on this principle which answers to the logic of the religious moment of consciousness. And this principle is at the basis of every religion, whatever form it may assume. In religious practice man oscillates continually from one pole to the other of the dialectic of redemption which assures him of perpetual happiness. At one moment "the soul cries out" [9] and despairs at the sense of its own nothingness, at the next it recovers the hope of salvation that is assured by union with God; and it exults in Dionysiac frenzy at the sense of its divine dignity and immortality.

But in the process of this mystic union there are grades and stages. Human nature, which at first sets man at odds with God, making him a being who is no true being because he is particular, finite, sinful, and in short mortal, does not give way immediately before divinity. It resists, it seeks compromises, it strives to save all that can be saved of its own natural heritage, and looks for a way of smuggling its own weaknesses into Paradise with it. In plain terms man tries to save what cannot be saved; even the 'particular interest' of which Guicciardini spoke,[10] which is just what must die

---

[9] *Anima ingemiscit.* I have not been able to trace this phrase.

[10] *Il particulare.* The word *particulare* often recurs in Guicciardini's *Ricordi politici e civili;* usually it refers to the details and special circumstances of a situation. But a clear example of the meaning that Gentile has in mind is found for instance in no. 28, where Guicciardini says that despite his disgust at the vices of the priesthood, "il grado che ho avuto con più pontefici, m'ha necessitato ad amare *per il particulare mio* la grandezza loro."

if man aspires sincerely and with all his might to the Kingdom of Heaven. But hope does not surrender easily in the face of the difficulties. Man says his prayers—and there is no natural inclination that he does not believe he can make acceptable to the divine will when he asks of the Father, "Thy Will be done."

Thus immortality, which we hope to merit by doing the will of God, will receive in its mighty bosom—a veritable asylum of the imagination—both saints and sinners, what is divine along with what is all too human. The devout lady trusts that there is reserved among the heavenly hosts in the other world a place not merely for her but also for her children, for whom she implores the Almighty most fervently and anxiously; and even—why not?—a place for the whole household into which her existence as an individual is woven—right down to the cats and dogs. Is it not natural that she should establish even with them, and even when they are dead, an "echoing of loving feelings"? [11] Here, in the orchard of the patrician villa that now shelters me, there is a funeral monument to a lap dog with an inscription which is the wish of a truly gentle soul, though expressed in two not very stylish verses:

> Diana, take unto thee the bones of the lively Lily,
> Who here fell victim to the unresting hunter.

Thus the dead survive with us. Why formerly did man desire to bury his dead in temple enclosures, if it was not simply to give to his Manes the place proper to them, along with the saints and the gods? *Deorum Manium iura sancta sunto;* [12] and great is the temptation to push everyone in among the Manes and not to leave anything out, neither soul nor body.

But religion gradually becomes refined, and ends in an intuition of the truth. This truth involves the necessity of the Cross and the death of the body [13] for man's resurrection into eternal life. From the naive primitive conceptions, with all their crude physical imagery, some 'clinkers,' as it were, remain; but they are continually broken down by the hammering of our consciousness, which is essentially spiritual and personal. As in the popular myth, even the body of Christ is made to rise and ascend into Heaven, so a dogma not less alive and eloquent in the imaginations of the peo-

---

[11] Foscolo, *I sepolcri*. The line is cited again in its context below.
[12] "The rights of the ancestral gods shall be sacred."
[13] Gentile says "the death of man" but the context makes his meaning clear.

ples promises in the day of the last judgment the miraculous resurrection of the flesh. These things are clinkers, on which the imagination feeds, for it too has its rights, which the mind cannot do away with, since, as Vico says, "it is overturned in the senses." [14] But speculative thought will not find it difficult to put its own fire into these clinkers and interpret them in a speculative sense.[15] Even these myths have a logic of their own, for they provide the answer to a question that is sure to be asked by a man who is being assured of immortality: "Am I then immortal with all that I find in me?" And the error does not lie in the claim that the body also is immortal, the body that every man has, and which is not an external adjunct to his Ego but its inner constitutive content. The error lies rather in the crude conception of this body, which the Ego does indeed possess, but which is not the material body that we ordinarily think of, but the ideal body, the body transfigured in consciousness, where it is given to man alone to meet it, the fundamental content of all feeling. It is transfigured by being despoiled of its particularity, spatiality, and materiality, and hence universalized or, in short, converted into spirit.

In any case, the faith inculcated in man by religion is that the divine element of man, and that alone, is saved in immortality. This is the salvation for which we hope, and for which we beseech God in prayer. One who wants to save his money box with prayers is not thinking of God, but of the robbers who in this world can steal it away from him. For God taught Buddha as well as Christ and St. Francis that no one can enter the Kingdom of Heaven unless he be poor.

Faith in immortality is put to a stern test by the myth of the Inferno where the sinner remains eternally and hopelessly locked in his sin. Immortality on this view would be not only salvation but also perdition, not merely life but also death—*mors immortalis.*

---

[14] *Si rovescia nei sensi.* I have not found this phrase in Vico, but it does represent his view of the relation between the mind and the senses; see, for instance, paras. 236 and 331 of the *New Science* (tr. by Bergin and Fisch, Ithaca, N.Y., Cornell, 1948). Vico speaks of the mind being "overturned in ignorance" (*si rovesci nell'ignoranza*) in para. 181.

[15] Gentile and his pupils are fond of comparing actual consciousness to a fire consuming the static substantiality or materiality of the world in the pure becoming of the spirit (cf. Chapter 2, p. 89, herein). The metaphor goes back to Heraclitus; but in this passage Gentile seems to have extended it. For he calls the myths and stories of religion *scorie,* the word that Italians use for the slag and clinkers left behind in a furnace.

In this too there is logic, but it is inadequate. It is true that sin, like redemption, is eternal—evil just as much as good. But these two terms cannot be paired in an irreconcilable dualism; the Fathers saw that it is necessary to regard evil as the negative of good, and good as a positive endowed with the power to negate its negative and annul it. Otherwise half of the world that God created would have been immediately yielded and abandoned to the Devil, which would not be consistent with the goodness or the infinity of God, and does too much honor to the Devil. Sin, then, is eternal also, but only as transcended and redeemed in the divine will; the existence of which excludes the possibility of a Hell beyond expiation.

In order to extend the ambit of immortality, the myth of the Inferno degrades the essence of the spirit, treating it as if it were a naturally immortal soul-substance [16] capable, in its native liberty, of good or evil alike. It is not the case that the spirit *is* immortal; it *achieves* immortality, and to this end it must struggle with its primitive nature and conquer for itself the liberty that will make it a participant in eternity. Through the fire of sin the spirit can, indeed it must, pass. But please don't misunderstand this. The spirit must pass through sin only in order to expiate it, because liberty is always a redemption from slavery. He who has never known what it is to be a slave will never be free, nor will he ever know, therefore, how to command.

The spirit must pass through the fire, but not be consumed, as it certainly would be if it remained there. In fact it would have to renounce the movement in which its life consists, a supposition which is absurd.

Nonetheless the determination to have an eternal Hell, and the life of the sinner immortal in it, proves one thing, and that is the unslakeable thirst that man has for eternal life.

But this myth, though it is not a necessary consequence of the essential religious moment of the spirit, is a clear indication of the inner conflict of religious feeling. For religion, as we have seen, involves the immortality of divine things, but also involves the denial of immortality for man, who is annihilated in the very act of presenting himself in the world of divinity. But he presumes instead, like Prometheus, to steal the spark of fire from Heaven,

---

[16] *Immortale immediatamente come semplice anima.*

and share himself in the eternity of the gods. And through this Promethean revolt he is impelled to break into eternity not merely by the grace through which it is granted him to achieve sublimity by uniting his will with God's, but even, if need be, by the violence of the satanic element of his nature, still untamed and prompt to resist the divine will.

This does not alter the fact that these waverings of religious thought on the subject of immortality all presuppose a basic tendency of the soul toward the divine, the source of the immortality toward which it aspires piously or impiously, in accord or in conflict with the gods, because of the dim but deep-rooted sense that it has of its own eternal value. For the spirit, when it looks upon itself from without, can certainly not conceive the possibility of its own withdrawal from the universal flux; but on the other hand, it cannot cast a glance into its own inwardness without finding there the resplendent light of things eternal.

3. The equivocation

But in all the concepts of immortality current—among the learned and the unlearned—there is a hidden equivocation that should be pointed out and clarified. It lies in the fact that immortality is sometimes understood as perpetuity in time, and sometimes as true and proper eternity outside of time. Perpetuity is a sort of disemboweled time, which, while bringing reality under its sway, respects it and abstains from carrying it away in the flux; just as the current of a river picks up and carries away with its waters the straws that fall into it, but laps round and leaves in their place the rocks, which, though they lie in the current, do not flow with it toward the mouth, but remain fixed in the bed of the river. Eternity on the other hand is something which has no relation with time. For a thing to be called 'perpetual' it must actually exist; but that is not enough. It is necessary to wait for tomorrow to see whether this thing will still exist; and then the next day and the day after that. One must stay there always to see the sun set and return again to rise, so as to be able to say that the thing remains while the days pass one after the other, and so many other things and thoughts pass also which the days bring to birth and bring again to death. Even as around us so many things come and go, yet it seems that the mountains stand firm and the sun circles on always according to its perpetual law, so also within us there is a continual succession and recurrence of images and feelings, among which there is one that is always there and never passes away: a dominant thought, a constant norm, a conviction rooted so deeply that it cannot be shaken. Perpetuity is commensurable with time through which it endures. So that the survival toward which the desire of men is turned is a perpetuation on and on beyond the day of death. The eudaemonist logic above referred to does not ask more than perpetuity of this sort—an indefinite prolongation of our existence into the future. It is something indefinite, not infinite. To what is infinite one can add nothing, while to what is indefinite one can always add more; the very concept of it consists precisely in the possibility of always adding more.

This possibility of further extension preserves the temporal character of perpetual things. For in the unity of what is perpetual there is implicit the multiplicity of the successive moments which do not succeed in breaking down the solidity of the perpetual object, and do not even touch it, but which are not therefore less necessary to specify the succession through which the perpetual object demonstrates its power of perpetuation. The perpetual object therefore is just as temporal as the things that are not preserved but perish in time. And the perishable things moreover, if they exist at all, as they must however fleetingly, exist in a unity of time, within which they are really there and conserve at least a minimum of their being, confined within the narrowest range of their perhaps variable capacity for individuation. Perpetuity is no more than the extension of this insistence on maintaining its own being that is proper to every transient existent. Hence the persistence of the perpetual object is a brute fact which does not truly imply anything for the future. Even mortals may long persist in their empirical existence as living creatures; but their longevity, marvelous though it may be, persuades no one to believe that it will never cease.

This means that the perpetual object is temporal and does not possess true and proper immortality. It lasts, it can go on lasting; it is foreseeable that it will last for an indefinite time, but without the *right* to last ad infinitum. It is a fact, with nothing necessary about it. Time always hangs over even the perpetual things with the iron necessity of death. And the mind, having begged from time a suspension of this destiny, and obtained an extension *sine die* of this suspension, is content to push it off into the dim twilight of the farthest horizon to which the imagination stretches; it gives itself up to a timorous certainty accepted through weariness as a sort of raft of salvation—a raft which is itself anything but safe, but which postpones the danger and opens to the longing of the shipwrecked sailor a parenthesis of hope.

Such is the immortality with which man is commonly satisfied; not eternal life but life which will continue after empirical death and not bring down the curtain on a certain day at a definite moment, cutting forever the thread of the Fates. The individual will still exist tomorrow, and the next day, and always, since we may hope for this reduced form of eternity called *sempiternity*. For if life can continue even after the dissolution of the body, there is no longer anything against supposing that it goes on indefinitely. But even in the life beyond, the days will pass, the hours, the instants, as they pass here; time will not be vanquished. And that other life which we have to imagine in order to conceive the continuation of this one cannot be much different from this one; time, space, multiplicity, and every kind of finitude there must be—so why not also error, sin, and matter as in this vale of tears?

The eternity men truly yearn for is quite another thing, and will not suffer a man who thinks, and possesses genuine moral sensibility, to content himself with mere survival for an indefinite time. I say 'moral sensibility,' but one might better say 'spiritual sensibility'—consciousness of the value and freedom of the spirit. And this is not an abstruse secret of the philosophers; it is the atmosphere in which every man breathes and lives, when he acts or even merely speaks or thinks—which is the least he can do to be alive at all. Action involves conformity to some duty, and we cannot speak without obeying laws which make us feel the value of what we say. And thinking? Who could think without a logic? Logic defines the duty toward which the thinker is quite conscious of his obligation, and in respect to which his thought either has the value of truth or falls into error. Truth is eternal, and when it rises on the horizon of human thought no one who grasps the worth and essence of it can think it is born at that moment, and that there will come a day in which it too must die. There is no when and where for the truth. If it is discovered only today, it was still true before and it will not cease to be so even if man, after discovering it, ceases to recognize it, forgets it, or no longer takes account of it. The skeptic may deny this truth on which all men universally rely; but he cannot help but have a truth of his own, which, like every truth, will not be merely his, or confined to that day and those circumstances, but simply *the* truth. Of course, philosophic thought may point out that this truth is not discovered but constructed by thought, that it is itself thought. But what follows is that the thought which is truth is itself independent of any when and where, independent of every condition; and therefore it is universally valid. John Doe thought of it, but not John Doe the particular son of Eve, who is a mortal like all his brethren; it is absolute thought, and when it shines forth it attracts the gaze of all who can see, living, unborn, and even dead, since we cannot suppose that if they rose again they could dissent. Truth then is not truth in virtue of the particular content that from time to time it has; whatever the content, it has a certain form because of which, in the actual moment of thinking it, one cannot but think it is universally true. That is to say it is such that in formulating that particular determinate judgment one cannot judge otherwise than as one does. There are great thoughts, exalted and splendid on the peaks of the human intellect; and it is easy for everyone to see that these are, so to speak, glittering with eternal light. But even the little thoughts of every day, which are the stuff of our inward existence, gleam with the same light. It is the light of all the beautiful and good things that we manage to produce in every hour of our lives. Not only Homer and Dante are eternal; for every humbler mortal, to whose heart Homer or Dante speak, is, so to speak, cut from the same cloth. Even the child who is still babbling is able to astonish us with some mangled but highly expressive word, and put upon us the spell of poetry—the spell that takes us out of time and ordinary life where all is limited and born to die.

"The poet's hymn remains," [17] said Carducci, but it was only a half-truth; for that 'remaining' is a matter of perpetuity, not eternity, and it is not properly perpetuity that belongs to the poet's hymn. In fact it happens sometimes that in the course of history the poet's hymn does not survive either the poet or Jove; it gets lost, or torn up and forgotten. But it is not needful that it should survive *in fact*, which is what perpetual things do. There is *a* hymn, and it is a *real* hymn, if it shines forth from its first appearance as

---

[17] *Muor Giove, e l'inno del poeta resta* ("Jove dies, and the poet's hymn remains") is the last line of the sonnet to Dante in *Rime nuove*.

a star of the first magnitude in the heaven of eternal things, without awaiting the applause of time. Like a landscape which on a sudden lies open to the contemplation of the spectator who looks out from a terrace dominating from on high a great valley, with the peaks of the overhanging mountains bathed in the glow of the sun; a magnificent spectacle that fills his mind with peace and a serene joy, driving out every present care of his own private life, every memory of the past, and everything of the future. In that moment outside of time, the world is complete in an ecstasy unconfined. Dream? Reality? It is simply the world of all poetry, and of art in general:

> Guido, I would that thou and I and Lapo
> Were caught up by enchantment. . . .[18]

But it is also the world of good and of truth; the world where the mind is at rest as in the infinite in which, as the poet says, "shipwreck is sweet." [19] Time disappears. The spirit arises in its glory; it affirms its own liberty, freeing itself from all the conditions by which it seems to be suffocated when one sees it fenced in and straitened among the phenomena of experience.

Into this world 'before' and 'after' do not enter. Time stands still; or rather it is halted in the thought that gathers, comprehends, and circumscribes it within itself. There is no longer the "series of years without number" [20] involved in the notion of perpetuity; but there is the period in which thought completes a story (from the beginning of the poetic cycle to its conclusion, a day, a year, or more); or the period of an epoch, of an event, the history of a people from its origins to the present or till its disappearance, a period whose bounds are clearly fixed by thought, which in the inspiration of historical construction encloses the whole web and frames the canvas of its history in a firmly established chronology. Time here no longer contains the thinker and his thought and his whole being, historically determined between a 'before' and an 'after'; instead it is contained in a thought in which the thinker assists—indeed he is its creator—enchanted, and full of wonder at the eternity of

---

[18] Dante, Sonnet XXXII (ed. by Moore), opening lines.
[19] Leopardi, sonnet "Sull'infinito," last line: *e il naufragar m'è dolce in questo mare.*
[20] *Innumerabilis annorum series.* The source of this tag—if it has one—eludes me.

the world that has arisen within him, and which reveals itself to him as the true world.

Let us take for example the poetic world of Ariosto. This world is not something that rose on the horizon of human consciousness in the first decades of the sixteenth century, and remains perpetually there on the horizon. This perpetuity is a false appearance. The eternity of poetry does not endure unmoved and immovable, withdrawn from the vicissitudes of time. The eternal beauty, which having once flashed forth remains always identical, so that it can be discovered and rediscovered by posterity, *in perpetuo*, is a self-contradictory myth. The poet is always born anew in the reader; and the world of poetry is an eternal creation like God's. Its existence is a continual self-creation *ex novo*. But in every creation it is resurrected, rising on high in the light of eternity. The new creation is the spark by which eternity is released. It does not follow from this that creation and the eternity that results from it themselves fall within time, as if all the single creative events to which the eternity of a work of art reduces could be lined up in a temporal sequence. Eternity on that view would be a mere label by which temporal events were evaluated or rather qualified. The truth is that creation is only a manifold if it is looked at from outside, as happens for example in the history of art when it deals with its own proper abstract content (an object considered apart from the subject who constructs it). Here the poet and the critics follow one another chronologically; one is earlier, another later in time. But if the historian of criticism considers his history from a strictly actual point of view, as his own act of historiography, it becomes a unique creation and resolution, true because it is unique and infinite.

The creative act is always unique, and is not to be put alongside others ('before' or 'after'). It is what it is, and is not to be compared with another act or spiritual reality. That is why it has value and exists on the eternal plane. It is beyond time, because it contains time and is not contained by it.

Is not this the eternity we are always experiencing within ourselves? Are we not assured of it by the fact that tomorrow we shall find ourselves to be the same person as today, and that today we are the same as we were yesterday? This fact is a consequence of the principle of personal identity; but the principle is already contained in the *fiat* of consciousness, the actual thought in which we cannot think of time, no matter how vast, immense, and immeasurable it may appear to us, without comprehending it as a definite or indefinite whole. So that we make of our own thought a power that overcomes time and annuls it. It is the air of eternity that we breathe as we live; and the thirst for immortality that man suffers as a torment that gives him no rest can be nothing else but this essential desire of the spirit which never is, but wills to be what it should be. It wills, it adapts itself, it strives eternally to be eternal; and it actually becomes eternal in this willing of eternity.

Must we repeat here the fable of the dog who in his gluttony opens his mouth and lets fall the piece of meat that he has between his teeth, in order to snap at the meat reflected in the water?

4. Illusions

The difficulty of distinguishing between eternity and perpetuity causes some pleasant and comforting illusions to flourish in the human imagination, all athirst for immortality; so that when philosophical criticism, toward which every man's intelligence has a spontaneous tendency, begins to awaken, the difficulties with which the idea of immortality is surrounded are multiplied.

The first such illusion is belief in the immortality of the soul conceived as a substance. The soul is taken to be a spiritual or thinking substance independent of corporeal extended substance, so that it can quite easily free itself at any time from its connection with the mortal body, and base itself on its own eternal essence.[21] But how much more difficult this substantiality is to understand, than just to talk about, is shown by the need, once the soul is saved, to find a way for it to be once more rejoined by the body. The body is dead but it is destined to rise again, so as to reintegrate in the world beyond the individuality that every soul achieves in its relation with its body; for we know of no life in this psychic substance that does not go together with the life of the body.

But this substantiality does not merely mean independence of the body; it means also independence from what the soul properly is, independence from its activities. And when it is ideally separated from them it withdraws into an abstract universality in which there can no longer remain any trace of its individuality; so that

---

[21] There is in this sentence an untranslatable pun on *liberarsi* (to free itself) and *librarsi* (to balance or base itself).

it loses its concrete content, the self which distinguishes every individual as a being with his own merits and defects, with a web
of relations that makes him just what he is, the center of a world
of his own—precisely *this* teacher, father, mother, son or soldier
etc. So that man would be saved, yes, but in a world in which he
would be destined, nonetheless, to lose his own soul.

Another illusion is the idea that what we call the *personal* soul
is immortal, where what is meant by 'person' is the individual as
he is immediately given in experience, one among many. Thus
every individual of every place and time, age and sex, race and
nation would be immortal; and the multiplicity that we find here
in our present experience is transferred, just as it is, to the plane
of eternity. We overlook the fact that personality means self-consciousness and unification; that it is not a substance but a process,
an act by which multiplicity is synthesized, and every empirical
person is united by means of society in the personality that is universal will, the unique and infinite law and value. We forget the
first maxim of the moral conscience which inculcates mortification
of selfishness and involves the negation of individual particularity
in a higher and wider self-consciousness; we forget what moralists
nowadays call *abnegation,* and urge on us most strongly as the virtue of sacrifice. Did not even Jesus say that in order to be saved
one must be ready to lose one's soul? And clearly he meant that
narrow soul in which the individual builds a barrier to keep himself separate from others, and says *mors tua, vita mea;* the soul
through which every individual is self-contained and feels nothing
outside his own skin, yet does not doubt that he is even so a person. Whereas really he becomes a person only on condition that
he sacrifices this self and burns away the various layers of scales
that form round his privacy and make him a windowless monad,
to use a phrase that is famous but certainly not morally elevated.

The basic error here is that of believing, after only a glance at
our inner life, that a 'person' is born. What was said of the orator
—that *poeta nascitur, orator fit* [22]—is true of every person. Not
even the poet is really 'born' unless we mean to refer to his 'genius'

---

[22] "The poet is born, the orator made." This proverb first occurs, apparently,
in the Horace scholiast, Ps. Acron; and, in the form which Gentile here cites,
in Badius Ascensius' introduction to his edition of Terence (1502) (see the
Journal of the History of Ideas, II, 1941, 497–504).

in the abstract; the concrete realization of this genius may well suggest that the idea of an 'art of poetry' is not altogether fantastic. Personality means self-consciousness; and the essence of self-consciousness is not to be an immediate datum, but to become, by negating one's own primitive being. We have to negate what we are at a given time, in a moment when we either regard ourselves as existing already or as existing in a fixed way. To deny ourselves, to die. To become immortal and not remain chained to ourselves like oysters clinging to a rock.

This death which is demanded by religion and morality, because it is required by the logic of the act through which our personality is realized, is something which the innate craving for eternal, or rather perpetual, felicity causes us to forget very easily; we give way instead to the blandishments of a most bounteous promise that assures us there is room for all as long as God wills it, and hence grants us His Grace. We might call this the illusion of the flock; in it man abandons himself to the lazy hope of the 'broadness of the gate.' Entry into eternity is to be granted not to the man who becomes sublime by sacrifice and attains the spiritual unity of the human family, but to the multitude rushing by natural inclination toward the green pastures pointed out by the shepherd's rod. For there is room for all in the verdant meadows of eternity as long as they still have the teeth and jaws they were born with, and the four legs they will need to run about with, and which they likewise possess from birth. God who of His Grace has given us life and maintained us in it, surely He, so good, so merciful, will not let us one day be cut off, saying, like Machiavelli's Belfagor, "That's enough."

This is what we might call the 'democratic' idea of immortality; and it is the most irreligious, immoral, and illogical illusion with which men swaddle themselves in their aspiration toward immortality, and their yearning for it as a comfort in this life.

A third illusion is the naive faith in another world where we can go on living after the death that seems to impose a limit on the life that we can live in this world.

This world is the world of experience; and the limit of experience is certainly not death, unless we mean precisely the death of the subject of the experience. For it is obvious that the death of others—which, strictly speaking, is the death of which we can really have experience—is well inside our experience, not on the outside edge. But within experience no one can discover what comes after death, if it is he himself, the author of experience, who dies. So that naturally, the man who talks about another world beyond the bounds of actual experience is not the one who is dead, but the one who is alive. The living man speaks, of course, in the name of the dead, and he refers to an experience concluded, which is not his, and an experience beyond, which is not his either. For, thanks be to God, these perplexing excogitations and arguments about the 'beyond' are no exercise in the Elysian fields, or dialogue among the mummies of Ruysch.[23] They are the concern of souls on earth, episodes of life in this world. The concept of experience is split two ways (and it might even be split three ways or any number of ways) into a 'real' experience and a 'possible' one, 'real' experience being in this world and 'possible' in another. Experience is split in the same way between 'waking' and 'dreaming'; and the world of dreams not merely does not coincide with the waking world, but is not even comparable with it. But this does not mean that our dreams do not have a place where they can be inserted in the 'reality' that results from the connecting of all the elements of experience into a compact whole, or that a dream is not dreamt by an empirically determinate subject at a definite time and place, who can therefore recount it as *his* dream, or as something that happened in the very world in which he really exists, and fell asleep and dreamed. Similarly the incommensurability of the other world—conceived as object of an experience different from our actual experience—does not mean that the other world cannot be inserted into this one as part of the system of thought established by actual experience. In other words, the other world enters into this world, where it levies recruits by means of thoughts that mature in this world, and are necessarily bound up therein with the living arguments of a rational life.[24] In short, the other world is a corner of this one. *Here* indeed there is room for everybody, both the living and the dead; and if the dead frequent the eternal seats of the gods, whose company they go to join as they die, we still must not think that this other higher world is so essentially unlike this world that it cannot be grafted onto it.

There are in fact two ways of understanding this world. We can take it as the world of existence with all its guilts and miseries;

---

[23] Frederik Ruysch (1638–1731) was a Dutch anatomist skilled in preserving cadavers.

[24] *Esperienza logicamente vissuta.*

and then a world that was pure of guilt and misery could not but be alien to this one. But there is another way, the true way of understanding this world. We must not take it as a finished production or as simply existing. It seems to exist, when we view it externally as an immobile dead weight of matter; but it seems so no longer if we spy into the inwardness of our own minds, which is where it attains to reality. Here its reality lies in the process of attainment. Here there is no fixed being that is not practically negated; there is no positive activity that is not the negative of its opposite, so that there is an incessant aspiration toward existence, toward the adequation of one's own being to its essence—an aspiration toward a world other than that which exists. It was said with an accent of profound humanity, "My kingdom is not of this world," precisely because in this world there is no place for the spirit, but only for matter and mechanism. But should we deduce from this that all liberty and all value are banished from our experience? From the content of experience, yes; but not from experience as a whole, in which the content is only the product of the activity that constructs experience. In integral experience affirmation is a logical act, and hence the implicit negation of the negative of what is affirmed; it is a continual transcending of what is given, in order to achieve the ideal and create another world that is the negation of the one in which we are born to a life of sorrow.

The transcendent character of the other world does not take us right out of our experience therefore, for that *would* bring us to a pretty pass; it is rather—and we say this with all solemnity—the celebration of our own experience.

5. *Fuga mortis*

In the minds that are farthest from this concrete conception of experience in which living involves dying, the imagination—or the abstract intellect which by definition operates with concepts that are self-contained and unrelated to each other—separates death from life and opposes the two of them; and it makes the living man shudder with horror by pointing out the corpse of the dead. Not, of course, his own corpse, which would certainly make a more horrifying impression, but which no one will ever be in a position to observe even from afar. The corpse that one may have before one's eyes is someone else's; the corpse of a man who in life was like ourselves, who but a while ago turned his anxious eyes toward us asking for our help. Then his eyes spoke; but now they speak no more, and our dear one no longer answers to our love. Alive, he was not alien to us from the moment when we embraced him with our love and made him part of us, another self. So that his death is really also a death for us. We are less than before; and that dead body is not so much someone else's (of whom we might say *mors tua, vita mea*) that we cannot almost see it within us as our own body from which life has fled—the non-being of our own being. Non-being, nullity; here is the root of piety toward the dead, and here too the origin of the 'fear of death'—which is the terror of nothingness into which suddenly it appears that not merely someone else's existence but even our own can be plunged in oblivion. An abyss opens before our feet and waits there to engulf us.

This shuddering over a body deprived of life, this horror of nothingness, this fear of death so that it cannot come near a man without turning his blood to ice until the pulse of life almost stops, is a very bad counselor in mortal breasts, as it is also the poison of all joys both sensual and spiritual. It is the shadow from which life can only escape with difficulty, so that it becomes sad and somber, and the faith in the future by which man lives and works is shorn away. Every other argument of pessimism is only a travesty of this fundamental fear of death which causes all our hopes to die away before our eyes as deceitful illusions, and drys up within us the secret fount of all rejoicing. The joy is desirable and alluring, but it dies; and even hope will die as the illusions that have sustained it perish. So the pessimist, convulsed always by this fear of dying, can no longer understand life as sacrifice, as a noble death, for he can no longer taste the sweetness of the finest death, the death that "fair appeared in his fair face." [25]

Under the arid breath of pessimism life's flowers wither. Therein lies its moral condemnation.

But even this feeling of abhorrence for death is susceptible of redemption and can be illumined by an ideal light that gives to it a positive moral value. This happens when it is grafted onto the sense of society which makes us feel that our own existence is bound up with that of others, so that our life is not wholly our own, but

---

[25] *Morte bella parea nel suo bel viso* (Petrarch, *Trionfo della morte*, I, 172).

belongs both to us and to others, and it is our responsibility to guard it and preserve it, as best we can, as a sacred trust to be restored in due time. The father who withdraws away from danger of death for the sake of the children whom it is his task to bring up; the man who in battle strives to keep his life safe so as to go on fighting for his country; and, in general, every man who knows that he does not belong merely to himself, or rather that he does not belong to himself at all except insofar as he carries his neighbor within him, and therefore God also; such men do not sin from lack of abnegation and disinterest. Indeed, as far as they themselves were concerned they might often be tempted by weariness to yield to the menace of the enemy, and in despair of victory, surrender. But when faced with this sort of temptation to cowardice they remember that they are not their own masters; and this single reflection is enough to enable them to conquer themselves, and resist the blind instinctive urge to abandon themselves to destiny.

But evidently this abhorrence of death because of the consequences that it may have for others, or for oneself as architect of a moral world, is an act of life, an act of abnegation and sacrifice, and not just flight inspired by fear. Here, rather, we have the virile courage of the man who distrusts destiny, but does not fear death like the one who loses his nerve on the brink of the abyss, and goes over it in a fit of vertigo.

6. The difficulty of the problem and the solution

Death, so far as we experience it, and the only death that we can say we know about, is, as we have pointed out, not our own but someone else's. But the knowledge is indirect and therefore it is not true and proper knowledge; for we can only really know what we can put to the test of actual experience in our own consciousness. The proverb tells us that it is one thing to talk of death and quite another to die; we might retort that we are indeed always talking about death and it is ever present in our minds, but that we who are talking of it never die. Death touches us, and we wither at its touch; it is there before us, but we cannot succeed in taking it to our bosom, so to speak. We feel it but we do not conceive it. It touches us because the people who die around us are our neighbors, part of ourselves; the 'other' within all self-consciousness, who as the partner of the self becomes at last identified with it.

But if someone else's death touches us in this way, and is even a kind of death for us, this withdrawal of others, once dead, into our own minds is also a kind of survival in a memory that is actual presence, illumined by the light of eternity. Herein lies the key to Foscolo's poem on *The Tombs*, the means and monuments of this survival that foreshadows an eternal existence—especially if, as the poet holds, Homer is the patron of the memories consecrated in the tombs.

> Does he not live perhaps, even beneath the earth,
> Though silent for him is the harmony of day,
> If he can awaken it with bittersweet memories
> *In the mind of his mourners?* Heavenly is this
> Echoing of loving feelings,
> A heavenly gift in men; and often
> Through it we live with the friend who is gone
> And he who is gone with us.

With us, or rather through us; just as the life ("the harmony of day") of the dead man is awakened "in the mind of his mourners." It may be mere survival (the "brief pause at the limit set by Dis"); or it may be eternity as in the harmony of the poet who "conquers the silence of a thousand centuries." But it is always in the minds of the living.

In the eyes of the poet who looks down from on high at this religion of the tombs, the eternity that halts the departed ones "at the limit set by Dis" appears a mere illusion ("why should man grudge himself the illusion ere time does . . . ?"). And the whole difficulty about the immortality that every man feels but does not succeed in understanding lies here: we have to comprehend the character of what the poet and common sense call an illusion, but which is in fact the genuine reality.

It must be an illusion, of course, if it is true, as Foscolo claims, that Hope herself flies from the tombs, along with all trust in the future, or even escape from the bonds of the present:

> Oblivion buries all things in its night
> And a mighty power wears them down
> Inch by inch, and man and his tombs
> And the death masks and the relics
> Of earth and heaven are carried away by time.[26]

---

[26] Foscolo, *I sepolcri*, ll. 18–23 (*Oxford Book of Italian Verse*, no. 305). The passage cited earlier is ll. 27–34; the other lines come from the intervening context except "conquers the silence of a thousand centuries," which is l. 241.

In this crude mechanical and materialist vision—which Foscolo professes openly, but which is concealed behind every spontaneous physical conception of the world produced by the imagination— there is no place for any form of survival, so that survival can only be an illusion. But even as an illusion Foscolo sees that it has incontestably been a real force in human history; it seems to him to be even a gift of the gods ("a heavenly gift"), something that gives value, a divine value, to human life, because of what life can be in virtue of its convictions and its faith. The faith that reawakens the life of the dead in the minds of the living is serious and deep-rooted. It makes him who is gone live again with us. And shall we not pass on ourselves? We shall die, but from this cult of the dead, lo, there arises the song of Homer, which conquers the silence of a thousand centuries. In the living heart that keeps the dead alive there is the spark that lights the lamp of the eternal.

The difficulty lies in this: the memory that perpetuates, the poetry that immortalizes, are merely subjective. Reality surely remains outside of it, unconscious and deaf to these movements of the soul which remembers and makes its memories eternal? This Ego in which I receive and keep alive that part of myself that was in others dead and gone, is it reality itself, or only an image of reality in a glass? Are we who are alive, we who among so many dead have all the decisions to make even "though the vault of heaven break and fall," [27] are we strong enough to carry on our shoulders this world in which no one lives more than one life? Rather than pure subjects of the world that we only mirror to ourselves in consciousness, are we the real principle, the solid and absolute foundation of the world itself?

That the answer to these questions is not easy is shown by the fact that everyone always seeks an external support for his existence, beginning with the truth for which he hungers, or with God who is his life. At first sight everything appears to man as external and alien; and it matters nothing if this way of thinking separates him from reality totally and makes him less than the shadow of a dream. But the difficulty is also shown by the structure of thought itself, which cannot achieve the inwardness of self-consciousness without first being self-alienated and fixed in its object as something extraneous and opposed to itself—so far opposed as to be

---

[27] *Si fractus illabatur orbis* (Horace, *Odes,* III, 3:7).

its negation. Thus estranged from himself, man can feel dimly the strength of his spiritual pulse, the solidity of the thought in which his own inward essence and virtue is poured out and made manifest, the thought that embraces all reality and contains it; but he is not in a position to form a clear and explicit concept of this his all-powerful nature. So he seeks outside of himself what exists only within him, and wearies himself over the impossible.

The search for immortality is simply the search for his own value, the dignity that he cannot renounce. But conducted *a parte objecti*, as he conducts it from his original *realistic* point of view, the search cannot but fail, or feed on illusions. Anyone who can get his eyes open will see clearly that the search must proceed instead *a parte subjecti*, and I would add that he must have the courage for it. This courage is not satanic pride, as some timorous people make out because they are terrified at the idea of the responsibility that is cast on the shoulders of man by this concept of the real infinity of his being.

In any case we must have this courage if we do not want to run away most shamefully from even the minimal responsibility that no man worthy of the name would wish to refuse. For the freedom of man as a subject who thinks or wills involves at least a minimum of responsibility; and it is impossible to make the active subject both free and conditioned without falling into a contradiction. Liberty *is* infinity.

Is man free? Is he infinite? He affirms that he is by thinking, inasmuch as he thinks always for himself; however humble his conception of himself may be, he speaks (or in other words thinks), no matter how submissively. And it is clear that think he could not, if it were not for him freely to choose the truth as against its contrary, to say *Yes* and reject the *No*. But this liberty would be a mere trifle if he could only call himself free up to a point; and beyond that point he were no different from something that exists mechanically, by brute necessity, determined by the conditions that were at the basis of its existence.

Man is then unconditioned, infinite; or in other words absolute and eternal, immortal, outside of time.

One should not seek for life in the tombs of those who have passed on, like Cavalcanti in Boccaccio.[28] "He is not here, but is

---

[28] *Decameron,* Day VI, Nov. ix. Gentile's reference is somewhat inaccurate since the whole point of the story lies in Cavalcanti's own implied assertion that one does not find life among the tombs.

risen." [29] Where is he? Not in Heaven, if Heaven is to be thought
of as a place and so, like all other places, external to us. Heaven
is spirit; and so it is in us or *nobiscum*. But this 'we' is able to
contain so much only if it is itself not looked upon *a parte objecti*,
as if it were to be found in the world of objects. The world of
objects must always presuppose the consciousness to which it is
presented; and this consciousness is a 'We' more true and real than
any we can represent to ourselves *in* the world. The objective
world is temporal, spatial, even conscious; but the thought in it
is already done, it is fully worked out and enclosed in the definable
range of abstract logic. "He is not here." Beyond the world that
thought constructs by affirming and denying, positing and destroying, there is the living thought, man himself, who never closes his
eyes because his being is thinking, and thought cannot abstract
from itself. He may, indeed, say for a moment, a moment only,
"God does not exist"; but he can never say "I do not exist." He
is the polar star that shines always at the top of the heaven, and
never sets; and his perpetual light is a confirmation of his essential
eternity, above all the stars that rise and set. He knows no dusk
because he knows no dawn; will not this eternity suffice man if
his essence is to think, and thinking exhausts his whole being?

7. Death

But does the soul think always? Is not sleep an interruption of
thought, that is of consciousness? If thinking is the essence of the
soul, then an interruption in thinking would be a hiatus in the
soul's life. But experience proves the validity of this conception
of thought, for we have the experience of dreaming, which is a
form of consciousness. Dreaming is proper to sleep; it may appear
to be accidental because when we wake, sometimes we remember
clearly that we have dreamed, and sometimes not. But it is sufficient
to reflect that a memory of this kind has infinite degrees of clarity;
between the dream that remains living in our minds and those
that are forgotten and submerged in the darkness of consciousness,
there are dreams which we remember, but which are more or less
colorless and confused, others which we can clarify and revive
with an attentive analysis of the fragments that survive and take
root in our memory, and others again that remain riddles without

---

[29] Luke 24:6.

a key that would help us decipher them, like a knot or a stain, something that weighs on the soul though we know not how to describe it. This experience is sufficient to confirm the a priori argument that makes thought the essence of the inner principle that keeps us alive and governs all our conscious being.

But does this movement of thought arrive at a final point at which it breaks down and ceases altogether? Experience offers us weak forms of consciousness (being on the point of falling asleep, or of fainting and losing our senses) in which the energy of thought is attenuated and made to lie quiet, until it seems to reach the margin of existence beyond which it exists no longer. Then it seems to a man that he is dying; he feels he is dying. But he does not die. What happens is described as 'losing one's senses'; that is to say the organs of the body are no longer obedient to consciousness and fused in the organic unity of the psyche. The whole body loses the warmth and movement of life, it becomes heavy, the soul no longer possesses it and therefore can no longer make use of it. In paralysis the body becomes foreign to the soul, mere matter that the spirit can no longer succeed in penetrating and dematerializing by its energy. At the point of death, at the limit of existence, the synthesis of self and other, which is what man is, is broken down; and the 'other' is no more than other.

For if man exists as consciousness of self (Ego), he exists as a unity of self and other, subject and object; and the first object is the body. In fact when we deprive an object of all the attributes that the subject confers on it, and seek to fix it in its pure opposition to the subject, every object reduces to this primary one before it disappears altogether. This object is the 'other' that is born with us; its relation with the subject is the nexus that we have called the 'transcendental society,' the principle of every association regarded as something organically connected with and immanent in the constitution of the individual himself. The approach of death turns out to be a crisis of the vital synthesis of the Ego, a dissolution of the transcendental society through the stiffening and estranging of the other in us.

But this crisis is foreshadowed, not absolutely realized; we see it from afar, but we do not reach it. The death we have experience of is, as we have said, not our own but someone else's; and this fact is of vital significance. Death presupposes always a society, and appertains to the history of the Ego inasmuch as it is a transcendental society, the principle of every form of empirical society.

Death is a social event. One who dies, dies *to* someone. An absolute solitude—which is impossible—knows nothing of death, because it does not realize the society of which death is the dissolution. Paradoxically, we might say that the solitary man does not die; he cannot die the civil or moral death which means becoming spiritually null for others. In this death man remains merely 'other' for his fellow man; he is deprived of that social link which makes him a 'fellow,' a man like us, another self, one who shares with us in the synthesis of our self-consciousness. For self-consciousness is always a unity of self and other, but the other is assimilated to us through the synthesis; he is an other who responds to us, and so participates in the internal dialogue by which our personality is generated. The dead man responds no longer. Similarly the man who is 'civilly dead' becomes equally mute to us, no longer a man but a mere object.

In the same way our own body, the object consociated with us, and so made intimate to us through the spiritual synthesis of consociation, suddenly stiffens and resists the offer of social assimilation; it is converted into mere other, pure object. It opposes consciousness in a completely negative way; it enters the agony that gives us a presentiment of death, and hints at death from afar. It becomes mute. It speaks no longer within us—and therefore we speak no longer. The body, which is all of it a language, whether in the word spoken through the articulation of the vocal organs, or in miming, the glance of the eyes, the contraction of the brow, the movement of the single organs, or the general carriage of the person, expresses nothing any longer. The expressive movement, through which the soul manifests its existence in the body that belongs to it, ceases. The body decays from spirit to nature.

This decaying, of course, is conceptual and not real. For this 'nature' to which the body, like every 'other,' is reduced when every characteristic that belongs to it in virtue of the action of the synthesis is taken away, is not and cannot be anything more than the result of an abstraction. It is the abstract logos, lacking even the slightest spark of the animation that belongs to it in the concrete logos. It is what remains before thought, when thought makes entire abstraction from itself: nullity.

This nullity is death, which causes shuddering and horror, precisely because it is the nullity of the thought that is trying to conceive it and fix it before itself. The 'other' who is *our own* 'other,' reduced to an 'other' without any relation to us—no longer ours. An other therefore that is colder and more silent than all merely *in*animate things—an *ex*animate thing, a corpse.

It remains, however, present. No longer ours, and yet always ours, because negated in its abstractness and brought back into the sphere of concrete consciousness. "He is not here, but is risen; he is with us, nay within us." This 'We' cannot be unhorsed without the experience of death itself disappearing—absolutely the only experience of death that is possible. The Ego therefore is immortal.

But this immortality belongs to the eternal process of the Ego, which exists through its own act as universal, infinite, and therefore immortal. It involves always abnegation and sacrifice of the lesser to the greater self, sacrifice of the reality that exists to the ideal that stimulates and goads the real self, making it feel that its existence as it stands is not yet true existence.

It is not the immortality of a photograph for one who prides himself on the good health of his youth, and loves to picture himself in the future with his head still covered with raven-black hair— even while it is inexorably going gray.

The immortality of the living man is that of the man whose life is a continual death to himself. Through a life of this kind he moves in the realm of eternity, he becomes immortal. Slight consolation, perhaps, for those who, like Narcissus, want to look in the mirror and find there their own youthful images. But alas, such things *are* only images and dreams, in which man seeks an imaginary refuge from reality. The man who prefers the consolations of true manhood offered him by reality will rather seek himself not in his own fancies and imaginings, but within himself at the fount of all imagination, which is also the fount of every real and substantial joy. To "know thyself"; that is what matters.

INDEX OF NAMES

225